Autism and Understanding

Education at SAGE

SAGE is a leading international publisher of journals, books, and electronic media for academic, educational, and professional markets.

Our education publishing includes:

- accessible and comprehensive texts for aspiring education professionals and practitioners looking to further their careers through continuing professional development

- inspirational advice and guidance for the classroom

- authoritative state of the art reference from the leading authors in the field

Find out more at: **www.sagepub.co.uk/education**

Autism and Understanding

The Waldon Approach to Child Development

Walter Solomon

with

Chris Holland and Mary Jo Middleton

Los Angeles | London | New Delhi
Singapore | Washington DC

SAGE Publications Ltd
1 Oliver's Yard
55 City Road
London EC1Y 1SP

SAGE Publications Inc.
2455 Teller Road
Thousand Oaks, California 91320

SAGE Publications India Pvt Ltd
B 1/I 1 Mohan Cooperative Industrial Area
Mathura Road
New Delhi 110 044

SAGE Publications Asia-Pacific Pte Ltd
3 Church Street
#10-04 Samsung Hub
Singapore 049483

Library of Congress Control Number: 2011930844

British Library Cataloguing in Publication data

A catalogue record for this book is available from the British Library

ISBN 978-1-4462-0923-3
ISBN 978-1-4462-0924-0 (pbk)

Typeset by C&M Digitals (P) Ltd, Chennai, India
Printed in India at Replika Press Pvt Ltd
Printed on paper from sustainable resources

TO GEOFFREY

for his

INSPIRATION and GENIUS

TO PAMELA

for her

DEDICATION and PERSEVERANCE

TO ROBERT

for his

COURAGE and CHARACTER

The cover picture and the photographs in Chapter 5 were taken at the Autism Resource Base at St Nicholas School, Oxford. 'The cover demonstrates the attention of two children with Autistic spectrum condition who can sometimes be distracted and anxious, finding it hard to maintain their concentration', wrote Sue Saville, Head of Base.

Contents

Acknowledgements

I started to write this book many years ago but the real impetus came in September 2005 when my late wife Ruth and I went to a writing course organized by Sharon Colback in the heart of the French countryside. The first chapter was started during that week and the other participants encouraged me enormously. So thanks to Sharon first and then to Penelope and Charles Rowlatt who were workshop co-participants and have watched and contributed comments over the past six years. I started writing again in 2008 after I had gone back to France to live amongst the vineyards of the Gironde. There must be something in the air or in the wine.

Thanks next to Bee Bee Waldon who generously gave her time and knowledge over a couple of long interviews and then directed me to the centres in Leeds and Oxfordshire. So thanks also to Terry Buchan and Richard Brooks who introduced me to their networks in Leeds and Oxfordshire respectively. Richard and the late Sheila Coates were also kind enough to let me have copies of the teaching videos they had taken during Geoffrey Waldon's workshops. Although these could not be included in the book they will be on the associated website as a rich source of learning.

Thanks most especially to Robert who encouraged me to write and has contributed freely of his memories, pain and joy as he emerged from his shell. It was often hard for him but he shares my hope that this book will be as helpful to others as the Waldon Lessons were for him. A special thanks to my daughter Debbie who found and gave me the beginnings of my first wife Pamela's book after she had also died too young. This made it possible to include her important voice in the first chapter. Debbie read the chapters as they developed and made useful comments and suggestions.

Thanks to Nigel Lawson who read the early drafts and kept me focused when I strayed along irrelevant pathways. Very special thanks to the long list of parents and students who have generously told me about their experiences and of their sometimes painful memories; without the interviews with them in chapters seven and eight this book would have been both less valuable and less interesting.

Thanks also to colleagues of, and teachers influenced by Geoffrey Waldon, who have given generously of their time and expertise. Interviews with many of them are the basis of chapter six. A special mention to Jiri Berger of Iceland who shared with me his important paper on the use of the Waldon Approach in a school setting, and to Anamarija Filipiè Dolnièar who organized for me a week in Slovenia where the Waldon Approach is in use in many clinics and special schools. My family and friends told me of their early memories of Robert which are included in chapter one; so thanks to all of them.

Warmest thanks to my co-authors Chris Holland and Mary Jo Middleton who have checked, corrected, written, edited and generally given structure to the project. The book would have been much the poorer without their input, and I have truly enjoyed working with them both. Mary Jo also produced the line drawings which appear in the text. Thanks also to my extraordinary webmaster Horst Kolo who designed the website and took the photographs for the cover and within the text.

At my wonderful publisher SAGE, Marianne Lagrange has been unbelievably supportive from the first day that she heard about the project. It could not have happened without her. Kathryn Bromwich has been an able administrator, Jeanette Graham and Thea Watson a very sympathetic team in the editing stages and Lisa Harper produced the excellent cover design. Thanks to Katrin Stroh, who was kind enough to introduce me to SAGE; she and Thelma Robinson contributed importantly in the final stages of editing and tightening the structure.

This has been a co-operative undertaking and Geoffrey would have been pleased at the way all those familiar with his work were excited to help and participate. The hugest of huge thanks goes to him.

About the Authors

Walter Solomon is the father of Robert, the autistic boy who is the first subject of the book. He was educated at St Paul's School, London and has a Master's degree in economics from Cambridge.

He is a passionate advocate of the Waldon Approach, and a speaker on the subject of autism. Walter now lives in the Gironde, a beautiful wine-growing area of South West France.

Chris Holland qualified in Medicine, Child and Family Psychiatry and Psychoanalysis, with special interests in early child development and in autism, from both neurological and psychological perspectives.

He studied the Waldon Approach with Geoffrey and other staff for several years at High Wick Hospital, where he was Psychiatrist-in-Charge, as well as participating in workshops in Manchester and on Geoffrey's French tour. He is convinced that Geoffrey was decades ahead of his time, and that the Waldon Approach has a great deal to offer in all areas of education.

Mary Jo Middleton is a physiotherapist and special needs teacher who has been using the Waldon Approach for over 25 years with a wide range of children and adults. She has a Master's degree in Philosophy and Psychology of Language.

She met Geoffrey through other Waldon practitioners in Leeds while volunteering as a literacy teacher. She was able to visit and observe him working in Manchester and was a member of a study group which he led.

The Foreword has been contributed by **Colwyn Trevarthen** who is Emeritus Professor of Child Psychology and Psychobiology at the University of Edinburgh, and is also a Fellow of the Royal Society of Edinburgh and a Vice President of the British Association for Early Childhood Education.

He originally trained as a biologist, before going on to study infancy research at Harvard in 1967, and has since published on brain development, infant communication and emotional health.

Author's Preface

Geoffrey Waldon developed in Manchester a theory of child development that included a carefully thought out philosophy and psychology of education. He refined this into a practical and reproducible system (the Waldon Approach), which can help children with a wide range of developmental delays.

Meaning from movement is an expression Waldon used constantly; it is foundational to his theory of learning. The Waldon Approach was developed in the 1970s but many of the ideas have since been validated, with increased appreciation of the role that movement plays in development by researchers like Stern (2010), Gallese and Lakoff (2005) and Sheets-Johnstone (1999) among others.

Dr Waldon – a neurologist by training – described the pathways followed by typical children; he described the steps by which children progress from one stage to the next (the learning-how-to-learn-tools), and then created a format for causing the developmentally delayed child to work through these developmental stages creating (in my opinion), neural neo-plasticity. The format requires a regular one hour Waldon Lesson, which can be given by a parent, performed in a manner which never exceeds the student's General Understanding,[1] and therefore avoids anxiety and the need for anxiety-avoiding behaviours which are expected gradually to fall away.

This approach has been echoed in the recent paper by Molly Helt et al: *Can Children with Autism Recover? If So, How?* They write: 'If the brain can be forced to engage in "exercises" that represent normal behaviour and cognition, there is more potential for these behaviours to develop neurological representation'.[2]

My purpose in writing *Autism and Understanding* is to provide a critique of the Waldon Approach and its effectiveness in helping children to develop their understanding.

I have adopted a three part approach to achieve this.

The first four chapters describe a particular case, that of my son Robert, who emerged from a seemingly hopeless case of remoteness (one might say autism), into a positive, constructive and contributing adult life. This was after many years of hard and devoted effort. It might be thought that any child receiving this intensity of education and dedicated support would emerge in a similar manner; but I hope to show that it was the early application of the Waldon Approach, with his unique analysis of child development, which made that possible.

Many people to whom I have recounted his story have said that he must have been one of the high achieving autists. He has become very high achieving eventually, although a Professor of Audiology reported at 15 months:

This most interesting little boy was seen here for a test of hearing ... the possibility of peripheral deafness can be ruled out.... It was interesting to see that he did not show any interest in speech when delivered at quiet or raised intensities. Affect in this child also seemed to be absent.[3]

At 22 months the educational psychologist reported: '*My view is that Robert presents a picture of general backwardness*'.[4] He advised us to keep Robert at home as long as we could and when it got too difficult we should put him in an institution and get on with our lives. There was little sign at that time of any intelligence.

As well as his weekly sessions with Geoffrey Waldon and daily lessons with my late wife Pamela, he also had three years of psychotherapy with Frances Tustin. She said that she would not have been able to work with him without Dr Waldon's previous cognitive therapy.[5] His charismatic teacher Joanne Beressi feels the same way about her important work with Robert.[6]

I believe that the conclusion is inescapable: Geoffrey Waldon's philosophy of child development distilled into the Waldon Approach and applied in the lessons was the catalyst which enabled Robert to emerge from his shell, to develop his understanding of the world, and to live appreciatively in it. Without Waldon he would almost certainly have become an autistic adult locked out of the world by a range of protective, self-delighting and disturbing behaviours.

Chapter 5 is a distillation of the many articles and papers which were written by Geoffrey Waldon but which he was never able to condense into an easily comprehensible text. Perhaps he did not wish to make it easy, writing: 'The job of the writer is to facilitate the effortful strivings of the enquirer much as the midwife eases the travails of childbirth. I shall try to be clear but the difficulty of the subject matter is a function of the reader's interest'. (Waldon 1985: 3)

Richard Brooks wrote: 'I can imagine him reworking the fifteenth draft, but not at a publisher's party' (In Commemoration: *Koine*, The Waldon Association, 1989, p. 10). It is, however, necessary in appraising its effectiveness that the reader should understand the principles behind and the methodology of the approach, and I hope that in preparing this simplified version I have not strayed too far from Waldon's thoughts.

Chapter 6 contains a series of interviews which illuminate the previous chapter. They are mainly with teachers who have integrated the Waldon Approach into their daily routines, one might even say into their psychology of education. They explain how Waldon has changed their method of teaching special needs children and adults, and how this has helped many students under their charge. The theory as set out in this and the previous chapter is a coherent whole. Geoffrey spent a lifetime working out the details, thinking over every point in detail and discussing each with many of the colleagues who speak in this chapter. At the time of Geoffrey's death a book was in preparation. Sadly none of the professionals have found the time or the energy to complete it. Perhaps only Geoffrey could have done this. What I have written is a simplified form of the theory but one which hopefully is true to the original and accessible to parents and to teachers. I started writing as a parent and over several years of reading, research and meeting parents and teachers have grown to understand the beauty of the approach.

What I find most persuasive is that the approach has worked in so many different hands in so many different places. In Slovenia, through the work of Katrin Stroh, Thelma Robertson and Alan Proctor it is widespread in the special education system; and the teachers there are amazed that it is not in general use in the UK. So too are the teachers in Oxfordshire. Also a study in Iceland by Jiri Berger, PhD, showed that it worked well there in a classroom setting.

Chapter 7 contains a series of case studies of students on the autistic spectrum and Chapter 8, studies of students with a variety of other physical and mental conditions. I have interviewed students, special needs teachers and class teachers, parents with success stories and parents where the children remain completely dependent even after many years of lessons.

There are three young men described, Peter, Dan and Larry, who also went from 'no hope' to college or to university and each of their parents feel the same way as I do about the approach – that it transformed their sons' lives. Then there are children who started life with severe physical difficulties and who after many years of Waldon Lessons and devoted care by parents are still completely dependent. Even these parents feel that their child's understanding has been expanded by the lessons and virtually all of them have reported that their child (often now an adult), is now able to communicate with them at some basic level. All report that their children are more relaxed, open and able better to enjoy their still limited lives. Then there is one parent of an autistic boy, Charlie, who started when he was young, did all the right things, gave lessons at home over many years and very sadly did not have a result on the scale of Robert, Peter, Dan or Larry. The mother cannot evaluate how much the lessons helped. So it does not pretend to be a miracle cure.

Chapter 9 contains the theory and practice of a specialized orientation of the Waldon Approach, called Functional Reading. This will be most easily appreciated by those who already have practical experience in using the learning-how-to-learn-tools described in Chapter 5 and they will find it instructive in helping slow readers to lose their fear of reading.

My position is clear: I believe in the efficacy of the approach. Even more now that I have met so many parents and teachers who have said unequivocally: 'Thank God someone is writing this book'. I leave it to others to judge, based on the evidence presented here, whether, amongst the many treatments for autism now available, the Waldon Approach merits further investigation and application.

I hope I will be forgiven for using some words from another era which are no longer in acceptable usage. I have done this so as not to alter medical reports or the words spoken to me by others. I am conscious that this may offend some and for this I am sorry.

Teachers and parents will find guidance on getting started which can be much simpler than it seems – providing the will and dedication are available. The cost in money is surprisingly small, although the emotional and time cost should not be underestimated.

A final word: ... any parent can do it. It only takes an hour a day and the materials can be found in any recycling box or attic. Some will be available through the website if a parent finds that easier than making their own. There will also be videos on the associated website showing how the lessons can be conducted.

But understand that it is a long-term commitment. Think of an hour a day for five to seven years. Think also of the emotional investment and the strength of mind and force of personality needed to give the lessons.

Then think of the possibility of helping your child to understand ...

Walter Solomon

23 June 2011

www.autismandunderstanding.com

End Notes

1. For Waldon's definitions of his specialized terminology please see Chapter 5 where they are all described.
2. Molly Helt, Elizabeth Kelley, Marcelle Kinsbourne, Juhi Pandey, Hilary Boorstein, Martha Herbert, Deborah Fein, 2008: 'Can Children with Autism Recover? If So, How?' *Neuropsychology Review*, Springer 2008.
3. Report from Manchester University Department of Audiology, dated 12 June 1969.
4. Report from Manchester University Department of Audiology, dated 29 January 1970.
5. See page 27, para 2.
6. Joanne Beressi, personal communication, 30 April 2007.

Foreword

Using an Imaginative Respect for the Hopes of Movement

Colwyn Trevarthen

This is a book about the work of a pioneer who discovered a new way of appreciating the child's *innate will to move* – by watching how a child grows, explores and learns in infancy and the early years, and by comparing this early moving with how an older person, struggling with a neurological disability or autism, tries to exercise his or her will. He realized that learning how to comprehend the world depends, from the start, on how well we test it with a lively body. Learning from teachers must try to support this self-generated knowledge of being alive.

Geoffrey Waldon was a neurologist. Clinical experience inspired him to make thoughtful observations of how young children and patients act, and especially how they choose to encounter and overcome challenges in moving in body-related time and space. What he saw led him to rethink his medical training about motor disabilities and psychiatric disorders, and to question standard educational practice, too. He devised a different way of placing himself *behind the child*, to support their discovery of ways of moving by gently guiding their repeated experimenting with intentions to use the world. He observed how young children transform spontaneous, non-reflex patterns of playful activity into self-created experience, mastering patterns of movement as 'learning tools'. He called this the building of General Understanding, and concluded that this self-discovery of moving is the essential foundation for collaborating in the social learning of the artificial Particular Understanding of a family, community and culture.

Waldon also noticed how human beings of all ages become inhibited, confused and emotionally unstable when they sense they cannot move as intended. He concluded that an acceptance of this defence of agency, and dismay, is something that teachers must take seriously if they wish to support the education and wellbeing of persons whose powers of movement are weak. He saw that a learner could be inhibited by instructive teaching.

Like the imaginative scholars, teachers and doctors Charles Darwin, Albrecht Peiper, Jerome Bruner, Berry Brazelton, Daniel Stern and others, Waldon was watching for creativity and learning in the early, inarticulate stages of a life. He saw how an infant moves *on its own* to master an active body and build

experience of how to use it more effectively, and more pleasurably. Every deliberate action of the naive intending self opens up new possibilities and invites
new efforts, new expectations and new goals. That must be how learning leads
to growth of understanding – understanding *how* to do, not *what* to do, or what
to *say* about it. He defined universal stages of childhood self-awareness in
action and the natural progress of intentions in movement, especially of the
hands, and put the principles he discovered in the service of persons, young
and old, who experience confusion, distress and anger because they cannot
move past a given stage of ability as they wish and hope to do.

Principles comparable to those of Waldon's method have been discovered
and applied in other forms of 'facilitated learning' and non-verbal therapy for
people with developmental disability, including autism: for example, dance
and drama therapy as a creative activity, non-directive play therapy, or the
interactive music therapy of Paul Nordoff and Clive Robbins. But the stages of
development of self-related actions and motor learning-how-to-learn-tools
were demonstrated with particular clarity by Waldon, and have been adopted
by practitioners in special education and child psychiatry for all ages and abilities. The realization that 'meaning comes from movement' has helped parents
support independence in activities and emotional satisfaction in children who
cannot acquire cultural skills by standard training, enabling them to become
both more self-confident and more open to others. Like the method of supporting action and communication developed by Phoebe Caldwell in her work
with profoundly autistic people, Waldon's approach encourages more skilful
activity and more open communication by sensitively following initiatives. His
'natural science' of learning through movement receives support from animal
and human biology, as well as from humanistic philosophy of education. It
questions reductive theories of cognitive 'information processing' and of
learning by instruction or 'conditioning'.

Over 100 years ago Charles Sherrington initiated modern neuro-motor physiology with his demonstration of the proprioceptive or 'self-feeling' integration
of awareness within a moving animal. By inventive use of film in Moscow's
Central Institute of Labour, Nicolai Bernstein proved in the 1920s that the
actions of tool use and locomotion are coordinated and regulated in time and
space by *motor images* generated in the brain, which employ the biomechanical
properties of the limbs and whole body with rhythmical efficiency, wasting
almost no energy. They must 'perceive' the experiences of the body, how it feels
proprioceptively and how it reaches its objectives in the world, *prospectively or
imaginatively*, not reactively. Reflex correction is too slow. With detailed
kinematic analysis of films, Bernstein also studied how the energy-efficiency of
a child's walking movements increases over two decades of development in body
and brain; and he measured how the toddler plays with the bio-mechanical
'degrees of freedom' of its clever body, experimenting how to hop, pedal a tricy-
cle, dance, etc., pushing the limits of deliberate control in gracefully risky ways.

Animal movement is a vital adaptive principle. As Roger Sperry put it in
1939, 'The experience of the organism is integrated, organised, and has its

meaning in terms of coordinated movement.' Similarly Karl Lashley, in a paper on the essential serial ordering of movement in speech published in 1952 concluded: 'Analysis of the nervous mechanisms underlying order in the more primitive acts, may contribute ultimately to the resolution even of the physiology of logic.' The vitality of the mind, and all that we know, is, as Daniel Stern has put it, 'the child of movement'.

So there are good grounds in motor physiology and motor psychology for believing in the imaginative creativity of movements, and on their capacity for learning new conceptions, and for making language about them. Their invention is also foundational for the development of communication and cooperative awareness or shared experience from infancy. In 1979 the anthropologist and linguist Mary Catherine Bateson, describing her research on 'proto-conversation' between a mother and 9-week-old infant, declared, '... we are suggesting that in addition to the advantages for learning given by intense attention and pleasure, the infant's participation sets the stage for learning: once he knows the "rules of the game" and can anticipate patterns, he can also deliberately and playfully vary them and he has a "handle" on what he is trying to understand. Here at the prelinguistic level we can see the child playing a "grammatical' game".' She was saying that the learning of language requires creative anticipation of movement and of the goals that can be found in the world, and perception of this imaginative project in self and other is how communication with words begins.

Waldon puzzles teachers with his claim that to assist the development of understanding, motor facilitation should be 'asocial'. What he is guarding against is didactic and verbal interference with the free mastery of intuitive movement. Attempts to instruct natural intelligence can provoke anxiety, the fear of failing. The Waldon method requires sensitive support, by the teacher positioned to one side or behind the person who is trying new mastery of movement in the space in front of them, making pleasure from it. This principle of *standing aside* has been endorsed by educational reformers for centuries. John Amos Comenius, Jean Jacques Rousseau, Friedrich Froebel, Lev Vygotsky, John Dewey, Rudolf Steiner, Alfred North Whitehead, Maurice Merlau-Ponty, Jerome Bruner, Paulo Freire, Loris Malaguzzi and Barbara Rogoff have all argued that the art of sympathetic and creative two-way communication is essential for 'intent participation learning' at every stage of teaching, from kindergarten to university. It must respect and be inspired by the initiative, enthusiasm or artful 'zest' of the learner. Alfred North Whitehead in his essay on *The Aims of Education* makes the point emphatically: 'The paradox which wrecks so many promising theories of education is that the training which produces skill is so very apt to stifle imaginative zest. Skill demands repetition, and imaginative zest is tinged with impulse. Up to a certain point each gain in skill opens new paths for imagination. But in each individual formal training has its limits of usefulness. ... The social history of mankind exhibits great organizations in their alternating functions of conditions for progress, and of contrivances for stunting humanity.'

Geoffrey Waldon's method of assisting Functional Learning, though not intended to be emotional therapy, could offer protection for the emotions of troubled people whose spirit is weakened by a too demanding social world. At High Wick Hospital, with the supervision of patients' care by the psychiatrist George Stroh, a comprehensive programme of care, combining psychoanalytic insights with the Waldon Approach gave treatment for both heart and mind to enable patients to escape from the trap of their mental and motor disabilities. As the account by Sheila Coates of the work at the Chinnor Primary School and in the Oxfordshire Service for Autism tells us, this way of interpreting affective difficulties of people with difficulties of development had support, not only from the Freudian theory of the development of an 'independent ego' as transmitted to Waldon by Francis Tustin, but also from the animal biology and ethology, the natural science of behaviour. Niko Tinbergen, Professor of Animal Behaviour at Oxford, took interest in the treatment of autistic children and materially supported the work at Chinnor. Animals are adapted to engage with the environment and to cooperate socially by finding patterns of experience or 'signs' that allow them to anticipate the consequences of moving, and to guard against fear. Waldon's method also attempts to respect similar reactions in patients.

In the past 50 years scientific understanding of how the mind and body grow in infancy, and how this growth is prepared for in development before birth, has been transformed. Although they know nothing of the particular world and society into which they have come, newborn infants make well-regulated actions that immediately attempt to extend conscious awareness and to form relationships with parents. From before birth, within the mother's body, a dialogue is established with the reachable world. And there is a 'co-adaptation' to engage with the mother's body. Thus a foetus responds to the rhythms of her life and actions, detecting and reacting to her states of pleasure or stress, even learning how to identify her from the sounds of her voice. Detailed observations of the spontaneous actions of the innocent mindful body of the newborn, have proved how rich is the natural adaptation of the human spirit for these two worlds, the self-created one and the interpersonal. The distress cries of the young child broadcast a strong defence against confusion and anxiety, appealing for support. But even a newborn is acting to discover gentle, pleasurable ways of using hands, eyes and mouth to make and use experience, smiling with satisfaction. They can provoke sharing of 'narratives of vitality' with an affectionate adult. We have collected evidence for this under the heading of *Communicative Musicality*, using detailed measures of the rhythms and melodies of proto-conversations and baby songs to show the natural talents of young infants for dialogue employing sights and sounds of human movement, acting with curiosity and sociability.

Perhaps the most important message coming from the success of the Waldon Approach is that we have to guard against too well-made plans to shape and educate young minds. The artificial techniques and regulations of complex social institutions to 'care for' them can stunt the creative spirit of the child, as Rene Spitz and John Bowlby proved by their studies of the crippling distress of hospitalized infants and institutionalized orphans. This changed paediatric practice. Beyond needs for food, care and comfort there are needs for shared creativity or companionship – for attachment and common understanding in our actions.

What holds a human body and mind together is *self-made imagination of movement, with feeling*. We communicate our motives and feelings by *how we move* – by signalling what Stern calls 'vitality dynamics', and by exhibiting a 'seeking' for understanding with 'emotional consciousness', as described by Jaak Panksepp. That, too, is an important message of the Waldon Approach.

Further reading

Bjørkvold, J.-R. (1992). *The Muse Within: Creativity and Communication, Song and Play From Childhood Through Maturity*. New York: Harper Collins.

Daniel, S. (2008). The therapeutic needs of children with autism: a framework for partners in non-directive play. Brit. J. *Play Therapy*, 4, 18–34.

Frank, B. and Trevarthen, C. (2012). Intuitive meaning: Supporting impulses for interpersonal life in the sociosphere of human knowledge, practice and language. In Ad Foolen, Ulrike Lüdtke, Jordan Zlatev and Tim Racine (eds) *Moving Ourselves, Moving Others: The Role of (E)Motion For Intersubjectivity, Consciousness and Language*. Amsterdam: John Benjamins.

Malloch, S. and Trevarthen, C. (eds) *Communicative Musicality: Exploring the Basis of Human Companionship*. Oxford: Oxford University Press.

Panksepp, J. (2004). Affective consciousness and the origins of human mind: A critical role of brain research on animal emotions. *Impulse*, 3: 47–60.

Stern, D. N. (2010). *Forms of Vitality: Exploring Dynamic Experience in Psychology, the Arts, Psychotherapy and Development*. Oxford: Oxford University Press.

Trevarthen, C. (2012). Born for art, and the joyful companionship of fiction D. Narvaez, J. Panksepp, A. Schore, and T. Gleason (eds.) *Evolution, Early Experience and Human Development: From Research to Practice and Policy*. New York: Oxford University Press. Expected mid 2012.

Trevarthen, C. (2000). Autism as a neurodevelopmental disorder affecting communication and learning in early childhood: prenatal origins, post-natal course and effective educational support. *Prostaglandins, Leukotrienes and Essential Fatty Acids*, 63, (1–2), July 2000, 41–46.

Trevarthen, C. (2005). Stepping away from the mirror: Pride and shame in adventures of companionship. Reflections on the nature and emotional needs of infant intersubjectivity. In C.S. Carter, L. Ahnert, K. E. Grossman, S. B. Hrdy, M. E. Lamb, S. W. Porges, and N. Sachser (eds). *Attachment and Bonding: A New Synthesis*. Dahlem Workshop Report 92. Cambridge, MA: The MIT Press. pp. 55–84.

Trevarthen, C. (2012). Epilogue: Natural Sources of Meaning In Human Sympathetic Vitality. In *Moving Ourselves, Moving Others: The Role of (E)motion for Intersubjectivity, Consciousness and Language*. Edited by Ad Foolen, Ulrike Lüdtke, Jordan Zlatev and Tim Racine. Consciousness and Emotion Series, Amsterdam: John Benjamins.

Trevarthen, C., Aitken, K. J., Vandekerckhove, M., Delafield-Butt, J. and Nagy, E. (2006). Collaborative regulations of vitality in early childhood: Stress in intimate relationships and postnatal psychopathology. In D. Cicchetti and D. J. Cohen (eds) *Developmental Psychopathology*, Volume 2 Developmental Neuroscience, Second Edition. New York: Wileys. Chapter 2, pp. 65–126.

Zeedyk, S. (Ed.) (2008). *Promoting Social Interaction For Individuals With Communication Impairments*. London and Philadelphia: Jessica Kingsley.

Colwyn Trevarthen, FRSE

Professor (Emeritus) of Child Psychology and Psychobiology, The University of Edinburgh

8 February 2012

1
Early Days 1968–1972

'Does he know he's in a different garden?'

In this chapter we trace Robert from birth, through the suspicion that he was not developing in a typical manner; to a series of documented visits to his GP and various specialists; and to the start of his lessons with Dr Geoffrey Waldon.

Walter

'Does he know he's in a different garden?' asked Hannah[1] as we sat in the shrub-filled garden of her Knutsford home one glorious summer's day in early September 1971. Robert was three and a bit, and had thoroughly inspected and flushed all the toilets in the house, and unrolled as many rolls of paper as he could get hold of; and he was now running happily in circles round and round the lawn. He was talking, but not making much sense, and it was clear that this good-looking, sturdy little boy had started life on a different track.

I was present at the birth except for the final moments of the forceps delivery and I will never forget the gynaecologist's impatience as he waited for the anaesthetist to arrive. It seems as though we waited for ever with him saying: 'Where is he?' 'Tell him to hurry'. But born he was, marginally underweight, which meant a week's stay in an incubator. But he and Pamela came home on schedule and I will never forget the pride of that day.

Robert was such a good baby. We thought we were blessed. He rarely cried. He went to sleep without complaint. He allowed us to enter and leave his room without protest. Of course these were signs but we were new young parents and did not know what to look for or what we were looking at. He walked late, talked late and failed to create the normal affectionate bond between mother and child. I so well remember Pamela hugging and kissing him and thinking the relationship somehow awkward and unnatural but did not understand that this was her response to Robert's seeming indifference to her.

In actual, and terrible, fact he gradually became a nightmare child. He screamed, he had tantrums, he ignored us. He was happy when he was alone, squinting sideways at the world or looking through his fingers, spinning a large multicoloured top, or splashing in the paddling pool. But he never intereacted with us, was never able to make any normal human contact. It was as if we, his parents, were just inanimate objects in his incomprehensible world.

Robert was our first baby and it is hard to express the anguish of having such an unresponsive, seemingly so unloving, child.

In another garden I had dropped in to see friends. Their nine-month baby clutched me, looked into my eyes and made my heart break. Home I sped to Pamela to describe the feeling and to express my fears.

Pamela

The first few months sped past. At three months he was sleeping through the night and was a model baby. His day was filled with feeding, bathing and playing. I spoke to him all day long, read stories to him, took him shopping and filled his days with a bounty of goodies. He grew and was content.[2]

By the time Robert was nine months old I had begun to make friends and I invited a friend over with her six-month-old baby girl. Two things stood out very clearly from this encounter. The little girl behaved incredibly well, whereas Rob screamed nonstop. But the most significant thing was the way this young six-month-old child reacted to her mother and the environment. Not for one instant did the baby's eyes leave the mother's face. There was constant eye and body interaction and to my amazement the baby actually put up her hands asking to be carried.

I asked Judy[3] if she thought that my nine-month baby was unusual as he had never displayed any reaction to me, but rather treated the world as of no concern or interest to him. He just spent hours watching his hands out of the corner of his eyes, looking at the ceiling continuously and rocking. He was getting to be rather an expert rocker and could move his cradle all over the room.

She replied that yes, Robert was rather unusual, and perhaps it would be a good idea to take him to the doctor. I was astounded. I had asked the question expecting her to say: 'Don't be silly. All first babies are different yet all first mothers are impatient'.

The family doctor at nine months
The next day I was at the doctor's. After waiting a lifetime, during which I repeatedly told myself that I was wasting his time and my money, but all the same wanting to be reassured that there was nothing wrong, we were finally ushered into the surgery.

'What appears to be the problem with young Robert?' Dr Casson asked.[4]

'Well' I began, hesitating to find the right words and trying to control the emotions that were building up, 'I just want to make sure that Robert is developing normally' and I recounted the worries that had arisen after the Judy episode.

'It is always wrong to compare babies' said the doctor, 'they differ enormously at this age, but let's be looking at the young man'.

With this I handed Robert over and watched with anxiety as the doctor performed the routine test for reflexes, gave him a very thorough work-out and finally put him into an adjacent room and, leaving him safely on the floor, closed the door. Robert was as happy as a lark and when Michael (Casson) sat down with me he was beginning to look concerned. 'Well he appears to be perfectly fine health wise; however it is unusual for a nine-month child to be so happy in a room on his own'. At this stage Michael retrieved Robert who seemed oblivious to all events.

'Why don't you play with him, stimulate him more, and bring him back at 12 months and we will see how he is doing.'

This was going to become a repetitive phrase 'Play with your child, Mrs Solomon' – what the hell did they think we had been doing? – 'and bring him back in x months'. However, I did not know that now; for this was the very beginning of my journey, and I was thinking in terms of a weekend in gaol rather than a life sentence.

Winter in Hale is a dreary time and the winter of 1968/9 was no exception. I would wrap Robert up warm, swaddle myself in rainproof gear and pram-push young Solomon all around the area. We visited the local farm, spoke to the cows, fed the ducks and stroked the ponies. We visited the local Fire Station where the firemen would indulge me and to Robert's delight sound the piercing bell. We shopped, we read, we played, and we swung. I brought sand into the house so that we could play in it and of course we had water play. I built with bricks, I painted and drew, in fact I did just about everything I could think of.

And what did Robert do? Well he did enjoy playing with his coloured beakers. He loved the swing, and he enjoyed running his fingers through the sand and water. For the rest of the activities I do not know. He screamed a good deal and otherwise appeared superciliously indifferent. He ate well but made no attempt to feed himself. Still I reassured myself that all adults I had ever met could feed themselves, so why not Robert. And with this logic I comforted myself.

One year old

At 12 months[5] I was back in Michael's surgery. He did the same checks and routine tests and asked me if I had noticed any difference.

'He appears not to listen to me' I began rather hesitantly.

'Let's arrange for him to go to audiology and test his hearing' he said.

'Robert is not deaf.'

'He does seem to have a hearing problem though. He does not respond to speech and he makes very few baby sounds.'

'That is true', I conceded. 'OK – let's give it a try'.

Walter

So we were referred to the Department of Audiology and Education of the Deaf at the University of Manchester. Pamela took him for a hearing test (12/06/69) and the report says:[6]

This most interesting little boy was seen here for a test of hearing ... the possibility of peripheral deafness can be ruled out... It was interesting to see that he did not show any interest in speech when delivered at quiet or raised intensities. Affect in this child also seemed to be absent.

Robert was referred to the Lecturer in Educational Psychology in the department who we saw about two weeks later.

Educational psychologist (15 months)

The educational psychologist's report[7] from that meeting on 26 June 1969 stated that:

It seems that Robert is not going through the normal mother/child reciprocal relationship. At this time his play is reasonably constructive and I was able to establish that he is well past the permanence of an object stage. He passed some Gesell Adaptive items at or near his chronological age, i.e. 15 months Cube/Cup item, 56 weeks Form Board, 52 weeks Cup/Tower, 52 weeks Releases Cube. Other examples of motor and adaptive behaviour place him nearer the 40/44 weeks level. In view of the well known poor predictive validity of sensori-motor testing at this early age it is not possible to say more than that present testing excludes severe sub-normality.

His parents are intelligent and tense, Mrs Solomon is particularly stressful. I have given them advice about the best way in which to handle Robert's developmental needs. At the present time he shows no understanding of speech and does not imitate gesture. A rating on the Sheridan scale places him at a six month level in respect of laughing, and screaming when annoyed. He is not at this level in terms of vocalisation or showing any evidence of response to different emotional tones in his mother's voice. *The possibility of additional problems consequent upon parental reactions to his retarded development must not be ignored.* [my emphasis.]

I have advised Mr and Mrs Solomon to read Bowlby's *Child Care and the Growth of Love*. I have given them advice about suitable play material. They are going to keep a developmental record for me and I have expressed my willingness to see Robert at intervals of three months until, at least, the diagnosis is relatively clear.

Although we did not see this report at the time, we came away with the clear impression that the psychologist believed his lack of affect was, if not caused by, then certainly reinforced by our failing to bestow enough love and attention on Robert. Most paediatricians and child psychologists had been influenced at that time by the writings of Bruno Bettelheim whose thesis was that the mother failing to bestow sufficient love and attention on the child caused much of child disturbance. 'Refrigerator Mothers' was the in-vogue phrase. This was absolutely not the case. No one could have tried harder to connect with and no one could have given more love to any new baby than Pamela. It was hurtful, damaging and distressing. No wonder that in his notes four days later Michael Casson states: 'T [telephone conversation] with mother. Psychologist at Audiology seems to have upset her and I tried to reassure her.' [8]

Meanwhile Michael Casson had referred us to a senior consultant paediatrician at the Duchess of York Hospital for Babies in South Manchester. We met him first on 12 July 1969 and our GP refers in his clinical notes to a report which he received on 6 August 1969 which says: 'Report from Paediatrician. No organic abnormality. Suggest condition is psychological due to stresses within the family'. This report appears to be missing from the records. I also remember a report (missing from the records) stating 'Robert is an odd looking child' which may be the same one.

Consultant paediatrician (1 year 8 months)

The paediatrician's report[9] following his second visit on 17 November 1969 states:

> The mother seems very satisfied with his progress. He is now playing with her, recognises and appears to want her as he comes around dragging at her clothes. He walks quite well. Speech: somewhat difficult. He copies sounds and makes other meaningless sounds of his own. Comprehension is difficult to decide. He never asks for anything by name nor does he point to anything. He never asks for food nor cry for it. He does not seem to be worried as to whether he gets it or not. He is exceptionally placid. His mother provides other children to play with him and he is not at all aggressive towards them and does not protect his toys from their depredations. Comments: there has been quite a considerable improvement in this child's behaviour and physical development. His emotional state has also altered and this was well shown when I started to examine him. He objected quite actively in the same way as a normal child. The mother certainly has a better appreciation of the problem than in the past and spends a great deal more time with him, which I am sure is the reason why he has improved.

– Here we go again. It was the mother's fault for not spending enough time with him in the past!

The paediatrician carried out a Gesell Developmental test with Robert three weeks later (9 December 1969) and reported on 22 December:[10]

> I observed him closely at Rodney House[11] which has a large reception area where the child romped around, played well, was happy and interested in everything around him. Clinically he did not behave like an autistic child. Details of the test were as follows: – Motor functions: 18 months. Adaptive functions: 52–56 weeks. Language development 56 weeks: Personal-social relations: 56 weeks. Comments: This shows a fairly wide

scatter which is often indicative of a child with brain injury. I intend asking our Consultant Paediatric Neurologist to see him and in view of the lack of overt signs, I propose having a chromosome study done at the Royal Manchester Children's Hospital.

Family doctor (fifth visit, 21 months)

Meanwhile on 15 December I had a consultation with Michael Casson about Robert. He noted:[12] 'Behaviour still abnormal and possibly autistic. Long discussion with father and advised not to start seeking further opinions at the special autistic centres which are in the south of England'.

On 29 January 1970 when Robert was 1 year and 10 months old he had his second evaluation by the Educational Psychologist who reported:[13]

> Robert was accompanied by his parents. I note that at the time of my initial investigation I commented on the fact that he showed some minimal amount of pleasurable reaction when stimulated by an adult. At that time he did not seem to seek physical contact. When I saw him today he engaged in a good deal of restless exploratory behaviour and showed pleasure a number of times. His parents confirmed an improvement in his degree of affect and stated that he seeks some physical contact, although intermittently.

> Pre-language development: I rated Robert's development on the Sheridan Scale. His range of vocalisation is very limited and places him below the six month level. According to his mother, he makes some responses to different emotional tones of his mother's voice, largely by showing a pleasure reaction (6 months).

> He does not vocalise deliberately as a means of inter personal communication and in this respect is not at the 9 month level. He is reported to imitate some playful vocal sounds and this is scored at the 9 month level. In addition, his parents said that he has attempted to imitate three words 'Mummy,' 'Daddy,' and 'Baby.' At the present time his only consistent attempt at imitation is in response to 'Mummy.' Mrs Solomon is of the opinion that Robert understands 'gee-gee' [horse for US readers] and gives pleasurable responses to words such as 'sweets' and 'biscuit.' Without being present during his responses to such words it is not possible to say that he necessarily shows any more than simple responses to tones of his mother's voice.

> Because of his restlessness and very short attention span I could not obtain some of the Gesell Adaptive Responses at the 15 month level which were reported after my initial investigation. By adapting the Merrill-Palmer Peg Board items I was able to demonstrate that he could complete these tasks but when a formal administration was attempted his attention span was too short for completion to be possible. This comment applies to several Merrill-Palmer items at the 18 months plus level.

With regard to sensori-motor functioning I am of the opinion that with special adaptations Robert could engage in some visuo-motor tasks at a level in some cases of 15 months. On the other hand, as rated on the Piaget model, the great majority of his exploratory behaviour is not at the sub-stage 5 level as I observed it today. This would place his essential exploratory behaviour at an age below the 12 month level.

My view is that Robert presents a picture of general backwardness. I have given his parents further advice about the manner in which they should attempt to help his development. I am going to see him again in six months.

It was either at this or at the prior meeting that he suggested that there was no hope of real recovery and that we should keep Robert at home for as long as we could, then place him in a home, have more children and get on with our lives. It was during this visit to the Department of Audiology that we first met Dr Geoffrey Waldon (first seen by me during hearing test)[14] – an event which was the watershed which enabled Robert to develop into the fine young man he is today.

First meeting with Dr Geoffrey Waldon (22 months)

Pamela

The next week found Robert and me in a large waiting room with chairs arranged around the walls. Robert was a bundle of uncontrollable energy and I had long ago reasoned that if doctors could not be on time for an appointment then it was perfectly alright for Robert to 'play' in his own way until they were. So I placed my son on the floor and watched him career around the room and tried hard not to be embarrassed in front of the other parents with their well-behaved children.

Soon I noticed one of the other men in the room was down on all fours trying to play with my son. A sort of peek-a-boo game. How nice, I thought, and picked up a magazine to flip through. When I looked up a second later Robert and his 'friend' had disappeared. 'Did anyone see where my little boy went?' I asked, feeling silly. 'The doctor took him in' was the response and very soon a nurse came in and asked me to follow her. I was ushered into a small room full of hi-fi equipment and there was Robert and his 'friend' from the floor. 'Dr Waldon this is Mrs Solomon', the nurse said and left us'.

'Well, Mrs Solomon', he said 'We have good news and bad news. The good news is that Robert is not deaf'. 'Of course not', I thought, 'How could my precious son be deaf?' 'However the bad news is that he is 98% deaf to the human voice and has absolutely zero understanding of what is being said to him'. 'No,' I said, 'Robert just chooses not to hear. He is far too busy playing in his own world, caught up in his own thoughts, to listen to us'.

'Mrs Solomon', Dr Waldon said more gently, 'I know this is hard for you to hear, but in order to help Robert you must fully understand where he is at. He cannot process human voice. Music, loud bangs and quiet sounds, yes – but voice, no'. He then proceeded to prove his point. He sat Rob on my knee and darted around the room making strange sounds. Each time he banged a drum or rang, ever so gently, a bell Rob's little head swung round instantly; but call his name or make a verbal sound he just looked straight ahead.

A lump started to build in my throat, but I forced it back, doubling it in size I'm sure. 'How will I ever be able to reach a child who cannot hear me?'

'Mrs Solomon', said Dr Waldon 'If no one else is helping you with Robert I think I might be able to. Go home, think about it, and if you are interested give me a call tonight'.

I hugged Robert to me and left. I strapped him into his car seat, pulled out of the parking lot and saw our first traffic light. It was red. Tears started to trickle and then pour down my face. I began to howl. How on earth will I ever be able to teach him what a traffic light is, that people stop on red, wait on yellow and go on green? The enormity of this simple concept overwhelmed me. I drove home and called Dr Waldon: 'When can we start?'

Walter

Paediatric neurologist (22 months)

By happy coincidence the first consultation with the paediatric neurologist to whom we had been referred by Robert's paediatrician was the day after our first meeting with Dr Waldon. He repeated many of the same tests and suggested we saw him every two months to review progress. At the same time he repeated the medical mantra that we should do everything we could to stimulate Robert.

We asked if he knew of Dr Waldon and he responded that there was little he or any of his colleagues in conventional medicine could offer us. He had heard of Dr Waldon and his unusual, even unorthodox, methods and thought he could not do any harm and might do some good.

The neurologist's detailed report in a letter to the paediatrician stated:[15]

There seems to be no unequivocal evidence of 'Brain Damage', the only possible point of significance being the low birth weight at full term. I would, therefore, classify the trouble as a developmental disorder, most probably mainly affecting language development. As I said to the parents I thought that the behaviour difficulties were, in large part, secondary to this.

Dr Waldon has said that he will see the boy again and work out a programme for him and I am sure it is justifiable to see how Robert responds to this.

The neurologist explained his views on autism in more detail in a letter to Dr Casson:[16]

I did try to explain to the parents that saying a child is autistic is only describing a behaviour pattern; just as one might say that someone is depressed. One is then left with the usually very difficult problem of why a child is behaving in this way. Is it due to a disorder of language development, brain damage, deprivation, mental retardation etc.?

I feel that children who behave in this way present some of the most difficult diagnostic problems, but pretending one has made a diagnosis by labelling them as 'autistic' usually adds to the confusion rather than helps.

First Waldon Lesson (1 year 11 months)
About two weeks later we went to the church in Wilmslow for our first appointment with Dr Waldon. This time after 'Hello Robert' he sat down and spoke to us.
  'Well' he said and the next eight years were encapsulated in that 'well'.

I would need to see Robert regularly. I will start by giving Robert a series of developmental tests to assess his level in a number of different areas and will give him exercises designed to equalize the developmental levels. I have to ensure that his development is balanced and that one area does not get too advanced or too left behind. Each week I will give a demonstration lesson and it will be your task, one or both of you, to repeat the lesson each day during the following week. Progress will be slow but if you follow my plan it will be sure.

Dr Waldon's notes[17] on this meeting describe an:

improving under-responsive child. Range of functional levels 3/12–12/12+ Modal point below 10/12. Aim at 6/12. In the play lesson he would work to (1) set up battery situation (2) encourage directed banging. Noted to be able to echo dental clicks and vocal-ortic sounds. In the second session (28/02/70) Robert accepted the Waldon Chair and sat for 20 minutes. Limited play. Banging. Picking up and dropping, leading towards purposeful dropping. Work towards (1) Handling etc. generally (2) restricted sitting with tray for solitary play (3) restricted sitting with tray for asocial lessons.

Educative play

Pamela

And so began what was to be years of educative play for Rob. Initially I would take Robert to Dr Waldon and he would sit him in a small sized chair and pull up a small table. Sitting close to him with his own chair behind Rob's he would present him with little games to master.

First it was the xylophone. Rob had to pick up a small hammer, hold it in his hand and bang when Dr Waldon gave the command. Robert did not want to sit in the chair, did not want to sit still, did not want to hold anything in his hand and certainly did not want to bang on command. He screamed, arched his back and turned away. Gently, with his hand over Robert's, Dr Waldon would guide him through various other activities, working with Robert in this way for about 45 minutes. He would later explain to me what was going on and why. I would then go home and every day give Robert a lesson similar to the one Dr Waldon had shown me.

We had a very firm routine. In the mornings we had 'our lesson'. We placed a large low child-sized table in his bedroom and Robert sat in his little chair while I sat beside him and presented him with tasks.

At first I would always do the task with my hand over his, so he would know what was required of him, together with the simplest of language so he would associate his action with the word I had used: e.g. 'bang' or 'wait.'

Very gradually he began to relax and even enjoy some of the games we played. From banging xylophones, we banged drums, beakers, small stones; we banged downwards, sideways, upwards. We banged with both hands, with each hand. In fact we banged everyway there was and gradually I could see Robert begin to loosen up a little and use some of the movements we learned in his lessons during the rest of the day. Each lesson had variety as he placed beakers inside each other, moved 'soldiers' in and out of boats and began some simple matching games.

In the afternoons we would sometimes have a second lesson, sometimes constructive play around the house, or in one of the nearby parks.

Robert was now nearly two and a half years old; I had been working with him for six months and saw good progress. I had decided about eight months before that what he needed was a brother or sister and what I needed was a normal baby. Beside which Robert was almost cured – or so I thought!

The park

I was about eight months' pregnant and feeling fine. Rob and I had had a good morning lesson. We munched our way through lunch. He would eat his way through everything that came his way on a spoon but never attempt to reach out and grab it or grasp his cup. I decided to take him out to a new park in Knutsford, which was a short 15 minutes away by car through the Cheshire farmland. When we got there I let Robert run around for about five minutes and then sat him on my knee as I sat on a swing and sang him his favourite lullabies. He loved to have his hair stroked while I sang to him and would lie like that happy for hours if I had the time. So here we were. It was a beautiful day, blue skies and June warmth. Feeling very close and at one with Robert after a while I set him down on the ground and watched him from the swing as he made his way slowly to the slide. There were a few other older children in the park, playing ball and chasing after each other.

Rob got to the bottom step of the 13ft slide and began to climb. He was a sturdy little fellow, and now enjoyed climbing and sliding. I watched him out of the corner of my eye.

When he was about four steps from the top of the slide my body jerked itself awake. I was on my feet and running the short distance to the slide. Why, I do not know – it was as if I was being pulled there. Robert was climbing the second to the top step as I began running up the bottom steps. He reached the top step, stood for a fraction of a second and then his body went rigid and he fell backwards.

I was about two steps behind and caught his unusually heavy body as it was beginning to fall. As I carried him back down the steps and laid him on the concrete floor I watched in horror as his little body jerked and twitched. This was the longest minute of my life. There was nothing I could do except wait until the convulsions stopped. I then picked up the dead weight of my son and slowly carried him back to the car, laid him gently down on the back seat and drove, trance like, home.

I called the doctor and told him what had happened. He said that I had done all the right things, that it sounded like an epileptic attack and that Rob would sleep it off in an hour or two. Meanwhile he would make an appointment for me to see the neurologist.

The neurologist again (2 years 4 months)

We had been waiting in a corridor for over one hour to see the neurologist and I was getting angry. Robert was running up and down the long hallway, running his little car along the walls and making screeching noises. He was nearly two and a half years old, as cute as a button with blonde curly locks. He still could not speak a word but could hum all five of the Brandenburg Concertos with absolute pitch and perfect rhythm. He was so sensitive to music that Beethoven's pastoral storm would terrify him and reduce him to tears. Speech however totally eluded him although he was beginning to understand some words. Through music I would teach him sounds – we would sing all day long. Instead of words I would use sounds, sometimes 'mmmmmmmmmm' or 'dadadadada' – anything and everything. I wanted to make sure that when he was ready to vocalize he would be able to make the sounds.

We were ushered into a small cubicle of a room and I told the neurologist of Robert's symptoms on the day of the slide incident.

He gave him the usual examination, tested for reflexes, and prescribed the drug Epanutin. He also ordered CT scans which thankfully proved normal.

We discussed at length the dosage Robert would be on and we agreed on a minimum dose – just enough to control the fits, not enough to cause him harmful side effects or slow him down.

I always was thankful for Robert's high energy level and felt that if I could in some way tap into it I would be able to help him use it for his own growth. So

I was really protective of his source of strength and did not want him to be overly sedated. I decided not to tell anyone about his fits as I felt most people would be overprotective of him and I wanted him to be able to experience everything. This was to backfire on me once he started school, but we will come to that later.

A baby girl

Soon after we saw the neurologist, Debbie, our daughter was born. She was lusty, impatient to start life and caused quite a scene by arriving on the trolley, in the corridor on the way to the delivery room.

Of course I had her checked out in all the ways there were and more again. Everyone assured me she was perfect and so we brought her home one July night. We bought Rob a bright yellow digger bulldozer which he still has and prayed that he might one day notice this new bundle of joy that had entered our lives.

I gave myself seven days' holiday while I rested, fed and enjoyed my daughter. Then on the eighth day it was back to work as usual as Robert and I started back on our schedule of effortful and carefully thought out Waldon Lessons.

He was just now beginning to make words – and it was oh so tempting to keep asking him questions, encouraging him to talk back. However his speech did not progress this way. When we asked him a question such as: 'Where is your shoe?' the reply would be an echo back: 'Where is your shoe?' This became both frustrating and bewildering. But if I gave him an action that required no speech: 'Point to your shoe' he could readily do it.

The fire engine

Geoffrey explained that the time was not right for talking; I must build up his vocabulary of understanding, yet encourage him to babble and sing sounds until he was ready for words. So we pointed, we touched and we bought a little red wooden fire engine that became Robert's teacher of language. It had four little wooden men who sat on bright yellow seats. Sitting at his lesson table first we would take out the men, wait, pick them up one at a time and put them back in their seats. We could take off the wheels and put them into beakers. Robert and I learnt about axles, chassis, steering wheels, nuts and bolts. Everything could be dismantled. It seems odd now, but not at the time, that he was learning technical words instead of baby words. We learnt by undoing and doing, and his language understanding was enriched by putting pieces in, under, above, in front of, behind, next to, etc. etc ... My days would be spent trying to introduce new words, new ideas and concepts through this simple toy.

Colours were discovered, yellow wheels, red axles, blue bolts all served their purpose. Quantities were explored – oneness, twoness, threeness, etc. I gave instructions like: 'Put three wheels into the beaker which is under the table' and would help him perform the task with my hand over his. But there was still little if any speech.

Robert was approaching three; 'time for playgroup', I thought. Perhaps if he was around normal kids he would pick up social behaviour.

Walter

The Centre for Educating the Young Handicapped Child at Home
(2 years 6 months)

One Thursday, Geoff told us that he worked directly for the audiology department and that the professor had decided that Geoff's work in child development was outside the department's remit.

Geoffrey resigned from the department and opened The Centre for Educating the Young Handicapped Child at Home in a large house in Didsbury. A small charity was set up and money was raised to support the centre.

His wife Bee Bee was headmistress of a local primary school and had worked with Geoff in the development of what came to be called the Waldon Approach. She was prepared to support his work and research as he left the security of the university and entered into the uncertain world of private practice.

So it was in this house that Geoff had his study. It was a large detached Victorian house. You entered down a path through the front and main garden, up a couple of steps and into a large and quite gloomy hall. On the right was the study/teaching room and behind it a small waiting room. This had a one-way mirror, which could be used by visiting teachers and students to observe the sessions. Otherwise it was covered by a black velvet curtain. The study was brightly coloured, crammed with shelves and boxes with a ladder to reach the higher shelves and various wooden apparatus for the children to use as necessary and as directed. At the centre of the room was the table, about three feet square with on one side a chair for the child and behind that a chair for Uncle Geoff as we had come to call him.

The Waldon Lesson

I remember the first. It was a lesson in banging. Afterwards Geoff explained – and more about his explanations later – that if you observed a baby, once it could sit, the first arm movement it made was to bang. It would bang its hand on the table; a spoon on the table; anything on anything; but banging came first and from the action of banging, all the other arm and hand movements flowed and these were both normal and indispensable in a child's development. Without the banging the development of the normal range of movements would be awkward, and a vital link in development would be missed. The result could be catastrophic for the child's understanding and could lead to the development of a range of compensatory avoidance and self-handicapping behaviours.

So bang Robert did. I had a white wooden table built at the factory, bought a child's chair and we set up a parallel workshop in Robert's bedroom. Here Pamela would give Robert his lesson for an hour, often two hours a day, repeating what Geoff had done in his lesson the previous week.

Geoffrey Waldon had not entered this field by accident. Trained as a neurologist he had decided to make a special study of child development. His nature was detailed and obsessive in pursuing every line of thought down every possible avenue. So our problem was in understanding the theory behind his actions. But the difficulty was that if a question was asked the reply might take five or more minutes before every avenue or facet or sub-clause or sub-category of the reply was exhausted, leaving us more confused than when we started. So each week after the lesson we would discuss and try to remember and understand both the instructions and the explanations for the following week.

Pamela's dedication

In giving the lessons Pamela was concentrated, determined and full of strength. No matter that she was feeding Debbie, she settled down each day to give Robert his lesson while I went to work. It was Pamela who gave single-mindedly of her physical and emotional strength to drive Robert through the programme. She was absolutely determined to bring Robert back to normalcy and at the same time determined that Debbie would not fall into the same pattern. So after Robert had had his lesson Pamela would give Debbie her own Waldon type lessons until she was absolutely certain that Debbie was well launched onto a normal pathway.

There was yet another problem, and one faced by all parents of special needs children. In a nutshell, we tried and I think succeeded in giving Debbie more attention than any normal child would receive. But this could never be as much as Robert received. So naturally and, I think inevitably, Debbie would always, if only subconsciously, feel that she did not get her share. So the circumstances affected the whole family both as a unit and as individuals.

For Pamela and me there was this deep feeling of despair, of sadness and alienation from the community in which we lived. Many of our friends with young children of Robert's age treated him, and us, as though he had some infectious disease so that the normal friendships and play dates developed at school with parents of other children failed to develop. We were very isolated.

Memories of Robert when young

The Manchester Evening News (2 years 7 months)

On Thursday 11 November 1971 the *Manchester Evening News* published the following article by Peter Harris, their medical correspondent, to mark the first birthday of the Manchester branch of the National Society of Autistic Children. 'Here', they wrote, 'our medical correspondent takes a look at a new form of treatment which is helping these children as well as children with other medical and physical handicaps'.

Nursery at Doctor Waldon's

Robert is a sturdy curly haired three-year-old who looks as though he might have stepped out of a Gainsborough canvas. He is physically strong and healthy. He lives in a privileged home in Cheshire. He knows all the comforts that intelligent, well-to-do parents can offer. He is also autistic.

His mental development age is at least 12 months behind his years and he behaves and reacts like a child of two. But in Robert's case, unlike that of many other autistic or withdrawn children, that gap is slowly being bridged.

Very gradually his mental age is catching up with what would be the accepted norm for his years and by the time he is five or six there is every chance that he will be able to take his place in a normal school.

It is being achieved by a Manchester doctor who has abandoned all the basic concepts of his particular discipline to practise privately what is an entirely new approach to the treatment of handicapped children.

His name is Dr Geoffrey Waldon and until recently he was working in orthodox medical circles at the Manchester University Department of Audiology. He works now from a modest consulting room in Palatine Road, Didsbury. Robert is just one of a small but representative handful of handicapped youngsters whom he lists among his current patients.

'Handicap', he says, 'implies that a significant part of a child's time and energy is continually consumed by activities which tend to meliorate his sense of emotional discomfort. The presence of this reserve [of time and energy] means that the child who is "handicapped" must always be potentially able to do a bit better'.

A trust has been formed to promote Dr Waldon's techniques and eventually to set up a school where [children] can be taught under his supervision.

Here are some excerpts from recently recorded conversations with family and friends which give a few snapshots of their memories of this time.

Bruce and Janet remember

We always felt welcome in Bruce and Hannah's house. Here is a transcript of a recent conversation with Bruce and his daughter Janet. Hannah had sadly died young of ovarian cancer.[18]

Bruce:	Robert had a whale of a time pulling all the toys out of the cupboards and spreading them all over the floor. I remember how he would scream at certain things and lose patience.
Janet:	When he got involved with something or started playing with a toy he got very focused on it. He was like a dog with a bone and would not give it up. He would do his own thing but with us around.
Bruce:	He was obsessed with the fan in the washroom and he used to spend ages watching it spinning and switching it on and off.

My sister Gillian remembers

He was staying with us at about 15 months old. He was in a playpen in our parents' garden with his back to me and I did what I often do with children, and said BOO! I remember very clearly that he just did not react.[19]

When he came into our house he would immediately go to the garage and for no apparent reason he would just sit and stare at the freezer. Then he would flush all the loos and unwind all the toilet rolls.

He also used to collect the keys from all over the house and every key would disappear. We had a small upright piano and at quite a young age Robert would sit at it and play by ear. And that was remarkable. I remember tantrums; I remember the need for instant gratification. I can remember at meal times at our parents' house he would tantrum for whatever he wanted.

He was very late in personalizing himself and to differentiate between things and people. He could always remember all the details of a journey especially any unusual bridges.

Cousin Hilary remembers

I remember this gorgeous little boy who sat on the floor who never had any eye contact with you, who looked at the ceiling almost permanently, who rocked himself to and fro. I tried to play with him but he showed no interest. I just remember him sitting a lot. He was like that for years – never looking at you in the face or the eyes.[20]

He was totally obsessed with keys and locks and would not sit down at the table and would spend the whole evening going round the house with a bunch of keys. He was not interested in us at all. Nothing changed for a long time – he was just remote and withdrawn.

Neighbour Valerie remembers

He had a fantastic love of music, even at an early age he used to rock backwards and forwards in time to the music and he really seemed to have a gift for it. I don't remember him speaking but I do remember that when he got annoyed he would bang his head against a wall in frustration.[21]

Grandma Ella and Uncle Stephen remember

Stephen: He was very remote. He was in a world of his own. And it was hard to get him out of this world unless you moved to something he was interested in such as his obsessions – cars or fridges.[22]

Ella: I remember his tantrums when Pamela and I used to go out on a Tuesday afternoon and when we got tired and returned towards home, as soon as he saw the church on the corner he would have a tantrum. He had to go home but he did not want to go home but to be pushed around more and look at things. He let us know by screaming and shouting.

Stephen: Once at meal time Pamela was upstairs with Robert wanting to give him a lesson. She would not start until he sat down and he would not sit down. It would take her perhaps half an hour. But Pamela would not give in and the lesson would not start until he sat down. I remember we left but Pamela had the patience to wait and the determination to enforce her will. It was on her terms and he was not free to do what he wanted until he had done whatever it was that she wanted. He learnt the rules, whether he liked it or not.

Heather Rawlins (a Norland Nurse) remembers

Pamela told me how difficult life had been when Robert was younger.[23] She would avoid taking him to friends' houses because she would never know what he might do next and this left her feeling very isolated. She described it taking all morning for him to dress himself. This was part of Uncle Geoff's programme and she had to carry it through. [Author's note: see discussion of continuant behaviour in Chapter 5.] She told me about the tantrums he would have. By the time I arrived Robert was at school all day and doing well. I don't remember his having any friends.

I remember Debbie with Robert and she was very good. You were always worried about Debbie because Pamela especially, was devoting so much time to Robert that you were afraid that it would affect Debbie. And I think she felt guilty about that but I never had any issues with Debbie being jealous of Robert at all. She reacted with him just normally. [Author's note: Debbie now says that it was never an issue for her but it was always an issue for us.]

I remember his keys. There were lots of keys on a ring. They were quite heavy. He carried them in his pocket and they went everywhere with him. At night he slept with them under his pillow.

Heather has found an old exercise book of Robert's from that time. He wrote over two entries:

Heather is going to look after me she is very kind woman. She reads me stories. She does not shout at me. She is very nice and good and she has got blonde hair. Danielle has come to school again on Saturday and Heather is going to look after me she is very nice and she is very good and clever to-day she is beautiful and pretty it is nearly my birthday I am nearly 8 years old.

2

School Years 1972–1987

'I am going to rat you round your head in a minute!' (Robert)

This takes Robert from his first nursery school at age three, into the special needs system and eventually into mainstream education at age seven. Waldon Lessons continued up to age 11, combined for three years with psychotherapy by Frances Tustin. We moved to the USA at age 12 where he entered the county education system and graduated from high school at age 18.

Robert's schooling in the early years

Church nursery school (3 years old)

My first 'school' memory for Robert is of a local church nursery school, which he attended from March to December 1971. It took children from the age of two to five. We informed the headmaster about Robert's problems and he said that he could cope. So Robert started mornings only school in March 1971 when he was three. Pamela continued with his Waldon Lessons in the afternoon.

Robert was now into the second year of his Waldon Lessons and was much calmer and more controllable. He was beginning to talk, certainly by age three he knew us and every time we visited one of the paediatricians we expected to be told: 'That's it – he's cured'! We still had no concept of the immense amount of work that would be needed to bring him to normality.

It was December 1971 and Pamela was walking down the path with Robert at the end of the school day, after nearly nine months there. The vicar/headmaster came quietly up to her as she was walking home, and said: 'I am sorry Mrs Solomon, but there will not be a place in the school for Robert next term'. Pamela came home in tears – all the work she was doing and this was the support from the local community.

Synagogue nursery school (3 years 9 months)

More enquiries, more visits to schools, and we settled on the nursery school attached to our synagogue. It was a 45-minute round trip twice a day but well worth the effort. Robert was there from January 1972 to July 1973, but all was not smooth running. This was the time that he was having fits although they were well controlled by the Epanutin. In June 1972 (Robert aged four years), the Paediatric Neurologist noted: [1] 'I was glad to hear that he had been free of all attacks and was making such obvious progress with the help of Dr Waldon'. But for some reason he had a fit out of the blue at school. We had earlier decided not to tell anyone about this particular problem and so had not warned them in advance.

Sheila Bernstein (his head teacher) remembers

Robert was a challenge for us. I had never trained in 'special needs' and I don't think that at that time there was very much around for people to learn. Children were either accepted locally or they were institutionalized or kept at home and people did not talk about it.[2]

Because we were a synagogue-based nursery I felt very strongly that we were there to serve our community and there was no reason why we couldn't bring children with difficulties into the group alongside other children.

We were very lucky with Robert because Pamela was a really hands-on mother. Because of her work with Dr Waldon, she wanted to know exactly what we were doing or how we hoped to deal with things and she also came with her own suggestions. We did not do anything specifically different for Robert but we learnt how to cope with his moods and we had enough staff on hand that when we felt it was needed Robert could be on a one-to-one with a teacher so that the group was not disturbed.

Pamela gave us lots of tools that not only helped with Robert but with other children as well. We had other children who needed help socially and getting on with other children, which is what a nursery is for. So we used some of the Waldon tools for other children.

I will never forget the epileptic fit incident. Robert went into a very deep sleep, almost like a coma, and I really thought he had died. Then as we were calling for an ambulance I saw Pamela arrive. I ran out and she saw my face and she knew what had happened and gasped 'I forgot to give him his medicine this morning'. She had a little giggle and I thought: 'I would like to strangle you guys'! It was a very frightening experience for all of us.

I do believe that in our own small way we helped prepare Robert for the next step and I am not so sure that it would have worked so well for him and for us without all of Pamela's help and suggestions.

The fit was sadly the cue for some parents to organize a petition against Robert's continued admission at the school. When we heard about this Pamela went to see the communal Rabbi, and in tears she asked for his support. He told her: 'This was an "Act of God", outside his province and there was nothing he could do'.

Not a comforting word, not a warm arm round her shoulder; but fortunately Sheila rejected the petition. Her final report from the synagogue nursery stated: [3]

> Robert has made tremendous progress since he first entered the nursery. He accepts the presence of the other children now, and acts as one of the group more readily. He still has plenty of problems; one being that he gets terribly upset when chastised.
>
> His group work is very good, the only drawback being the need to hold his attention all the time; this leaves little time for the other children. He is not yet ready to take part in formal work with a fixed group – he seems more suited to an open plan atmosphere where some element of choice of activity can be maintained. He doesn't like change of routine or staff – he will take time to settle at his new school – but will continue, I am sure, to progress.

The local education authority (5 years)

Robert was coming up to five and now the local education authority was taking an interest in his schooling. The educational psychologist initially recommended a unit attached to the children's hospital for Robert but we did not want him to go into the special school environment, believing that once in, there would be no escape. We discussed educating him at home where he could have both his Waldon Lessons and Pamela, as a trained and registered teacher, could also take care of his early school learning.

Next we were notified of a vacancy arising in an infant unit, with the educational psychologist writing: 'The question of home tuition does not arise in Robert's case, since it is considered that he would benefit from full time school attendance'. He was determined that we accept a place at this unit and in the letter inviting us for a visit he added: 'but I must insist that this is done by arrangement, so that I can accompany you'.[4]

County infant school (5 years 6 months)

This was part of a new concept in special education where a 'special needs' class would be in the same building as a mainstream primary school and the 'special needs' children could be integrated with the normal children for certain activities. They would gradually come to be fully integrated in mainstream education. It was a good story, well explained, but in the event it was a pipe dream – at least for this child in this particular school.

Robert attended from September 1973 to July 1975 (aged 5 ½ to 7 ¼ yrs.). From the outset Pamela and I decided that we would restrain ourselves from being 'pushy parents'. We would be laid back, non-interfering and would let the experts get on with what they officially knew best. He was picked up from home every morning and brought back in the evening in good time for a Waldon Lesson from Pamela. We went regularly for parents' evenings and were shown all the nursery equipment and reassured as to how well he was doing.

During these two years Pamela was giving Robert his daily lessons and teaching him to read and to do elementary number work. And he did clearly improve in all areas. His understanding grew and with that his speech was developing well. His avoidance behaviours were diminishing. He still had his obsessions, had no friends and no after school play dates. He remained difficult to take to restaurants, because he would wander off to 'explore', would disturb other diners and still had his habit of taking off the tops of the pepper and salt pourers and making his own melange. But both he and we were learning to cope.

At a school meeting in June 1974 we were discussing Robert, his progress with Dr Waldon, his ability to read (which surprisingly his teachers had not noticed), and suggested that the next year perhaps they could start to integrate him into a normal class. The headmistress responded that they did not think Robert was ready to be integrated into a normal class and, disappointingly, it was not possible for anyone from the school to visit Dr Waldon.[5] We had no alternative but to leave him there for the following year.

Recommendation for school for children with severe and complex needs!
Just before the end of the summer term we were notified by the school that as he was going to be too old for the next year, they had us taken him to a school for children with severe and complex needs, and that was to be his placement for the next year. They not only took him there without informing us but clearly were unaware of all the things that Robert could actually do. So we decided to find a private school which would accept him as we felt this would be the only possibility of his being able to enjoy any kind of normal independent life in the future.

Preparatory school

'Dad, I didn't know before that school was for learning!'

We were very fortunate to be able to find a small local private school which accepted Robert and which assigned him to the class of one of their most gifted teachers, Mrs Beressi.

The first day (7 years 5 months)

Robert started in September 1975 and I will let Mrs Beressi take up the narrative: [6]

J.B.   On his first day when he came into the class I said: 'I am Mrs Beressi'. 'Oh' he said looking me up and down. 'Yes', I said, 'I am Mrs Beressi and you sit there please'. He said: 'Alright', came in, sat down, looked around at everybody else and I said: 'Robert would you like to come and read to me?' He said: 'No, I can't read'. I said: 'Robert would you please come here. I know you can read because you already told me you can read'. 'No I can't'!

I thought: 'He is going to be difficult' so I said to this little girl: 'Please go and get the first reading book from the nursery class because this boy says he can't read'. She brought the book and I said: 'Robert go to the first page. This is a Rrrrrrrr we get the phonetical sound first. This is a Rrrrrrrrrr'. He said: 'Rrrrrrrrrrrrr'. I said: 'Rrrrr Aaaa Tttt – would you say that to me?' He looked at me and said: 'Rrrr Aaaa Tttt – I am going to rat you round your head in a minute'! I said 'Pardon?'. He said: 'Yes – I'll rat you round your head in a minute'. Well I said: '*How dare you*. Don't you ever do that to me again. NOW READ. From your own book that I've given you – *properly* – never mind RAT or any other – READ'. Well, he took the book and he read.

W.S.   Picking Robert up that first day is imprinted on my memory. I came to the school and he came out and I asked him: 'How was school?' And he said, and I will never forget this, he said: *'Dad, I didn't know before that school was for learning!'*

J.B.   Next day I said: 'Good Morning Robert'. He asked: 'Can I go back to my place?' 'No', I said: 'I have really got used to you sitting next to me. Please sit here'; and that was when we really began to have a friendship. I didn't go too quickly and by the end of the month he was giving out the books and he grew. He must have grown about two inches in that time. I was relying on him. He was really settled in and when you came to see me and asked: 'Are you going to keep him?' I said: 'Of course'. He was intelligent. He really was.

Once or twice when he came back from Dr Waldon he was very upset. On one particular day he came in obviously very frustrated as if he had not been able to do something and he said: 'I don't like Uncle Geoff. I am *not* going back to Uncle Geoff'. So I said: 'Come and have a hug first', so he had a hug and I asked: 'Are you better?' He said: 'Yes – but I'm still not going to Uncle Geoff'. I said: 'But he is really nice. Let's have another hug' and we had another hug and he said: 'I'm all right now'. But he was so adamant.

He had an excellent end of term report from the school summed up as follows: 'Robert has settled down in the class extremely well and always does work of a high standard. He has made excellent progress'. We were overjoyed. This was the end of our problems. A school report any parent would be proud of.[7]

Two years later at the end of Summer Term 1977 his new form mistress reported: 'Robert is well behaved in class. He tries very hard with his work and is making steady progress. Robert's sociability is improving as he matures'.[8] An undated special school report from about that time says revealingly:

He usually plays on his own at play-time but he generally brings something mechanical to play with e.g. a car or propeller. He never joins in the football either on the Games Field or in the play-ground. The only child he chooses to play with in the play-ground is his sister.

Robert does not bother the children by playing with their hair anymore. He gets very annoyed when others touch his things, especially his case. He doesn't talk a great deal to others but he talks to himself and he seems happier this way. He does share well, e.g. the class crayons and equipment and he sometimes borrows from the other children. He has not a special friend but there are some children he seems not to like i.e. one or two of the younger ones. He derives great satisfaction from his piano lessons.[9]

He loved to play the piano and one report from his piano teacher said: 'Robert is very gifted'.[10] He had always related to music and as mentioned earlier he could hum the Brandenburg Concerti before he could speak. He had perfect pitch and it was sad that for personal reasons his teacher had to give up in April 1978.

Passing the eleven plus exam – what joy! (11 years)

By the spring term 1978 Robert was aged 10 years in a class of which the average age was 9 years 9 months. The head teacher and now his form mistress, reported:

> Robert has settled into the form quite happily although he finds it hard to accept the discipline of 'listen, think and then apply' after the less exacting approach of 'watch and do'. I feel he is beginning to come to terms with being treated as one of a group.[11]

Socially, however, he remained very isolated. He talked to himself for years (and still does), hated anything competitive, and was always happier with things rather than with people. At our urging he joined the local scout group, but without much enthusiasm or active participation.

In his last year at this school he did make friends with Anthony. We would quite often pick up Anthony and bring him back to our house.

Robert was now coming up to age 11. He sat his 11+ exam and passed both for entry into the state grammar school for boys and a private grammar school. We were overjoyed at his success. This was the first time that he had achieved an entry into a school on his own merit and not by parental persuasion. Not just one, but two schools of an excellent standard.

We rang our parents and our close family to tell them the news, but when we came to friends who would be excited for us the list was overwhelmingly short. We were part of the community, but in reality we were isolated, on our own.

We chose the private boys' grammar school, and he started there in September 1979.

Grammar school (11 years 5 months)

The grammar school was a great success. Again his first report was excellent and the headmaster summed up: 'A very pleasing first term. He has settled down well and his work shows a good deal of promise'.[12]

Off to the USA August 1980 (12 years 4 months)

Robert only spent one year at the grammar school before we moved to the United States. He made friends there but only superficially. I remember one boy, James, tapping his glasses and asking: 'Is there anyone at home?' He went there and back on the bus, was liked by the masters, did well in his exams and came 16th in a class of 26. The headmaster said in his end of year report: 'He has had an extremely good first year in the school. We have enjoyed having him here, and we are truly sorry to be losing him so soon'.[13]

Frances Tustin and psychotherapy 1976–1979

During 1975 Pamela had come across a book called: *Dibs: in Search of Self.* This true story, written by Dibs' therapist, Virginia Axline, is about an autistic boy who through psychotherapy found his way to a school for gifted children. Through that work he found and developed his true self, having previously been described by his paediatrician as: 'a strange one, who knows? Mentally retarded? Psychotic? Brain-damaged?'[14]

We found this story both inspirational and deeply encouraging. We had always known that Robert would 'get better', that one day he would be 'normal', that is, like other children; but this knowledge was like faith – lacking proof or rationality. With Dibs we had evidence that recovery was possible and it made a deep impression on us both.

Robert was then six years old, in his second year in the special needs class at primary school, speaking a little and reading a little. However he was still highly dependent on his obsessions. He had a large wire key chain with about 50 keys on it, and he carried this with him wherever he went. He still flushed every toilet when he visited other houses, and remained uncomfortable and isolated within his peer group. He had no friends at all.

But he was doing well and had improved immensely after four years of Waldon Lessons. These had given us a boy with developing General Understanding, but he was still very different from other children of his age. We thought that perhaps he could be helped socially and emotionally by a course of psychotherapy which might be adjunctive to the Waldon Approach Lessons which Pamela continued giving to Robert when he came home from school.

Pamela researched psychotherapy and autism and came across the name of Frances Tustin who had practised at the Tavistock Clinic[15] in London. We found that she had retired from the Tavistock, was living in Buckinghamshire and was a leading UK authority on psychotherapy with the autistic child. We duly made an appointment to see her and drove down to Lee Common, a tiny Buckinghamshire village not far from Great Missenden.

Mrs Tustin invited us in, heard our story, and started to explain that she was in retirement and that although she was still seeing children she had decided not to take on any new patients. However she had a student whom she recommended highly and promised to arrange for Robert to be seen by her.

However, with some considerable persuasion we eventually convinced Mrs Tustin to take on Robert herself and left quickly before she could change her mind. We were once again on a journey – both literal and metaphoric. We would travel from Hale to Lee Common every weekend for the next three years.

Mrs Tustin lived in an old cottage with a swimming pool at the front, and to the side a brick built shed with a stable door which was set up as her therapy room. Arriving for our first session, she welcomed us, said: 'Hello' to Robert, directed him into the therapy room and asked us to come back in an hour. We had Debbie with us and did not know what to do but fortunately found a pub in the village which allowed children in with their parents. Over the next months and years we spent many hours in that pub, reading, talking and getting to know the locals.

We arranged to come every weekend for two sessions, one on Saturday and one on Sunday. We bought a caravan and found a friendly farmer close to Lee Common who allowed us not only to leave the caravan in one of his fields but to use the farm as a huge play space. That worked extremely well. There was a large hay barn in which the children played endlessly, we could cook our own food and generally use the caravan as a base from which to explore the local area. So we went for walks, often went to the swimming pool in Aylesbury, found lots of pubs for lunch, and even, in 1977, joined in the local village Queen's Silver Jubilee celebrations.

Tustin worked under the rules of patient confidentiality and would never divulge what happened between her and Robert. Robert would just tell us that he 'played with animals' or he 'drew pictures'. He always went into the sessions willingly and came out quite normally so he was obviously not in any way upset or alarmed by whatever was happening. We did have occasional meetings with Mrs Tustin when her husband, a retired professor of engineering, would entertain the children – even giving them the rare privilege of a dip in the pool. At these we would discuss his progress.

Tustin devotes most of Chapter 16 'Thinkings' in her book, *Autistic States in Children* (1981), to Robert, and the whole of Chapter 17: 'The struggles of a psychotic child to develop a mind of his own', is about her sessions with him. There are also many references to him in earlier chapters.[16]

One thing was certain: he gradually gave up his dependence on the key ring, which Tustin refers to as his 'Autistic Object'. Asking Robert today about the keys which he still keeps as a souvenir from his autistic days he agrees that they made him feel like a grown up. He does not accept Tustin's deeper and more psychological explanations. However this does not invalidate them. The story of Robert and the yellow daisy may illustrate this point.

A psychotic child called Robert, as he left the therapy room, pointed to a tall yellow daisy and said: 'I'm inside that flower – it's the yellowness I'm inside.'

He was at a loss to explain his experience any further. His whole body was taut with heightened responsiveness, the pupils of his eyes were dilated and his eyes shone with preternatural brightness.

I talked with him about this experience in a quiet, non-intrusive way. I said that perhaps he felt bathed in the yellowness. I said that perhaps he felt that it was a beautiful feeling and so the gap between himself and myself did not feel so sharp and frightening. Perhaps he felt that beautiful things could be around him and go in through his holes, rather than the ugly and frightening things he sometimes felt were there. I also said that perhaps he wanted to go inside me to feel safe because it was frightening to feel that there was a gap between his body and mine. As I talked his whole body relaxed, his pupils stopped being dilated and suddenly he said: 'I'm ready to go home now'.

I do not pretend that what I said interpreted the whole of his experience, but it helped. It is a great comfort to me that much goes on in the therapeutic situation of which I am not aware. I understood enough for Robert to feel that I was in touch with him and that he could come back to an ordinary state of awareness and find me waiting for him. (Tustin, 1981, pp 140–1)

Tustin reported:

I had the following conversation with Robert, it was two years since he had begun to talk and he was in his third and last year of treatment and he was grumbling about some nasty thing which had happened to him, so I said, 'You've got to learn to take the rough with the smooth, haven't you?' To which he replied, 'Would that mean to be reconciled to it?' When I said, 'Yes', he said, 'We had that word in spellings the other day and I thought about what we had talked about here'. (p 176)

Altogether Robert saw Tustin for three years having two sessions a week.

Dr Sheila Spensley, a retired NHS Consultant Clinical Psychologist and specialist in psychoanalytic psychotherapy, who trained at the Tavistock Clinic both as a clinical psychologist and a child psychotherapist, wrote about Frances Tustin's life and work. Spensley devoted one chapter of this book to Robert: 'The Keeper of the Keys'.[17] She writes that she had seen the clinical material relating to Robert in Tustin's book and has drawn on this as well as other published sources and supplemented the whole with observations based on her clinical conversations with Tustin. She also notes that she had privileged access to Robert's treatment records. Spensley reported that Tustin began with a child who gave little indication of being interested in anything she had to say. He hardly spoke in the early sessions and she was faced with the problem of engaging his attention and, literally, of making her presence felt. Robert, like many autistic children, totally ignored the therapist and Tustin describes: 'feeling as if she did not exist in Robert's eyes. His averted gaze and his concentration on his keys, examining them and counting them, was capable of extinguishing her as a live object in the room and this drew immediate attention to her primary task which was to find ways of making her presence felt'. (Spensley, 1995, p. 77)

How the therapy actually worked was not absolutely clear to Frances Tustin but as her approach succeeded with other autistic children she continued with this method. We have seen above Tustin being thankful that changes occur without her quite knowing why and notes that: 'She is rewarded one day, three months into treatment, when he moved on from handling and fingering the keys to using them like a template to draw around. It was a significant for Robert to start to use the keys as representable on paper by their outline'. (Spensley, 1995, p.78)

In considering the relative places of the Waldon Approach and the Tustin psychotherapy in Robert's recovery I am sure that Robert's progress would not have been achieved without the Waldon Lessons but that the adjunctive psychotherapy had an important place in his development. It helped him to drop his obsessions and to better relate to his feelings. Perhaps also she was instrumental in helping him to resolve his internal 'me – not me' conflicts. Dr Chris Holland, who knew Frances Tustin from the world of psychoanalysis, remembers Tustin saying that she did not think she could have worked with Robert if he had not first worked with Geoffrey Waldon and his method.[18]

Frances Tustin and Geoffrey Waldon

Frances Tustin in her book (1981: 221) described the work of Geoffrey Waldon in the single sentence: 'Prior to coming to see me, Robert had had some cognitive therapy'. In fact when Robert first went to see her, Waldon had already been seeing him for over four years. Waldon in his turn was doubtful about psychotherapy believing that his own approach would solve all the problems.

However, Frances Tustin contributed a warm piece about Geoffrey Waldon and his work in an issue of *Koine* – the magazine of The Waldon Association (June 1992):

I first met Geoffrey Waldon as the result of my taking into psychotherapy a six year old autistic boy who lived in Manchester. Robert had been taking part in Dr Waldon's cognitive learning programme and had been helped by it, but his insightful Jewish parents felt that he also needed help with his feelings so they brought him to me.

Dr Waldon was good enough to come down from Manchester to meet me in the cottage in which I lived in a remote corner of Buckinghamshire. Dr Waldon conceived of his work as being based on engineering concepts, and so he was very interested to meet my electrical engineer husband. As for me he was quite willing that Robert should have psychotherapy but he did not seem to be much interested in it. However his cognitive work with Robert never interfered with my psychotherapeutic work with him. Indeed 'Uncle Geoff', as they called him, helped it to proceed in that he gave the mother and father commonsense advice, particularly encouraging them to be firmer with Robert and to set limits.

After a time I introduced Dr Waldon to Dr George Stroh who was then the Psychiatrist-in-Charge of High Wick Hospital for Psychotic Children and the two of them embarked on collaborating over a book about Functional Learning. Unfortunately this project did not come to pass due to Dr Stroh's sad death. But Functional Learning, as Stroh called his adaptation of Waldon's cognitive methods, became an important part of the programme at High Wick Hospital. Dr Stroh's widow, Mrs Katrin Stroh, continues to be influenced by Dr Waldon's ideas in her private work with disturbed children. It is also used in the Chinnor Unit for Autistic Children.

Waldon was a unique and original individual whose pioneering work has had an important influence on the method of others, particularly those workers concerned with autistic children. Like such children he was a loner. Perhaps if George Stroh had lived and he and Geoffrey had collaborated over a book ....[19]

Richard Brooks, an educational psychologist in Oxfordshire, recalls going to a lecture by Waldon together with Anne Alvarez, a lecturer on childhood autism at the Tavistock Clinic and a student of Frances Tustin, sometime in the 1970s. At a later date Alvarez said to him that she: 'had changed her approach to the treatment of autistic children having heard Waldon speak'. Alvarez has since confirmed this comment to me.[20]

In August 1980, leaving behind Geoffrey Waldon and his lessons, Frances Tustin and her therapy, the grammar school with its traditional rigour and our families and friends, we moved to the USA. Amongst many reasons for going was our belief that even a fully recovered and 'normal' Robert would never be accepted within the community in which we lived.

Robert's Barmitzvah and the USA

But we did go back to Manchester for his Barmitzvah[21] the next spring. In March 1981 Robert would be 13. We had joined a synagogue in Georgetown and asked the Rabbi there what he thought we should do. He recommended that we return to England as that was where all our family and friends lived and so we did.

It was a very special event. Robert sang beautifully, and it was so moving to see him performing, making a speech, and generally being a typical Barmitzvah boy. For me it was an emotional weekend seeing Robert stand up and be counted – like any other 13-year-old Jewish boy.

Progressive School Washington DC (September 1980–December 1980)

It had been a wrench taking Robert out of the grammar school where he was doing so well, but we persuaded ourselves that he would prosper at a progressive school we had found in Washington DC.

Robert's condition and academic level at that time is best described by the following report by Geoffrey Waldon to the Washington school director or headmaster when we were considering placing him there:

Dear Head Master[22]

Robert's basic education has been unusual since unaccountable circumstances put such strains on the form of his early development as to necessitate very particular countermeasures. Robert was in fact what psychiatrists call 'autistic' – delayed both in his general development and more obviously in the realm of social interest – but, thanks largely to the ministrations of his mother, he has developed from an undoubtedly very backward and socially remote child to one who has settled very satisfactorily into a normal school environment of fairly high academic standard.

The nature of Robert's basic difficulty has occasioned his learning the behaviour of others not only tardily but also by way of the more difficult route of reason and interpretation as opposed to the more normal way of a child's being conditioned from an early age to respond 'appropriately'.

His social behaviour continues to approximate more and more closely to the usual and acceptable, but while he is fully capable of becoming a secure social organism in due course, Robert is still oblivious of the more subtle nuances of social intercourse. He certainly recognizes himself as a novice in this respect and sometimes 'opts-out' from attempting to understand.

I have been teacher and adoptive 'uncle' to Rob for nearly ten years and so feel that I am less ignorant about him than most. Should it be agreed between parents and you that Robert goes to your school, I would be very happy to communicate to his teachers my views on his needs and my own attitude to their supply in due course; also the mechanism which has modified his development, perhaps not only negatively.

Yours sincerely

Geoffrey Waldon

Unfortunately this school was a severe disappointment and Robert left after his first term. Illuminating conversations with Robert will form an increasingly large part in the developing story. He was 13 years old, settled in mainstream education at his chronological age level, a lively and contributing member of our family, but still socially isolated from his peers. Robert had come a very long way but there was still a very long way to go.

Robert describes his school experiences from his year at the Grammar School in England followed by his experiences in the USA.[23]

'Uh oh, here comes this storm cloud!'

Walter: I was struck when you said, after reading in one of my chapters how your mother and I felt isolated when people didn't want you in their houses, that this mirrors what you feel today about your life. Could you tell me that again?

Robert: Well, it is because I'm the weirdo. I do admit that is how I come across, because I have been rejected, teased a lot, you know … I have a very intense personality and I get angry easily – and I am not the easiest person to get along with, and I am aware of that. People sense this about me and they say 'Uh oh, here comes this storm cloud!' And they run away from me. And as a result, I have great difficulty participating in the conversations. I am very good at talking one on one with somebody, however I have great difficulty participating in a group and trying to take an interest in what the group is discussing. People didn't really care about me and that is basically the way it goes. It is a pain in the butt! But I've learnt to deal with it, and I don't like social situations very much anyway.

Walter: You said you remember a lot about your last school in Manchester.

Robert: Well I know basically the teachers. I was much better off with the teachers than the students. I remember my beloved headmaster, some of the other boys didn't like him. They called him 'the bin' for some reason and I really got upset because I thought he was a wonderful man, and even at that age, I knew he was, and when everybody put him down, I really was angry. My form master, very nice man – he was tough but he was a good honest Lancastrian kind of guy. One of my favourite teachers was my French master, and I got along famously with him, I really liked him a lot! A sad thing is that here I am in France [the interview is at my French home] and the only French I know is due to him. My geometry master was really nice. I liked him a lot. He was funny and he gave us Mars Bars when we did well.

Now as far as concerns the pupils/students of the school, the boys were not so cool, there were a few nasty ones. One called Nigel who, I didn't know if he actually would beat me up, but he was threatening to do so. I remember asking you to take me to judo classes so I could beat him up. However that didn't last very long and I lost interest in judo. I did do about 4–5–6 classes but then said Naah, I don't want to do the prep, because I do have a lazy streak and it was very difficult for me to commit to practising it.

I basically hung out by myself. I didn't have the pleasure of having Anthony with me. He was my best friend from my previous school. I did hang out with a boy called Justin and another one, Steve – I actually went to his house once – and another guy called

David. The friendship was kind of tentative, and they never missed an opportunity to take the mickey out of me, tease me, or call me silly names like weed, wimp, or something.

I also remember Matthew. He was a nasty guy who always called me a weed, meat-head or spaz because of my nature. I was probably strong enough to beat them up, but I never got into any fights. At the beginning I used to, but every time I got into a fight (the boys would call my fights 'epis'), I don't know why they called them epis – perhaps I was acting like an epileptic – I would punch and lash out blindly in a rage. My opponent would be in control of the fight and know when to counterpunch, wrestle and pin me down properly, and I couldn't get out, so I always lost my fights despite my strength – that was really horrible! Even though I knew deep down I was strong. Because of this, I hated PE and backed out when they wanted me to play soccer [football in England]. I am glad they didn't make me play American football or rugby!

However soccer is tough – you have to learn how to control that ball and I couldn't for the life of me control that stupid ball. The other kids did 'footies' and managed to keep the ball in the air ... I really had zero control over that football, I couldn't do anything. When in those extremely rare situations I actually got the ball, I blindly kicked it because I didn't like all those other boys ganging up on me! So basically during PE, I just walked off and la la la'ed and avoided the games master, because the last thing I wanted was to be in a game. Many years later in America, I tried to redeem myself by joining a soccer team. Let's put it quickly, it didn't work out and I quit because it was just too painful.

It was the same with all team sports. I hated basketball, hockey, I hated them all because I couldn't play the bloody sports. So I stuck to solo activities. I liked skiing much better, and biking – so there you go!

Walter: You were talking a bit about Anthony. Can you talk more about him.

Robert: Oh he was an amazing person! He is a Greek Cypriot. I met him at school when I was about eight. I don't know why he wanted to hang out with me, but he did! He really is an amazing guy! We had sleepovers at his house and we basically hung out together. I never had any other friends but him except for Jan Wise, the son of my father's best friend, who is now a successful psychiatrist in London. We first met when I was a baby. Jan actually was inspired by yours truly to do psychiatry.

Walter: What did you and Anthony do together?

Robert: Oh we went to his house, we kicked the ball around. We didn't play any games because I think he was sensitive enough to realize I hated competitive sports. So we just kicked and threw balls at each other. He tried to teach me how to skateboard, but I never got the hang of it! We went to movies together, we didn't do much I just hung out with him and it was really cool. Hey Anthony, if you see this book, please give me a call and get in touch!

Walter: Then we made the decision to live in America. And the first school we sent you too was the progressive school.

Robert: Oh yeah, the play school.

Walter: Yes the play school! But that was not the idea. We chose it thinking it would give free reign to your imagination, allowing you to grow in a lot of different directions because they were so free thinking, fun and, in a word, American! So what was it like in reality?

Robert: Well, I kind of vegetated in the class. I don't remember much about them – they were a bit weird. I spent most of my time in the basement with some kids who were playing electric guitars and synthesizers. I wanted to be cool and become a rock star like them! Also roller skating was big there, and I basically spent most of my days roller skating and that's it really.

The next school (January 1981–July 1982)

Robert: Yeah, and there I ran into a different problem – girls! I didn't notice this before, and since I am now an Orthodox Jew wearing a yarmulke[24] I'm embarrassed to say that I found myself looking at women's legs and their short skirts. I was very distracted. I developed a crush for a charming young lady called KR who rode my bus. I just didn't have the courage to ask her out or to even talk to her. Nobody taught me how to talk to girls ... nobody warned me about this! Anyway I was frustrated, distracted, and would not concentrate on my homework. I spent most of my time in study hall. I was there all the time. This went on until the principal decided she had enough of me and threw me out of the school (politely of course)!

Robert's reports from this school are full of his inattention, failure to complete assignments and the disappointment of his teachers over his lack of application and concentration:

Robert's performance on the final exam was a pleasant surprise. During the second semester and especially during the fourth quarter he has not participated in class and showed minimal signs of being interested in science. His exam showed that he understood and learned the material even if he did not answer questions in class or spend much time reviewing in class before the finals. (Science, June 1982)

Robert needs to concentrate himself a bit more during class discussions. When he does participate, he usually does get a firm understanding of the material. However, most of the time, Robert prefers to observe, and thus he misses out on an important part of the class. (History, April 1982)

Robert can do this preliminary algebra work successfully when he sets his mind to it. Most of the time he is not paying attention in his work in class and often his homework is nonexistent or too messy to read. As long as his behaviour remains as such he will continue to be sent to study hall. (Math, April 1982)

Despite repeated study halls and constant reminders, Robert was continuously late with various parts of his final project of the quarter – a report on the Arab–Israeli war of 1967. In many ways his constant forgetfulness was indicative of a problem Robert has had all year – his inability to focus for any long period of time on a particular subject. Robert is a very capable student when he wants to be. Unfortunately his self discipline still needs work. If he can build on this aspect of his learning skills he should be able to make progress on a regular basis. (Composition, June 1982)[25]

The picture is clear. Robert at this stage is an intelligent boy who could do well academically, were he not so wayward in class. Neither his teachers nor we his parents had any idea that he was so distracted by the presence of girls in the classroom. He was just 14 so the hormones must have just started to kick in!

Simon Baron-Cohen, Professor of Psychology and Psychiatry at Cambridge, and a well known researcher into the causes of autism, suggested following Asperger 1944, that: 'autism may be an extreme [example of the] male brain', and Tordjman et al 1997 say: 'in one small scale study, men with autism are also reported to show precocious puberty correlating with increased levels of current testosterone'.[26]

Whilst this is an unproven hypothesis it might well explain both Robert's distraction at school and his later obsessional attitude towards women. Robert loves this explanation!

So we were back again looking for an appropriate school and, having failed to get him into another private school in the Washington DC area, thought that perhaps a boarding school with its structured atmosphere might be a good environment for him. There seemed to be none close to home and the ones we found were in the more conservative areas of New England.

His maths teacher was kind enough to complete an assessment (and let us have a copy), for a boarding school for which we had entered Robert. She recommended acceptance and it is a very fair summary of him at 14 years:

I taught him basic algebra. His capacity for academic growth is very good, yet presently he is easily distracted. He is very curious and his academic achievement is satisfactory. He does not use the classroom opportunities to the fullest, yet he picks up the content being presented satisfactorily. He is a neutral influence. Robert has a high native intelligence from what I can see but he is just very disorganized and sloppy. He is often anxious, sometimes flustered, fidgety, non focused, bright (underneath it all), but withdrawn.

Although I do not know much about your school I feel that Robert would become a lot more focused if he were in a situation where the organizational expectations were high and strictly enforced. In this atmosphere he would excel.[26]

Again Robert has the best memory of this period:

Robert: So then you and Mum tried to get me into other schools. We tried loads of the good private Washington schools – all close enough to where we lived. They all said something like: 'Well we think Robert is a wonderful little boy howeeeever we feel that he won't fit in here'. We even tried boarding schools in New England. It was the year of getting rejected from school, and then Mum, God bless her soul, threw in the towel and said: 'We're going to send this boy to public school!' Problem was the best public schools were in Bethesda, Maryland, so we had to move house.

Junior High School 1982–1984 (aged 14–16) and High School 1984–1987 (aged16–18)

Robert: I was accepted into the Junior High School and spent the rest of my schooldays in the Montgomery County public school system. However I was still distracted, I still looked at girls, and the legs got longer and the girls got sexier.

Walter: Did you make any friends at Junior High?

Robert: Not really. I was friendly with a guy called Marco. We actually went to Cape Cod together when I had my first car ... One of the reasons why I liked Marco was that we had this really stupid English teacher and we would make fun of her. I think we also did this with another English teacher in High School. We made fun of them, and the friendship started from that!

Walter: Did you hang out in the playground?

Robert: It wasn't much of a playground. It was more like a social ground. I think I was just too hung up with girls and didn't do much else.

Walter: You did do reasonably well at those schools didn't you?

Robert: I was about average: C+ to B- average. Wasn't what I could have done. One thing that really discouraged me was that I decided to go into honours Algebra2/Trigonometry course and for the life of me, I just couldn't do well in that course! I tried and tried, but eventually I threw in the towel and said I can't take it anymore! I went into a much easier course but I lost the drive to do well at math, and that put the nail in the coffin. Actually there was one other teacher that I worked really hard for – but for the wrong reasons – because she was gorgeous. She taught Anatomy and Physiology and I kept thinking of her all the time! I made sure that I studied HARD for her classes ... she was married but I wanted to impress her nevertheless! But the right teacher makes all the difference!

Walter: Yes in all schools for all children. No question! What do you remember of your Barmitzvah?

Robert: [Sings the blessings in a falsetto voice.] I remember all those boring lessons with the Rabbi. In synagogue I just went up and did my stuff and then I came down and everybody loved me. The rabbi made a speech and told me how I should be the best Jew I can be and yadayadayada.

Walter:	And a few years later you followed his advice.
Robert:	Boruch Hashem [with thanks to God]. Actually a few decades later!
Walter:	Going back to Washington. Do you have memories of Nostalgia – our sailing boat?
Robert:	Yes. I didn't like the boat. It was very small, too poky. It always needed cleaning. Basically we spent more time cleaning the bloody thing than sailing it. I always thought you were so dumb not getting a power boat. It was too small and tiny. There were some days when it was really nice and I remember taking it down to Solomon's Island. It was pissing down with rain. It was just a motor boat with a mast. 'Hey – we're sailing'!
Walter:	Winston?
Robert:	The best dog in the whole world. I don't think there could be any dog like him – beautiful, a perfect head, very friendly. One thing I envied Winston was his ability to be always in a good mood, to be able to welcome people like that. If I had Winston's capabilities I would have a lot more money!
Walter:	And your Jeep?
Robert:	It was great fun until I totalled the thing. I loved driving it. I drove it to Cape Cod as well. I loved taking the roof off. It kept breaking down all the time but I loved it. I don't think any car I had came close to it. And finally that day when I had eventually got everything fixed I put a little tiny steering wheel on it and I took it on the beltway and it was raining and – I got a new roof for the car, a new axle, a new four wheel drive – everything is new on the car and what do I do? I slide, get out of control in a lot of traffic; hit a tree, total the car and it is history! Junk!
	It had previously been my psychologist's car and mum had persuaded him to sell it to me. The psychologist was awesome. He was the kind of guy I wanted to be. He was tall, strong, he had a commanding presence, was really nice to be around. A fun guy. I started to see him when I was at High School, mid eighties. I had a session with him every week. We talked mainly about girls and dating and we would talk while we played video games and focused on kicking each other's butt. He became more a friend than a therapist.
Walter:	What else do you remember growing up in those years in Bethesda?
Robert:	The cheerleaders in the short skirts – that's one. Same problem with gym except there was no soccer … I tried to do flag football and baseball but with similar bad results! I was a good swimmer but I hated competition! I really did. Whenever I lose I really feel bad and like a loser. However when I win, I also feel bad because I know what it feels like to be a loser, and I just don't like beating people. So no matter which, I'm going to lose and I don't like that. Also in group biking, whenever I am overtaken, especially by a woman, I hate it because I feel like a loser! But on the other hand, when I am doing well, I can't allow myself to overtake the lead biker. I don't want the pressure of the competition, but also I do not want to humiliate someone else!
Walter:	So you lose out both ways?
Robert:	Yes I lose out both ways! I just don't speak the language of competition. That is why I am in a job and not in a business because I just

	don't want to compete against anybody! Maybe against my dad, because I like to kick his butt!
Walter:	Ha ha! And tell me if you can what autism meant to you.
Robert:	Autism, it was a pain in the butt, but one thing: it makes one realize how important it is to treat other people well. When you, my friend, have been teased and when you have been the butt of many jokes, and when you have been rejected and nobody wants to be your friend, and when you realize how horrible gossip is, when people say stuff behind your back, you realize you don't have the luxury to say nasty things about people. You don't have that luxury, and you get sensitive and you feel and that's probably one of the greatest gifts that autism has given to me.

Robert spent five years in the Montgomery County school system for which we had moved to a Maryland suburb of Washington. After high school his grades were high enough for entry to an excellent college in upstate New York. We were all absolutely delighted.

3

College Years, UK and Israel 1987–1998

'Wow – I got a date!!!!!' (Robert)

Robert goes to college with good academic but still poor social skills and this chapter traces his college and postgraduate career in the USA, the UK and in Israel. Increasingly the story is told in Robert's own voice and provides insight into his deepest feelings.

Robert had written to 'Uncle Geoff' on his acceptance at College and Geoffrey wrote to him in reply:

25th June 1987

Dear Robert

Thank you for your letter of – oh so long ago – and for the enclosed examples expressing your varied interests.

I had intended replying to you immediately and do so promise in connection with your next letter which I hope will arrive soon, your having forgiven your adopted uncle and not chosen to emulate his dilatory response to your most welcome letter. I can only cite the process of work and an uncertain temper of mind as my excuse.

Your essay on Parkinsonism was of considerable interest to me and I was struck by your allusion somewhen [sic] to a similarity between some forms and phases of the condition and some manifestations of the catatonic state of schizophrenia, a resemblance which struck me whilst working as a nurse during my medical school studies. Have you any suggested explanation for another curious phenomenon which I have witnessed on a number of occasions, in which the afflicted patient imprisoned by frozen rigidity can when caught 'off guard' move with lightening speed and agility, for example, to catch a ball?

Your poems too I found particularly pleasing. I could vicariously share in the excitement of a ski run (even though I have no experience of the sport), and sympathise in your hymn and invitation to the erstwhile virgin, a somewhat more familiar pursuit.

Do write me something of your first impressions of campus life and something too of your choice of subject matter.

I shall not bore you just now with my own exploits and adventures about my own field of study into learning and the development of adaptive understanding, the exploitation of some of which I like to think may have influenced your very early career.

I sometimes wonder how much you remember of your primeval struggles with coming to 'know' the world; of my 'bullying' you unmercifully and your fluctuating ambivalence towards me.

I do recall many years ago when in high dudgeon you had retreated, at my command, to the waiting room. Not aware of being overheard you vented your indignation in the form of a vituperative argument. Having recently recognized the natural 'law' of increasing size with increasing age and growth, you verbally expressed the wish that the process might be confounded in my case so as ultimately to achieve my absolute extinction from the chronic shrinkage which should accompany reversal of maturation! This was, no doubt, the most dire malediction you could wish upon anyone at that time.

Luckily for me your temporary ire proved not to be a very potent curse and I so far seem to have survived the imprecation!

Yours

Geoff

Geoffrey must have been so proud of Robert and his achievements and of the immense part he had played in Robert's development.

College USA 1987–1991

Robert did exceptionally well educationally at College, majoring in biology and graduating on the Dean's List,[1] but these four years were not a particularly happy experience for him. Robert takes up the narrative.

Walter: What do you remember about College?
Robert: My teachers again. I liked my teachers and didn't really care about the students and the students didn't really care about me. I had virtually no friends in college. I basically stuck to myself and … I tried to go to parties, I tried to go to the Dug Out bar, but for some reason I did not master the skill of standing for long hours in a very crowded bar drinking kegs of beer. I didn't understand the need to go to every football game to scream, and to cheer the team along.

The only time I was interested was when College was playing in the Stagg Bowl (the Super Bowl for our college league), otherwise forget about it! We won by the way!

And it was nice having my own room. I wanted to live off campus but I ended up living with a bunch of guys I had nothing in common with!

Walter: So it wasn't particularly a happy time for you?

Robert: Very bad! Finally for my last year, I ended up in the College Circle apartments and that was a nice rental place very close to the college. So I did enjoy my senior year. It was really nice.

Walter: Because you enjoyed the work and you enjoyed where you lived. But, you were still quite isolated socially?

Robert: Yeah, I lived with three other roommates. There was a guy who was into aeroplanes and I think he was in the army or the air force. Really nice guy, but I didn't really hang out with any of them. Actually, call this Divine Providence, but I actually managed to get a date somehow. Now the area is famous for its parks – it's the Finger Lakes area – with waterfalls and gorges. I visited them all the time – on my own of course! However I always dreamt of taking a girl out there ... and finally the opportunity came. She was a sort of la la girl and not but you know ... reasonably attractive, I screwed up the courage to ask her, and she said: 'Yeah why not?' so we had a date for the State Park – the best one!

I was dancing! I was saying WOW I GOT A DATE!!!!! Finally my life's going to change! And you know what happens? The time comes, I don't see her ... I sit by the phone, I was crying ... do you remember that?

Walter: No. What happened?

Robert: What happened was the silly girl was playing Ultimate Frisbee, which is yet another form of American football played with a Frisbee. And what does she do? She twists her ankle and couldn't go! That fell through, and I never had a date. There was an urban legend about the ball sculpture on the campus that if any guy would graduate a virgin, the ball would roll off. Well I'm living proof to say that that statue is still there! I went on the internet site for the college and the statue is still there, so the legend is BS.

Walter: Do you remember our journeys to and from College?

Robert: It was so nice being in the car just you and me on the road. That was really enjoyable It was good for us to bond together, sometimes you embarrassed me when you criticized my driving, I was very sensitive about it then. We tried to take the Beemer up over 100 – the speedo only went to 85 mph but we certainly went much faster than that! It was just fun taking that German battle-axe all the way down the roads and stuff. What do you remember about it Dad?

Walter: I remember your teaching me to love The Who and Pink Floyd.

Robert: At that time the whole world was getting back into classic rock. Before, we were listening to 80s bands like A-ha, Duran Duran, Michael Jackson – New Wave stuff – and then some people decided to bring back not just the fifties Doo-wop music, but the sixties bands like Paul Revere and the Raiders, The Who, Pink Floyd – it was amazing to hear that old music again. I was buying CDs and wanted to get a collection. I got into *Tommy*, I got into *Quadrophenia*. One of the reasons why I forced you to listen to the Wall was because I felt I had to get into this music but there were some songs in it which were pretty scary; some songs in *The Wall* – we all know: 'We don't need no education' and all those but there were some lyrics which were very scary like: 'I'll put you in the shredder in front of my friends – oooh babe – to beat you to a pulp on a Saturday night'; and the court trial where the poor guy is being tried by the worm because he has built this wall and he has to tear it down. They were very disturbing lyrics and I felt I had to get into it. And I played it to you. I wanted you to listen and to ask: 'Am I crazy for listening to this' and apparently you liked it!

Walter: Not only did I like it then, I still love it and often play it when I am driving. I play *The Wall* and I play *Tommy*. They are the two that have stuck with me. Tommy has a remarkable, amazing cure from autism! Those journeys were special for me and they were obviously special for you.

Robert: Oh yes. I wish we could do it again.

After I came back from Israel I started to see Sandy Weinstein [another psychotherapist]. She was much more serious, very kind, very gentle, very helpful to me. She was also like a friend, in a way like a mother – she was like a mother when mum got too difficult to be around.

Walter: I remember that after your mum died I told you to become self reliant and to stand on your own feet.

Robert: mmmmmm......

Walter: Was that a good thing for me to have said, or not?

Robert: mmmmmmmm......... On human beings, yes, but we are all dependent on Hashem [God].

The divorce

Although Pamela and I separated and then divorced in 1989, we did stay friends until, sadly, she died of ovarian cancer in 2006. After the divorce I moved back to London and eventually married Ruth, whose husband had been a friend of mine until he died at age 36 in a car accident. Ruth had remained a friend of ours, had been both to Robert's Barmitzvah and our going away party, and in fact, after the divorce, Pamela had suggested that I marry Ruth. Always obedient (!), I did and Pamela was always our first stop for tea on our frequent trips back to Washington.

Working life starts – with some stutters

Robert graduated from College in 1991 (aged 23). But what was he going to do now?

Robert: Well what happened was that I graduated from College and while I was there, I was contemplating moving back to England. Originally, my goal was to get into medicine – however when my guidance counsellor told me that I would have to be on call 24/7, I decided quickly that that life was not for me! Therefore, I decided to go into chiropractic. There was this school in London that taught osteopathy – which was similar to chiropractic, but gentler. They accepted me on the spot while I was in the US without an interview! I thought: 'Man, I got it made! I'm going back to England, my old country'. I wasn't religious yet and I considered England my true home! 'And I will go, settle down, get into the osteopathy profession and live the life of a successful Englishman'.

However, when I came to England, the principal wanted to see me for a 'friendly' interview. We started talking and – I don't know what happened, but I suddenly got really scared and suddenly, they rejected me! I remember that period well, don't you Dad?

Walter: I remember exactly why they rejected you! You were talking with the principal about osteopathy and he was describing what you would have to do as an osteopath. And, you asked him: 'What happens if you get sexual feelings when you are treating a client?' And he said: 'I'm sorry, if that's the sort of thing that you are afraid of, I don't think this is suitable for you'. He sent you home, and of course you were very upset. I remember giving you a lecture about how you have to filter what you say and not blurt out the first thing that comes into your mind.

Robert: But I was miserable! MISERABLE! I then spent that year hanging around the house trying to figure out what to do next, polytechnics, universities, and it was a miserable time for me!

Robert produced a letter he received from his sister Debbie at that time:

Hi Rob!

I'm writing you from school[2] where I'm trying to write a paper about Modern Culture and Media. I thought of you because I've been staring at a poster above my bed that I 'borrowed' from you after you left (I figured you didn't want it). It's about a storm with a picture of lightening in a red sky. It says 'When I heard the storm I made haste to join it; for in storms nature has always something *extra fine* to show us'.

You must be very disappointed about not getting into osteopathic college – and I'm very sorry that they couldn't see how great you are. I just want you to know, and maybe it's a small consolation, but you are one of the most incredible people I know. I don't even mean getting out of autism and all that – I mean that right now, you are funny, sensitive, caring and deeply loving in a way that few other people are.

The superficial nuances of behaviour and decorum will come in time – I'm sure of that because I've seen how much you have improved already.

But always remember that your core personality – your sweetness and humour – are *extra fine* just like the storm in your poster.

Hang in there

Love

Debbie ☺

Becoming religious

Robert: … uh did I mention about meeting Malcolm? You had given me some Deepak Chopra books on dieting because I was into health and weight loss at the time and I was into comparative religion as well since I learned that at college. Then I went up to stay with my grandparents in Manchester. I showed them this stuff which seemed pretty cool to me; stuff on meditation, transcending body limits, etc. They then said: 'Why don't you see what your own religion has to offer? You could learn a lot! Come on, there is a group of young men learning in the Synagogue every day, and for the hour before the evening service, they invite the community in to learn with them'.

Well, I reluctantly went, just to humour my grandparents, and I was outside looking at a poster, or a bulletin board, and Malcolm, a rabbinic student – he is a rabbi now and runs se•ed[3] in Edgware – saw me. Well, he seemed like a cool guy and he talked me into joining in. Pretty soon, I was hooked.

That year I also went to stay with Grandma and Grandpa in their holiday flat in Israel. I met a rabbi and asked him some questions and he suggested that I spend some time in Yeshiva Or Sameach[4] after the family had gone back to Manchester, and I said that I would love to but could not because my Grandma would not be happy if I did that. I really wanted to spend my life there at that time, but obviously could not – but it was an amazing time.

So I came back from Israel and went to Nottingham to work in a place for young people with disabilities. That was depressing. After Israel Nottingham was a joke. It was full of ugly buildings and it was very difficult. I was freshly religious; I was living on my own and was very depressed and I was trying to keep all the strict religious laws. They had a whole bunch of chocolates and sweets there and I was so bored I ate them all. They gave me a flat of my own which was very nice.

I stayed there for one or two months, came back to London and I worked for a company that sends people to third-world countries. They had a place in South London. I got bored with it quite quickly and the idea of being sent to a third-world country like the Peace Corps put me off so I quit. I spent a lot of time in Regent's Park just jogging and in the other parks and just bumming around London trying to keep myself amused. I would do anything to keep occupied.

More stutters

Next Robert went to Glasgow where he spent a year (1992/93) on a BSc Physiotherapy course. He rented a flat in Glasgow, made some contact with the Jewish community there but dropped out of the course after a year, largely because it involved touching women and that was hard because of his increasing infatuation (his word), with orthodox Judaism.

Robert: When I got accepted it was awesome at the time because now I could get my life in order again. When I went to Glasgow I was still newly religious. I wanted to make sure I lived in the Jewish area and did not want to live near the campus which was a non-religious area. I needed rabbis around me at the time big time. I needed to be in a Jewish environment. So I lived in the religious area which was Giffnock in south Glasgow. The flat I lived in was owned by the University Jewish Society (JSoc), run by a rabbi and I stayed there with three non-religious Jewish girls. That was not really a very good situation for me, but it was free, I had a nice room on the ground floor. But being newly religious and trying to keep away from women but living with three women was quite unsettling. But the three women kept to themselves, watching TV and doing their womanlike things and I was basically alone in that house.

     Fortunately, I was walking distance from the synagogues and the rabbis at the Glasgow Kollel [a place of learning for married Jewish men]. There was a group of young men, just graduated from the Yeshiva and newly married and they learn all day and they welcomed me. So I was in close contact with the people at the Kollel. I used to go to the house of the rabbi who was one of the heads of the Kollel every Sabbath and it was like a second family for me. One thing really annoyed me with the girls in my house; because they were not religious they had the television on all over the Sabbath and it really pained me. The rabbi had pity on me. He had a spare room in his house and allowed me to sleep over during the Sabbath afternoon. I was very grateful to him for that.

As I said, Robert dropped out of his physiotherapy course in Glasgow for religious reasons and I was furious with him. Robert kept and has now given me the letter I wrote to him at the time:

June 27th 1993

Dear Robert,

Now that your course has ended and you are embarking on the next phase of your life I thought it appropriate to let you know my thoughts and feelings about the past year and your plans for the future.

I should first let you know that I am angry; angry both with you and with the religious influences which seem to me to have blighted your chosen career. You were so happy and excited to have been accepted at Queens that I can only believe – no matter how fair minded I try to be – that it is the religious inhibition about being with – let alone touching – single women that destroyed your interest in physiotherapy. Perhaps it was not the best course for you. Perhaps Ruth, Pamela and others were right that you were not suited to this personal kind of treatment. But you and I both believed that it would help you in developing confidence and that you would have been able to overcome your fears and inhibitions. Unfortunately the religious dogma gave you the perfect opportunity to hide behind your fears of and fascination with women.

And I am angry that you would take my money or Camden's money with no conscience that you were failing to attend your classes. It would have been alright to fail the course if you had not been capable of passing. It is absolutely not alright to have failed without even trying. You tell me that you lost interest in physiotherapy and found it boring – you never gave it half a chance.

Now it is time to look to the future. I understand even if I do not agree with your adoption of orthodoxy and will support this as long as you fulfil the same three conditions on which we agreed at the outset.

1   You stay within the family as a full supporting and supportive member
2   You pursue a secular profession or career to support yourself and hopefully in the future to support a family
3   You remain tolerant of others – both Jewish and non Jewish who do not share your fundamentalist beliefs.

We have agreed that a career in computers may be a good option. Camden will pay for your course and now you are twenty-five for your living expenses so long as this leads to an HND Diploma. See their form which makes this clear.

I know that you want to spend time in a Yeshiva. I agree that you should do this once you have a computer qualification. I see little reason why I should support you on a course which gives you less qualification than one which Camden would approve. This would be a soft easy option and one which I will not take. I suggest therefore that you actively look for a course (one or two years) which will lead to an HND [Higher National Diploma].

Please be patient about your Judaism. The Yeshivas will still be around in 1,000 years. With a computer qualification you can enter for a year or more knowing that you have a career to take up again when you are ready. Then you will be in Israel, hopefully speaking Ivrit and understanding whatever computer discipline you choose.

Robert, please understand that this is written sincerely, from my heart and with love.

Dad x

Robert went back to Manchester and rented an upstairs flat above a religious Jewish couple who were very kind to him, inviting him for meals and generally being very supportive. He enrolled in September 1993 as a BTEC HND student in software engineering and in July 1995, aged 27, successfully completed a two-year course with two distinctions, two merits and two passes.
Shortly after starting the course he wrote to me:

November 3rd 1993

Dear Dad

I have to admire you for your uncanny gift of observing people. You are right in thinking I was nervous. However when a person tells me how I'm doing I get nervous, even if I am doing fine. I have a rotten habit of downplaying my virtues and achievements and focusing on negative things. Yes it's illogical and I'm working on it, but I can't become a tzaddik[5] overnight!

I have though gone to the library and done 60 pages of reading on systems analysis. I hope I remember it! I have done some work in programming and started on my business ops assignment. Remember, Dad, I feel nervous & I have great difficulty in saying 'I love the course and I am doing great and keeping up' EVEN IF I AM TELLING THE TRUTH although I do admit it is easier when you are telling the truth – but it is still hard!

Really I had little to tell you. We've only just started and we haven't had any assignments since we last met. Also I get a bit hesitant because I know how you can be very sharp with me.

Please, I beg you dad, don't frighten me with failures! Yes, I know I can pass the course, but the fear of failure is high in me. My big fear is: I TRIED MY BEST AND STILL FAILED !!!! Now this is probably highly unlikely, but I'm still scared of this feeling; and if – God forbid – this happened, how would you react to it?

I thank you for so continuously and righteously supporting my Jewish commitments. I will try hard not to make it an obsession. Nevertheless it is HARD. The Torah is just so full of light, riches, joy, simcha,[6] and challenges, that it is hard not to be obsessed with it.

Well I hope I said the truth. I am very frightened of your rebukes and I guess you know this! I am afraid and terrified of you when you rebuke me. Then I feel so helpless I have difficulty restarting again! Nevertheless you mean the best for me since you love me very much. I hope I can give my children the same excellent love you've given me!

I now sign off. How is everything going with you? Hope your life and your business are coming along great.

Please write back soon. I love you Dad but I am scared

Thanks for the rebuke – Take care

Love

Robert

Well as you saw he did pass with good grades and I tried to be more gentle with my rebukes!

By now he was seriously religious and wanted to go to Israel where he had spent a fair amount of time while we lived in the USA. This was a time when I had a marketing consultancy with an Israeli company and was going there quite often.

One day Pamela phoned and reminded me of Professor Yosef Bodenheimer who was President of the Jerusalem College of Technology (JCT). This is a Yeshiva (religious college) in the mornings and a high level technical college in the afternoons. She suggested that I meet Prof. Bodenheimer next time I visit Israel and discuss the possibility of Robert's going there after Salford. So I did and Robert was enrolled after the Professor had written to me to say that:

We had discussed Robert's special circumstances and would be able to design a custom tailored programme to meet Robert's needs and that the coursework would include the courses required to complete Robert's degree in computer sciences in addition to courses for improving his Hebrew language skills.[7]

Robert's move to Israel

So Robert's next adventure was to study at the JCT. He enjoyed it there for a while but his Hebrew was nowhere near the level he needed to succeed there. For example, he failed his calculus exam twice, and was very frustrated that he could not understand the Torah lectures there.

The students were up at sunrise for the morning prayers, and spent the morning in the large study hall where they paired up in the traditional manner and studied Torah (the book of Jewish history and law). After lunch the afternoon was devoted to technical and scientific studies. The days were long, the intensity great and the pressure enormous. I think that the pressure was more than anything Robert had previously experienced and it was just too much for him.

Robert: I did not succeed there firstly because my Hebrew was nowhere near the level I needed. Even for Israelis it is a difficult place. Taking calculus in your native language is in itself very difficult. Now try taking it in a language you don't understand. I never ever failed my exams. If I did not try hard I would get a D. Ever since Junior High School I never failed an exam. I made sure about that. But here I worked really hard to pass the exam and I failed it. I could not answer the questions. It was horrible. I hated it.

Also I was so depressed because I felt excluded from JCT society because everybody spoke Hebrew and I found the Ulpans (Immersion Language Schools) very difficult because it felt like going to kindergarten and learning the Aleph Bet (ABC). On the one hand the teachers were teaching us as though we were in kindergarten and on the other hand they were speaking so fast that I could not understand what they were saying. I felt myself being swallowed up by Hebrew but not understanding a word. It was very very frustrating and to top that I did not understand the other subjects, like calculus, that I was taking in Hebrew.

The best thing about JCT was that I had a truly wonderful roommate for the first year at least. He was Yoel, a lovely boy, who was younger than me. I am sure he is now graduated and doing really well and I pray that is the case. He helped me so much trying to get to grips with the study and I spent many hours just talking to him about my problems. I really miss him. He is a lovely, lovely person and I pray the best for him.

During all this time Professor Bodenheimer took a great interest in his well-being and it is not overstating the fact to say that he acted in loco parentis. Robert spent most Friday nights and Saturdays with Yosef, Rachel, their children – mostly daughters, and whoever else happened to be in town and needed an invitation for Sabbath dinner. Robert lived in college so could not get back home until the end of the Sabbath on Saturday evening because of the prohibition against driving on the Sabbath. I also benefitted from many of those invitations and remember with great happiness the warm feelings that Yosef had towards Robert and indeed to me. That has continued to this day.

So Robert left the JCT after a year, decided to make Aliyah (immigrate into Israel and become a citizen), and found a job in Ramot, a northern suburb of Jerusalem. I helped him find a tiny room in an outbuilding next door to a sofer (a writer of sacred Jewish script). Unfortunately he was laid off after three months but continued to live in Ramot whilst he was looking for another job.

Pamela went to visit him at that time and phoned me in horror at the dreadful conditions he was living in. She found him a much nicer small flat in a pleasant and more central suburb. So during 1997, aged 29, Robert continued to improve his Hebrew at many different Ulpans, all of which he says he hated; looked for jobs but failed to get them, but also enrolled and successfully completed various different computer courses to try to improve his chances of getting work. At the same time he joined a small morning Jewish study class at Machon Daniel in Har Nof – this area, far from where he lived, and where he had studied at Dvar Yerushalayim, seemed to have a special attraction for him.

Now Robert met and became a friend of a Vietnam veteran called Reuven. They biked all over the country together, from Jerusalem to Netanya (95 kilometres) and especially around Bet Shemesh between Jerusalem and Tel Aviv. He enjoyed the risks of biking through Arab villages but never had any difficulties with them. I can imagine that his conversations with Reuven, a guitar playing free thinker, would have influenced Robert quite considerably and in fact he quit Machon Daniel in favour of biking. He was starting to lose the religion.

Then, as a new Israeli citizen he got his call-up papers. This caused a deal of consternation and whilst I thought that the discipline of army life could be the making of him, Pamela thought that it could be a total disaster. Robert himself was none too keen and went to a medical board which declared him unfit for service. Soon after he decided that as he was having no luck finding a job it might be better to go back to the USA where the economy was strong and he would have no problem with the language.

4

Work and Marriage 1998–2011

'This lady made chicken and lasagne for me' (Robert)

Now age 30 Robert returns to the USA and his story continues in a series of interviews through his jobs, his increasing interest in religion and his attempts to develop a social life. It ends as he becomes a family man with a career, a wife and baby daughter. The story concludes (so far), with the insights of a psychoanalyst friend who has known us all from the time before Robert was born.

Back to America

Aged 30 Robert went to Bethesda to stay, in the first place, with his mother. He had a number of jobs with software companies until, in 2004, he moved, yet again, to be in the website support group for an American trade association. He stayed there for three years, until, in 2007, he got married and moved to Baltimore.

So there were plenty of moves as Robert adjusted with some difficulties to the working world. He and I talked about those years next time I visited the USA in May 2010:

Walter: I want you to talk a bit about what it was like to come out of autism. I have been reading a lot of books about autism and some of the psychological books say that people want to hang on to their autism because they are scared to leave it behind.

Robert: Well, I'll tell you something, it is very hard for anybody – but especially me – to mature. For example: don't tell this to my boss … shall I talk about my work habits?

Walter: Yes, why not?

Robert: I think my former teacher, Dr Geoffrey Waldon, may he rest in peace, said in one of his videos that one of the natural behaviours is that a person wants to get the most pleasure for the least effort possible. And that basically describes my work! I want the pay check, the golden goose, the money. But hard work scares me. It's part autism, laziness … however maybe it is not laziness, it's fear … you see I am a programmer and with God's help, I have successfully completed all the assignments that I have been given. The problem is that when I don't know the solution, I panic, I can't relax, and it is very difficult for me to get the confidence. So I don't like getting assignments that I don't know how to do. Therefore, I passively wait for somebody to give me a new assignment, and while I am waiting I spend too much time surfing the internet. I just want to do the least I can to get away with, because I am frightened to put my neck on the chopping block! This is an example of where it is very, very difficult to give up the autism because I like my cocoon. I like my womb-like environment. I like a predictable place where I get a pay check and I don't have to worry about starving.

However one major problem with that is that life becomes very very VERY BOOORING! And I know I'm rotting. There was one job where I was rotting away for three years in an office basically doing nothing! I really hated it! I wanted to move on and do more challenging things, but I was frightened and was pulled in a tug of war of pleasure versus pain.

It is the same with dating! I so badly wanted to go out with women, but I didn't want to go through all the pain of rejection and ridicule! Especially since my social skills were so bad! I wanted the pleasure of having a girlfriend. Not marriage ... that's too painful, but to have a nice relationship. The pleasure of having a girlfriend is so awesome, but the pain of going through that rejection is so scary that I just didn't do it.

Walter: Is the pain of getting a hard project still so difficult that you run away from it?

Robert: Not as bad as it was, it is getting lesser and lesser and lesser, and actually in my present job, I have basically managed to crack this thing and figure out what's going on. I still don't understand everything – it's a very complicated program. But I have been able to figure most of it out. Well stuff that I needed to work on anyway. I have been quite a guru on it, but yes, I still have the PROBLEM and IT WON'T GO AWAY AND I WANT IT TO GO AWAY. I want to grow. I do want to overcome it. But .... bottom line is that I want to also get away with the least effort and that it is very hard to break that habit!

It is also true that when I have an assignment I get stuck in and concentrate until it is done. In my present job I have been begging for more work and get frustrated when they don't give me enough. Now I use the spare time to learn more computer languages and skills that hopefully will be useful in the job.

As I write in spring 2011 Robert has been in a good job for nearly two years, has learnt Java and is more and more self motivated and less and less scared of new assignments which he receives on a regular basis. He tells me that his bosses have been impressed with his abilities and he is enjoying work probably for the first time ever. One of his bosses with whom I spoke said that his confidence level has been boosted by his successes in learning Java and that he is much better able to take on new assessments without his old fears getting in the way.[1]

Multi-level sales opportunity!

In 2002, whilst Robert was employed at one of the software companies, he met a young woman in a gym who introduced him to a multi-level marketing company and persuaded him to go to one of their meetings. He joined and was taught how he could become financially independent in three years by working a couple of hours a day during the week and then at the weekends. I found it amazing to watch Robert, with his difficulties in being social, approaching waiters in restaurants, people on the street, family and friends and trying to persuade them to come to one of the company meetings and join the band of hopefuls.

Back to religion

Robert was at a regional company meeting and the leaders were explaining that the programme worked best if you had God on your side. This struck a chord with Robert and he decided to become religious again, but in his own Jewish faith. By now he had moved out from his mother's house, at her urging, and had made a downpayment on an apartment in another part of Bethesda. He joined a local congregation located in Rockville about half an hour's walk away. This was a very happy choice. The synagogue has a warm and welcoming ambience and Robert became a stalwart member, loved by the congregation. He made many friends there and perhaps for the first time friends of his own age group. So once again Robert has become religious and this time without the zeal of the new convert but with the maturity of one who wants to study and learn and delve deeply into the writings of the rabbis of old.

Our conversation again as we talk about relationships (or lack of), with women:

Walter: There was a whole period of time when you were really bravely putting yourself out going to activities like dating cruises. You really went on one?

Robert: I took a singles cruise. I wasn't just looking for women; I also wanted some male chums. However I found the men extremely boring so obviously I much prefer being with the ladies! But it didn't work. We went to Belize and Key West. I remember going mountain biking through one of the jungles out there. The thing I remember the most about that cruise unfortunately is when I caught my bunk mate having sex with one of the girls in our cabin. I was really upset about that!

Walter: Were you upset that he was doing that in your cabin, or were you upset that it wasn't you?

Robert: Both actually! So I went up and had a good sulk at the top of the ship. I had a rather crappy day in Key West because of that … it really soured the holiday. Also, I just couldn't get into the social stuff. I tried to join in the Halloween dance, but I couldn't blend in with the other travellers. It was like oil and water – being unable to mix together! They didn't want me, and I really didn't want them! And that was that. I also remember when Mum picked me up from the airport, and told me about a cruise she went on, when she had a similar problem.

Walter: Do you remember last night, you were talking about something quite strange – about comfort zones, and how you don't like to succeed, how you don't want other people to be happy, that is, you are happier when other people are miserable.

Robert: Yeah. It sounds pretty grotty doesn't it? If you think I am a bit of a killjoy, then you are probably right. I realize that I have the ability to understand that this is not the right way to think. We really want the best for other people. It's just that it is human nature that when a person is upset, it's not enough that he is upset ... especially somebody with a sensitive nature like me. If that person is upset and everybody else is ignoring him, then he feels left out and therefore he wants people to understand that at least he is upset. The saying 'misery loves company' is unfortunately very true! It's not that I want everybody to be miserable, but I want people to understand that maybe this guy is not feeling too good let's give him a little attention, help him out, and maybe give him something to get him out of his rut. However a funny thing with me is that sometimes I am locked in a weird situation where I want people to know that I am miserable, but I don't want them to come over and talk to me! It is sounding quite confusing and it is very hard to find a solution to get out of that tailspin!

Walter: And you were also talking last night about the difference between important and urgent things, and how you react to that.

Robert: Yeah, well a definition that works for me is that urgent things are things I have to do right this second, and if you don't do them – you're in very bad shape. However in the long run, in the whole realm of things, they're not really that important. And I said that things that you do in a job are usually urgent. You HAVE to do them, but in the long run, no-one's going to care – yeah my boss will care if I write this program that will for example sort out this list, or help that website work. But at the end of things ... when you are on your deathbed ... who cares? The important things, though, are the things you want people to remember you by when you leave this world, like being a good husband and father, learning Torah. However they are not so urgent! You can put them off, but you will have to get them done eventually!

Walter: And how does that affect your work life?

Robert: Not too much actually. When there is something urgent that needs to be done, I do it. In the office, I definitely focus a lot more on urgent things than important things.

Walter: When you were in your most remote – your most autistic – phase; before you started your lessons with Uncle Geoff, you used to do things like spinning, head banging, or rocking. Do you remember those things and why you did them?

Robert: A lot of that period before school and what happened with Mrs Tustin is a big blank to me. If I knew what it was, I would be the first one to throw it all out. But I do know one thing: I loved watching fan blades spin. It was fascinating to see this big metal/plastic thing spin into an invisible nothingness! You can see right through the blades – it's thin air! There were times when I was tempted to put my finger in, but thank God I had the common sense not to do that! Otherwise I would have no fingers. I also remember spinning my toy car wheels; I loved spinning them BRUM BRUM BRUM! These activities relax the mind. I still do silly things like chewing straws, fiddling and feeling things because it takes the stress out of life and that they are so soothing.

Walter: Psychologists would think that was breast substitute.

Robert: Yeah well they just think too much. I don't know, maybe it is. I wanted a nice pair of breasts but I didn't get any dates!

Walter: You've always been very open with your feelings. And I have always thought that perhaps you learnt to express your feelings at Mrs Tustin's?

Robert: Maybe, maybe – I know I love to talk to myself a lot and it helps me plan everything, my day. People think I'm weird, but I say: 'Sod them', because it really helps me organize everything ... my thoughts, plans, etc. And I like talking to myself. I still do it all the time.

Walter: What does that do for you?

Robert: It helps me express myself. I'll tell you one other thing I do, I carry pictures around. They used to be women, but I stopped doing that. They are now usually pictures of Rabbis I admire very much and I like it when they look at me when I talk to myself and it gives me some sort of attention and social recognition!

Pamela develops cancer

From 1996 to 2006 Pamela fought the second intensive battle of her life, this time against ovarian cancer. She also ran a support group for women with ovarian cancer. Eventually she became resistant to everything on offer and knew that she could not survive much longer, so on one of my visits took me to the Jewish cemetery and then the undertaker, to choose the style of her funeral, boldly introducing me: 'This is Walter – my ex-husband'!

These were difficult years for her relationship with Robert. Perhaps Bowlby, quoting the analyst Melanie Klein, was right when in discussing the phenomenon of ambivalence in psychic life he wrote of: 'this inconvenient tendency we all have to get angry with and sometimes to hate the very person we most care for' (Bowlby, 2005: 10). This tendency worked in both directions. Robert felt pressured by his mother and responded by behaving 'inappropriately' in her presence. Their rows were frequent and upsetting to both.

It was at the end, when Pamela was in the hospice, that Robert showed his true and deep love for his mother by sleeping in her room so that she would never be alone – especially at the moment of death. Knowing when this was imminent, he phoned Debbie and they were both able to be with her as she passed away.

Robert meets Yelena

Robert has grown enormously since his mother's death. Inge Wise, a family friend and a psychoanalyst, when I was having the conversation with her which follows, said to me that we all grow when our parents die. Within a year he was engaged to Yelena.

Robert: Yelena was far different from all the other girls. For the rest, I either had to drive to New Jersey and back paying for tolls and gas. The cheaper option was to pay for a cramped seat in a Chinatown bus for about six hours, and then taking the girl out for a meal in one of NYC's kosher restaurants. Those meals would run me up $50–$60 – it was very expensive. And then I would shlep on home knowing that either I was not interested in her at all, or I would be, but she wouldn't be interested in me. And in the end, I would come back to Washington feeling like junk to put it mildly! Yelena, do you want to be on tape, baby?

Walter: Yelena, you told me this lovely story about when Robert first dated you. Could you tell me that story again? To remind you what you said is that one day this lady rang you up and said she had someone who was interested in meeting you. Well he took you out and it was the 25th of March [Robert's birthday] and you didn't tell me where you went. What did you do?

Yelena: We went to the park.

Walter: And then he took you home?

Yelena: Aha, and then Robert called Devorah [the matchmaker] and he said that he was ready to get married with me. She called me back the next day, and said the thing, that he wants to get married, and I wanted to throw the receiver through the window! I then hung up and started yelling to my mother: 'Come out, come out wherever you are! I have to tell you something!' When I told them I am going to get married, they said: 'Get real, you just met the guy!' I said: 'I think I am actually serious this time! At least one time in my life, I am serious! That's it! The End'!

Walter: Then what happened next?

Yelena: We planned the wedding!

Walter: How do you remember that story, Robert?

Robert: Well it was – I felt that ... Dad, you're trying to get me in trouble aren't you?

Walter: Yeah, ha ha ha.

Robert: Devorah, that shadchan [matchmaker] was amazing! I wouldn't have done that without her because going from singlehood to marriage was very difficult ... Hashem made sure that I would get a really powerful shadchan that would – she did do a bit of twisting here, and she was very powerful but I was really impressed with Yelena! It's just that I am a guy and Yelena was ready to be married when she was in diapers and I was not ready to get married. Same thing with the kids – you know as soon as Yelena came into the world, she was ready to be a mother and I am still wondering 'Oh my God! Now I'm going to be a dad???' So Yelena and I come from totally different mindsets. So Devorah really pushed me and Yelena was far different from all the other girls. When I went out with Yelena, we went biking, and also she was unlike the other women who I had to fete. This lady made chicken and lasagne for me! She actually made food for me, God bless her.

Walter: Well you know what they say; the way to a man's heart is through his stomach!

Robert: But you know what really clinched it? We went to the park and then she told me stories about her other boyfriends. If Yelena hadn't shared with me about them, then Devorah would have had a much harder time persuading me. So that's basically that!

Walter: Well good for Devorah! And good for Yelena! Teaching you how to catch a man!

Robert: She sure did! .... And good for Hashem, because Hashem orchestrated everything perfectly!

They were married less than six months later (August 2007, Robert aged 39), and what a wedding that was! It was a traditional orthodox Jewish wedding. Many things happened that celebrative weekend because Pamela's family all came from England and there were two important ceremonies. And for me it was an even more emotional time because my second darling wife Ruth had died of complications associated with her dementia, just two months before. We had had 18 absolutely wonderful years together.

So that wedding weekend we had Sabbath dinner at the home of Robert's best man and his fiancée. Robert was called up in Synagogue with a festive lunch there to follow on the Saturday. On Sunday we had the stone setting at Pamela's grave where Robert gave an unrehearsed, deeply felt and extremely moving speech expressing his gratitude for all she had done to prepare him for this point in his life, a point which so sadly she had not lived to see.

Tuesday was the wedding day. I have never been to such a joyous event. My two closest friends, Leslie and Nigel, had come from England for the celebrations and Professor Bodenheimer had flown in from Israel. In his speech he quoted from the Hallel, a prayer said only on festive occasions: 'This is the day the Lord made. Let us rejoice and be glad in it'. He said he had never fully appreciated the meaning of that verse until this day.

So Robert set up home with Yelena in Baltimore, in the heart of the religious community there and close to Yelena's mother Galina and great aunt Bina. Yelena had come from Russia and Robert from England to meet and marry in the New World.

Now Robert resigned from his job in downtown Washington DC, with its long commute, and found a new job in Baltimore. After a couple of moves, he has found a good programming job with a downtown Baltimore company.

In September 2009 he and Yelena, expecting their first child, took their belated honeymoon to Europe. They travelled to Manchester where Robert took Yelena round all his old haunts and to meet the people who had been important to him in his early years and then to Paris, to my cottage in south west France and then to London to show it to Yelena.

Robert and Yelena become parents

To Robert and Yelena Solomon a baby daughter, Rachel. I thought, Debbie thought, many of my friends thought they would need a lot of support as they adjusted and so we arranged for a nurse to come for the first two weeks. After two nights they fired her saying that they could manage perfectly well on their own and did not want a nurse to boss them around! As I write, 15 months later, Rachel is beautiful, is doing well and is bright and very connected with her parents. Yelena is truly embracing motherhood and Robert has entered this new stage with an ever growing maturity. I am proud of them all.

The rabbi comments

Rabbi Paysach Diskind who knows both Robert and Yelena well said:

> Among the many rabbis who have come to know Robert there is a whole-hearted recognition of his sincerest desire to become a better person. This is also evident in the beautiful relationship that Robert and Yelena have as they build a Jewish home together. Robert has a deep sensitivity to Yelena's needs and does his utmost to meet them.[2]

A psychoanalyst friend remembers

Let me finish this section of the book with a conversation with Inge Wise, a psychoanalyst, whose husband Leslie was one of those who came from England to the wedding and who has been my very best friend for over 60 years.

Inge: It seems to me that Robert has done very very well. My own thoughts about what happened to Pamela looking back and even at the time – I think that her relationship with Robert was so intense and so prolonged. She just had to get this child to where she might imagine he might get to. There was no choice in it. She had to do it. But I think in a way she never got over that. With Robert I think she had had a purpose in her life and she achieved it magnificently. I think she poured herself – all her efforts, all her purpose went into setting Robert off the right way and getting him to develop. As he began to develop and be himself at 13 and 15 and older I think she felt left behind. She never found another purpose like that in her life. I call it a tragedy because she had so much to give. It is very sad that she could not find something else.

In a way the two of you paid the price because it was too much effort for the couple. I am now separating the couple from the parents if you know what I mean. Between you I think all the effort had gone into getting Robert to become a full member of the human race as it were. It took the expectations for him not to be outside the broad spectrum of people – to fit in somewhere there. So much effort had gone into that, you each got depleted inside. There was just not enough of a couple to continue because so much effort had gone into that relationship with the child.

Talking with Pamela about what she was doing – this was her aim and everything else came second. Her training as a teacher gave her the right preparation for it. Then there were Robert's obsessions – first this thing with the electric toothbrush or it was puzzles. He would get one and be obsessive about it. Doing it and redoing it over and over again. He would take an object and it was as though he wanted to get inside the object. Psychoanalytically there is a wish to return to mother, to get inside mother which we all carry. We all have to manage and cope.

I remember watching the way in which a closed mind, which is what one saw in 18-month-old Robert, develops; also hearing Pamela talking about Robert when he was six months and eight months and she was beginning to notice things. From being the non-responsive child and seeing the first sparkle in his eyes – suddenly his attention was caught. You saw him inside the shell which seemed like a closed system. Suddenly there is this small opening and that is what I saw on the first visit when he was 18 months old and increasingly so by three.

There were sad occasions. At one time I was seeing patients and Robert was not in the consulting room and not liking the attention my patients were getting. He made a lot of noise, disrupting the session. I had to go out to him and say: 'Robert you can't do this. Go and play in the garden. Do what you like but you cannot disturb my patients'.

Our second son Adam saw that and he talked about it, whether with Robert or not I don't know. I heard later from Pamela that Robert had said that he saw that Adam had a very close relationship to me that he thought he did not have with his mother. That was something which felt very sad because I think it was a moment when Robert realized that there was something missing in his life. I thought that it was both very sad but also very exciting because he noticed a lack. When you notice a lack, you can do something about it.

There were many years before that when Robert did not know something was lacking, of give and take and the easiness of relating to each other. That was not there for him. Adam has a talent for relating to people. He is amazing in his ability to reach out to people and to relate to people. This was something which Robert saw and understood. And now he has developed – becoming able to have a girlfriend, to get married and to have a child.

Walter: There was a whole period, talking about his adult days when I would say that the umbilical cord between him and Pamela never got cut, which was extremely painful for both of them.

Inge: Yes absolutely and I can sympathize with that. From it being your new born baby, the child you bring up, the youngster and so on – when they go to nursery school that first day you lose them. When they go to school and when they go to university, and come back for the holidays and they go off – it is always painful. And our umbilical cord got cut many years ago. But it is a sort of elastic which gets longer and longer and I think that Pamela and Robert just couldn't cut it.

Walter: They couldn't because Pamela always had expectations of Robert which Robert could not fulfil.

Inge: I don't know actually – I think it was mutual and in a way she was an auxiliary ego for Robert in a way that you are not for other children. She was always there for him and when you have a child like Robert it is always an emergency. It ALWAYS is an emergency.

Robert has done so well because of what Pamela has put in and what you have put in. Even writing this book you did not need to do that, and you don't have to. This is so intense and so wonderful at many levels that it is very difficult to see the cost. There is a cost because what you put into the child, what you put into the relationship with the child, is what you can't put into other things in your life. And you would not have it any other way. It is a sacrifice and it needs to be recognized as that.

Walter: There are costs. There are costs to everything. It is hard to say this but since Pamela died he has grown enormously.

Inge: This is not surprising. We do, all of us do, when our parents die. Winnicott said: 'the adolescent wants to kill the parent in his life'.[3] In a way Robert remained 'wedded to his mother'.

Walter: It was so difficult. You could see them rubbing up against each other and you could see Robert behaving in front of Pamela in ways that he did not behave in front of anybody else. He was regressing and Pamela reacting to that and the whole thing deteriorating.

Inge: That sounds right. Remembering now the lessons Pamela gave Robert. I just know that it was every day, at the same time, it was ongoing and I was amazed at their perseverance. It went on and on and on and Pamela never tired of it and Robert did not tire of it. When I sat in, it seemed to be very mundane things, they were repeated and they were done again and again. They seemed to have a calming influence on Robert.

Walter: They were calming because the lessons were designed never to take Robert beyond his level of understanding, of his knowledge and his abilities. And the other thing I did not talk about earlier is the difference between the intrinsic disability and the defensive behaviours. These defensive behaviours are developed by the children in order to escape the pressures placed on them by parents and teachers. By the time Robert was two he had all these defensive behaviours and you had to work your way calmly and gently through them, through the asocial lesson. What I saw was Robert developing almost from the day he first went to Waldon and started the lessons at home with Pamela. He got better and better and better.

Inge: The routine of it, the everyday of it, Saturdays, Sundays, weekdays – because we saw him only periodically we could see the difference. It was quite startling. What I admired greatly was the application with which Pamela would do this every day. It was extraordinary. How could she maintain that sort of energy and application when on a day-to-day basis I am sure you could not see the difference? It was easier for us to see. You might have had moments when suddenly there was a spurt. You might look back and say that three months ago he was not doing this. It must have happened almost imperceptibly.

Walter: It was imperceptible but I remember clearly that every time we had, perhaps a six-monthly visit to the paediatrician we thought: 'Oh he is doing so well we are going to be signed off now'. Of course we weren't. There was always still a long way to go. But we always believed that the end of the road was in sight.

Inge: You had to believe that of course to have the strength to carry on. What of course one knows nowadays with the scanning of the brain is that the repetition and the doing of things can re-structure the brain. That is the basis of many things including the basis of analysis. You create new connections in the brain.

Walter: That is what everyone is talking about today – the neoplastic capability of the brain. I have always believed that what we did was to develop new pathways in Robert's brain. Perhaps there was an area of his brain that was damaged and we bypassed it with new connections.

Inge: I would be very interested in Debbie's view. When she was little, perhaps two three and four, she must have thought many many times: what was so special about Robert that he got all this attention that he had this closeness with his mother?

Walter: I can tell you clearly what Debbie thought because at the time Pamela and I were very conscious of the fact that she might feel neglected. And of course it was impossible even though she had more attention than most children in the world; it was never the same as Robert. And she says: 'I didn't want the kind of attention he got. I was happy to be (relatively) left alone to do my own thing, without constant lessons or having my behaviour corrected all the time'. I really wanted her to speak about it and whether it is suppressed or not, I don't know.

Inge: It may not be suppressed – but never mind. There must have been something. It is perhaps some kind of childhood amnesia.

Walter: I asked her what about all those weekends going down to London, destroying your social life with your friends at school. It is impossible that there was no effect. But no, she says she did not mind at all.

Inge: Debbie was a very cheerful child. I am smiling. She was a solid, not very tall, a contented child. Round faced, round bodied – not obese or anything like that – with very curly hair, and giggling, and never a problem.

Pamela and I had a bond because of what I saw of her intrinsic value as a person, especially what she was doing for Robert. I had come from a country with a troubled history. Even as a child I had an understanding that life was difficult, that you have to be committed and you have to get on with things. Pamela could not walk out on Robert – it was not an option. It was something you had to live with 24 hours a day every day, and I think it made for empathy and an understanding that did not need much talking about. It was very low key and basic. You knew that if you really needed support it was there. I was very sad that you went to live in America. There was a lot of hope that things would be easier in America for Robert – I don't know if they were. I thought you were trying to get away from the very depressing atmosphere in England at that time. I felt it was a manic movement.

Walter: Sheila Spensley said that Frances Tustin said that we had said that Robert would never have been allowed to grow up normally in his own community and that it was important for him to go somewhere where there was no record and he could start afresh.[4]

Inge: And now you have the next generation – very exciting and scary.

Walter: I was scared at the beginning, but Robert and Yelena are such good parents. They are calm and they are responsible and they are very loving.

They met on a website for young Jewish people with special needs. And Robert, fine as he is, still has some relationship difficulties. It is not easy for him. And Yelena has always been a little young for her age. So Robert is the leader and the master of the household and Yelena looks up to Robert as being her guide. It is absolutely marvellous and together they are an ideal couple in a loving relationship. I have to say 'Baruch Hashem'.

5

The Waldon Theory of Child Development and the Waldon Approach

'All understanding has its origin in movement' (Jonas Torrance)[1]

This chapter summarizes the Waldon Theory of child development. The Waldon Approach (sometimes called Functional Learning), utilizes a very particular form of lesson based on this philosophy. Robert and the other children[2] in the case studies in Chapters 7 and 8 all had lessons based on the Waldon Theory of child development. So what follows is not a 'recipe' for the use of his method but an explanation of the theory. Parents and practitioners need to understand the philosophy and work out the best way to implement it in each individual case.

The Waldon Theory

Geoffrey Waldon developed, directly from his own observation, an original theory of the growth of understanding. Although he sometimes suggested that his work be compared and contrasted with that of Piaget or Gesell, the ideas are neither derived from nor a continuation of their work. A study of the Waldon Theory and its place in the literature of child development would be a fruitful area for further research.

Geoffrey Waldon resolved in about 1960 to learn something about the development of young children and spent several years in 'casual but careful' observation of children in public and private places, on buses and trains, in parks and waiting rooms, in nursery and infant schools and in the houses of friends. During his everyday work as a neurologist he was also able to work with 200 or so developmentally delayed and 'brain damaged' children in whom variations on the more usual pattern of developments could be studied.

By observing both typical and atypical behaviour, and by speculating on possible behavioural growth mechanisms, Waldon began to build and test hypotheses about atypical development.[3]

Meaning from movement

'Meaning from movement' is an expression Waldon used constantly; it is foundational to his theory of learning. Waldon believed that movement is the most consistent and regular source of experience and provides the structure of understanding, which develops alongside the movements. Objects, or the environment, are said to 'inherit' interest from movement; without bodily integration and organized movement patterns, children will not be able to develop the usual capacity for action and subsequently for more abstract thinking.

The Waldon Approach was developed in the 1970s but many of Waldon's ideas have since been validated with increased appreciation of the role that movement plays in development. Researchers like Stern (2010), Gallese and Lakoff (2005) and Sheets-Johnstone (1999), among others, confirm this. Even Einstein said that, for him, thinking in mathematics involved sensations of bodily movement (quoted in Stern, 2010: 20).

Stern continued: 'Movement is our most primitive and fundamental experience. Many thinkers have long argued that besides the fact that movement comes first in animate evolution and in development, it has a primacy in experience throughout life' (2010: 20).

Professor Maxine Sheets-Johnstone (2009: 168) writes: 'Though we may have forgotten what we first learnt of the world through movement and touch, there is no doubt but that we came to know it first by moving and touching our way through it, in a word, through our tactile-kinesthetic bodies'.[4]

Jonas Torrance, a dance and movement psychotherapist in the Oxfordshire Service for Autism, said:

> 'although I did not meet Geoffrey Waldon I have read various things he has written and agree with him that movement is the foundation of understanding and that all understanding has its origin in movement. I put Waldon's teachings within that context of movement analysis which was originally pioneered by Rudolf Laban'.[5]

Bodily integration

Waldon hypothesized that understanding is derived from effortful movement and that the earliest learning is derived from the infant's earliest movements. He calls the fundamental drive to move 'motivation' and infers that this 'motivation' is in some way self-reinforcing, possibly from the pleasure children experience in performing the movements. These rhythmical early movements generate regular patterns of activity from which new patterns, that is, new experience, may be developed, leading to the development of what he called General Understanding (1980).

From birth, and probably even before birth, babies explore and make sense of their environment, by moving their bodies. Soon they are able to move their heads and limbs. In the early weeks babies get bigger, stronger and heavier and are changing shape as their limbs get longer in proportion to their trunk. They move more during their waking time which is also getting longer. As they grow larger and gain more control, their movements expand to fill the available space. As they grow, the effort required to move against gravity increases so the amount of motive power required gets progressively greater day by day. Waldon suggests that the movements themselves provide reinforcement which in turn leads to an increased supply of motivation. The larger and more effortful the movement, the more feedback or reinforcement it provides, and the better it is for this purpose.

By six months babies are capable of focusing interest through their head, eyes, ears, arms and hands into one direction. At about this time they start to put their hands on things in a very deliberate way, guided by head and eye movements. By the end of the first year babies can both sustain and vary the focus of interest at will. They can easily shift attention from the area of space on one side of the body to the other, or from near to further space and back again. Their bodies are becoming integrated.

Spontaneity

Babies move spontaneously and for the evident pleasure that they derive from the activity. They move effortfully and the effort forms a part of the pleasure. Babies will start to act on objects in the environment as a by-product of their repeated and rhythmical patterns of movement.

They can grasp things dangling or lying on surfaces around them; they learn to roll over and then to crawl, all the time expanding the space available for exploration. As they explore, objects are encountered and pleasure is found in picking them up and putting them down.

They may by chance find that a distant object can be manipulated by some other nearby object and so find that an object can act as a limb extension. They repeat the action. They bang something on another object and enjoy the noise, or the feeling, or the movement, or the result. Perhaps they reproduce the movement for pure pleasure. They may place one object on top of another. It may stay or it may fall off. Later they pile up many objects. All the time they learn, especially through actions which do not have quite the expected result, and as they notice the discrepancies they continue to learn. The limbs reach across the midline discovering the regions of space normally inhabited by the contralateral limb as they explore the available space using both sides of their body on both sides of their environment.

Early child development

Gradually they will develop the rhythmic and ongoing repetitive behaviours which are crucial to later development. They will learn to combine the use of different body parts, for example head and eyes with head and ears, arm with hand, eye with hand, etc., and to develop the ability to shift the focus of attention from one area of their reachable space to another.

In a rhythmic manner babies reach things, get hold of things, then transfer attention away from the hand doing the holding so that that hand releases the object, and so on. Over the second six months children will learn to reach into the whole region of their own space, discover more about that space while fixing on and, both manually and optically, 'acquiring' different objects. Children reach for objects, lose interest in them and release them, picking a second thing up, and so on. At around six to eight months children are able to hold on to two objects and a bit later are able to transfer an object from one hand to the other; not in a very deliberate way, but rather one hand reaching for the object beside the other hand and the object very often getting transferred across.

There is reaching and picking up, but not putting down or deliberate dropping at this stage; but a great deal of picking up and translating with the object often released in a different place from where it was first picked up. As children's capabilities in holding on to objects increase they will frequently reach for an object without previously releasing an object already held by the hand, as if they had forgotten this first object. So the first object drops against the second object.

Beginnings of tool use

Before long we actually find children experimentally pushing and pulling, tapping and scraping other objects with a held object. Waldon saw this as being the beginning of all hand tool usage.

Children actually handle a variety of objects, which stick out of the hand, may have heavy ends, and so on. By the time they are about nine months they can hold a projecting object and touch other objects with it as if it has become an extension of the hand. At this time the tool use is generalized and one can see it as knocking on objects or banging and holding one object firmly against other items.

During this time the objects are generally in the children's hand, within their grasp, and this occurs in many different ways. Children learn to vary the hand pressures and to use different parts of the hand in accordance with the shape of the object and the direction in which it happens to be held. They have to get used to a very wide range of grips and uses of fingers and fingertips. All this is going on in the second half of the first year and by the end of the first year children will typically have an enormous capacity to use both hands separately and to use an object held in both hands together.

From the accidental holding of an object that may turn into a tool for more distant exploration they start to hold objects in a sustained way and deliberately use them to produce specific effects. So a rake may be used to bring distant objects closer or a spoon used to create a banging sound against a metal object.

All this leads on to general use of hand tools. We might imagine that we have taught a child to use a spoon, for example. But that is not really the case. All we do is to allow children to play with a spoon: they soon use the spoon in the same way that they have been using tools for the past five or six months and are soon able to tip the contents onto the floor and move things around not just into the mouth but increasingly around their own personal space.

Acquiring and disposing

By the end of the first year children have capacity to pick things up and to release them into vessels of various kinds and during the early part of the second year to put objects back onto or into specified places.

Towards the end of the first year children can usually acquire and dispose in what Waldon describes as 'a kind of rhythmic non progressive' way. They drop something into a vessel; see something in the vessel to take out; take it out; look at it and put it back; then see another object to take out and so on. The pleasure is not so much in the objects themselves but in the taking out and putting in. Waldon also described this as 'Eeyore behaviour'. In A. A. Milne's story, Pooh takes a jar of honey to Eeyore for a birthday present but eats it on the way, while Piglet bursts the balloon that he intends to give Eeyore. However, Eeyore combines the empty jar and the burst balloon into the perfect toy: enjoying placing the balloon in and out of the jar in a deliberate and repetitive manner.[6]

This is pre-continuant behaviour which soon changes into continuous or ongoing behaviour where children pick up an object, dispose of it in a certain place and are able to go back and get another object and dispose of that and then go back again, and so on. This behaviour is rarely seen until early in the second year.

Continuant behaviour

Continuant behaviour arises early in the second year when children gain, by 'haphazard but effective experimentation', the preparedness necessary to develop their understanding.

Waldon describes continuant behaviour as: 'one of the most fascinating tendencies in development – it arises early in the second year and together with striking and scraping provides the main source of the experience which founds the learning-how-to-learn-tools during the third year'.

Continuant behaviour is related to children orienting themselves in relation to their environment and being able to go back to a particular place at will. It is characterized by the continuant transfer of objects from place to place, or 'picking up and putting in'. This is well demonstrated at Pennyhooks,[7] a care farm for young autistic adults which has been influenced by the Waldon Approach. There, amongst a whole range of farm activities designed to help the student workers to develop their continuant behaviour and their General

Understanding, they move wood from a woodpile on wheelbarrows to where the wood is needed. The wheelbarrows are placed some distance from the woodpile to encourage the rhythm in the movements.

The learning-how-to-learn-tools

These tools and their precursors are fundamental to the sequence of learning that Waldon observed. Fundamental Understanding, he hypothesized, is a sequential process starting with movement, and leading on to bodily integration, continuant behaviour and the development of the learning-how-to-learn-tools. The learning-how-to-learn-tools are seriation, sorting, matching, drawing, brick-building and coding. Ultimately these are abstract mental operations which underlie our capacity for logic and reason.

Each tool evolves from a simpler precursor version which emerges within continuant behaviour and depends on a developing interest in objects as traces of movement.

Rhythmical placing of objects with slight changes in location, leads to sequencing, the precursor of seriation. Other early sequences include banging with increasing force or scraping in larger or smaller movements. Happening to put things on top of other things leads to piling and thence to more complex brick-building which involves making hypotheses about three-dimensional relationships. Putting something with something which happens to resemble it leads to separating objects into sets and eventually to mature sorting, where incoming information is scanned for its resemblance to existing sets or categories. Trying to find something leads to pairing and eventually matching, where attention is given to differences. Early scraping gives rise to scribbling and then to drawing which leads to understanding of two-dimensional space. At the same time, tool use becomes ever more refined and pervasive. Coding develops differently from the other learning-how-to-learn-tools in that it is an applied version of simple association which starts at a pre-continuant level. Mature coding which is essential to speech and reasoning depends on the development of the other learning-how-to-learn-tools.

All of these developmental steps are necessary for all children and how they can be restarted or strengthened where they have appeared only patchily in a child's development is the foundation of the Waldon Approach. More detail on the learning-how-to-learn-tools is available in the description of the Waldon Approach later in this chapter.

Atypical development

From his observation of the development of typical children Waldon developed his approach to the teaching of children who have failed for whatever reason to produce these typical movements and behaviours. Where this happens the children can become locked into a series of problems with a vicious circle of reduced motivation leading to reduced movement. This can lead to failure of bodily integration and an inability to develop a sufficiently unified bodily space. This in turn produces problems in focusing attention through the body and in shifting attention between areas of space. The child's space will be more sparsely structured, leading to a reduced ability to scan the environment and to notice things. During the second year this can also lead to a reduced ability to orient oneself in the wider environment, and thus to difficulties in developing continuant behaviour. Where the problems are less extreme, more stereotyped behaviours may arise with a failure to generate a normal level of variety due to the reduced level of motivation.

Primary and secondary impediments

Waldon distinguishes between the primary impediment which is the intrinsic problem affecting development, and secondary impediments which are described as learned problems or learned behaviours arising as a result of the primary problem.[8]

Primary impediments

Primary impediments can be thought of as anything which interferes with the system of motivation and reinforcement and secondary impediments are behaviours which try to compensate for this.

The human body develops in such a way that typically the increase in body size and weight is matched by an appropriate increase in General Understanding. Where this is not the case a disharmony can develop which can lead to further problems. Those actions that would naturally lead to later developmental stages very often do not do so under these circumstances. Or individually learned skills may not come together in a typical manner because they have not been learned in synchronization with each other.

Secondary impediments

These are the child's learned behaviours which interfere with the growth of General Understanding. They are described as anxiety-avoiding (or as Waldon called them self-handicapping), behaviours and as effort-saving behaviours.

Anxiety-avoiding or self-handicapping behaviours
Anxiety-avoiding behaviours may start as a reaction to a perceived sense of over-demand and are designed to avoid the stress and anxiety derived from expectations placed on children which are often beyond their level of understanding. They can become addictive habits which cocoon the children in a familiar and predictable world of their own making and prevent their engaging with the world around them. There are many variants of these anxiety-avoiding behaviours, for example having a tantrum, stiffening the body, averting the

gaze, indulging in annoyingly inappropriate social behaviour or in appealingly inappropriate social behaviour.

Self-delighting behaviours

Anxiety-avoiding behaviours also include 'self-delighting' behaviours, such as rocking, spinning and hand flapping which are typically seen briefly in early childhood, and which give the child the greatest feedback for the least amount of effort. They fill time with repetitive activity which does not lead to any gain of experience.

Where there is a primary impediment affecting motivation, the failure to develop typical movement patterns leads to the proliferation of those patterns which do develop. Those movements become habitual, through the cycle of reinforcement and motivation described above. As they are among the child's most familiar behaviours and generate much familiar feedback, they are engaged in at the expense of the development of less known movement patterns, and fall into the class of self-handicapping behaviours. They cocoon children in familiar experience and lead to stereotyped repetition. They are defensive, anxiety-avoiding behaviours and this anxiety is not purely evoked by the pressure of others but also by the relative unfamiliarity of other activity where the child has an awareness of the possibility of a less familiar pattern emerging and a consequent sense of potential over-demand.

There are also many children who are 'over-social' in moulding themselves to please or to elicit social responses from the surrounding adults, while their understanding lags behind. Social behaviour is one of the most potent generators of social reward, and external rewards for behaviour give children the wrong messages. In the case of the overly social child the over-social behaviour is rewarded and is thereby encouraged to the child's disadvantage. Their internal motivation is neglected and the real learning suffers.

Effort-saving behaviours

These arise from a cycle of inadequate motivation and reinforcement and interfere with the typical behaviours which encourage the growth of experience. Adults will generally find short cuts and easy ways of doing things but these are against the interest of developing children who need effortful activity to maintain their motivation. Short cuts save on effort but prevent the child from creating variety or from fully exploring space. They compound the initial problems of inadequate motivation or lack of reinforcement of the pleasure derived from the performance of an effortful activity. Typical effort-saving behaviours will be the use of one side of the body only, or the use of smaller and fewer movements. Sticking to familiar activity, which is characteristic of anxiety-avoidance, also saves on effort.

Effort-saving and anxiety-avoiding behaviours are therefore those which are adopted by a child with any primary disability to guard against or distract an expectation to perform tasks which are perceived as over-demanding.

Waldon believed that learning can only be derived from exploring the outer edges of what is already understood, which is achieved through doing what is already understood in a more effortful way. This allows more variations to develop more frequently, with a virtuous circle of reinforcement. He thought that the anxiety-avoiding and effort-saving behaviours are often more harmful to the child's progress than the original problem. The Waldon Lesson is designed to minimize these behaviours by reducing the child's need for them whilst enabling their understanding to increase, through the repeated use of the learning-how-to-learn-tools and their precursors.

With time, patience and perseverance there is a real possibility of achieving a positive outcome through the Waldon Lesson. In Robert's case it took five years of daily lessons to reach the stage of his going to a mainstream primary school. Earlier chapters have described his problems even after that. But the results in our case and in the cases of virtually all of the parents I have interviewed for this book which are included in Chapters 7 and 8, have far outweighed the time, effort and energy that were expended.

General Understanding

Waldon regarded spontaneous, effortful, undirected activity as universal to all babies and infants irrespective of their race or culture. It is simply how the human child learns. He called this learning the acquisition of General Understanding. According to Waldon, General Understanding does not change according to the social environment, country, climate or relative social position of the family in which the child is growing up, but is basic to all human beings. General Understanding is not taught but is acquired internally by children as they play and explore the environment on their own. Waldon's hypothesis is that General Understanding is gradually acquired in the typical child but that it levels off as competition with cultural rituals and social demands distract the older child. General Understanding can continue to develop during the whole of a person's lifetime, whatever their starting point. Whenever individuals move away from their usual routines their General Understanding will tend to be enhanced. Waldon used to say: 'The businessman who goes rock climbing in his holidays is reinforcing his General Understanding – his learning about the world through movement'.[9]

Particular Understanding

General Understanding is the necessary foundation for the acquisition of what Waldon called Particular Understanding. This is acquisition of particular skills and behaviours taught by adults around children in order to help them fit into the particular culture into which they happen to be born – be they Roman, Sioux, Japanese or British children, living in a high-rise apartment, a mud hut or a palace. In order to take their place in society children need to learn the particular norms of that society. So Particular Understanding is moulded by external requirements and changes enormously according to circumstance. It varies according to country or region, between social classes within the country or region and will be affected by the gender of the child. It is meant to prepare children to fit into the society in which they are growing up. It is actively taught to children by the people around and supporting them. Table manners are an example of Particular Understanding, as is arithmetic and potty training.

Some examples of the differences between General and Particular Understanding are:

General Understanding	Particular Understanding
No right or wrong	Lots of rights and wrongs
There are no rules	Rules must be followed
No adult teaching	Adult directed
Full of experimentation	Full of directed learning
The long effortful way is best for the gain of maximum experience	The shortest route is best for maximum efficiency
Powered by child's own 'motivation'	Powered by adult direction
Reinforced by pleasure	Reinforced by adult approval
Adult approval not required or requested	Adult approval unrelated to effort but to socially acceptable behaviour

Of course both types of understanding are necessary for survival and success in life; but Waldon believed that the later the rules of Particular Understanding are applied, the less they are applied during the first few years of life and the more children are allowed just to play on their own without direction or correction, the more solid will be their foundation of General Understanding and the more easily they will later be able to successfully integrate and manage the rules of their particular culture.

The Waldon Approach

Not only for autism

Although the early chapters of this book are about the history, treatment and ultimately the recovery of an autistic child it is important to recognize that the Waldon Approach is appropriate to people with all kinds of learning and physical challenges, and of whatever age. Although the case studies in Chapter 7 are of young people on the autistic spectrum, those featured in Chapter 8 have had a range of different problems so that the potential of the students described is immensely varied. Success is not defined, but I see it simply as exceeding expectations – sometimes marginally but often dramatically!

The assessment

The Waldon facilitator will assess developmental levels in the first meeting. The chronological age is irrelevant; what matters is the assessment of the child's developmental age in terms of bodily integration, range and type of movement, continuant behaviour and the learning-how-to-learn-tools. The assessment will consider the student's level of motivation and how broadly based the General Understanding is, how the student manages frustration, how tolerant and adaptive the student is to imposed movement and the constraints of the lesson and how easy or difficult it is to introduce new activities. Crucially, the assessment will try to identify the secondary impediments or learned habits that are likely now or in the future to obstruct the satisfactory creation of necessary experience.

The Waldon Lesson

The Waldon Lesson seeks to recreate, albeit in a somewhat concentrated form, the conditions encountered by typical infants as their own motivation takes them through the learning processes, and they naturally and without external direction develop and apply the learning-how-to-learn-tools and their precursors discussed above. For the developmentally delayed children all of these indispensable developmental steps are introduced at the appropriate time in the lesson which becomes the vehicle or framework for them to encounter and practise all the development stages which they have missed.

The lesson is designed to create the natural environment of the infant as closely as possible. The student's motivation is the pleasure derived from the action. The teacher/facilitator sits or stands behind or to the side of the student and does not give any facial or verbal clues of approval or disapproval of the child's actions. There is no success or failure. There is simply doing. The facilitator will often place a hand over the student's hand as a guide. This is used as an aid and will be used sometimes when unnecessary so the student never feels the guiding hand as a correction. There are no rights or wrongs. Frequently items will be removed before a task is completed to remove the possibility of an endpoint being falsely interpreted as success and to discourage dependence on that endpoint.

Ideally a lesson of about one hour will be given to the students each morning, and as they become used to and accepting of the routine so the activities practised in the lesson will begin to spill over into their spontaneous activities during the rest of the day. The Waldon Approach does not depend on a team of willing helpers to occupy the child throughout the day. On the contrary it will be most productive if the child has long periods of time when he is left to play alone and hopefully to rediscover some movements or activities introduced in the earlier lesson.

For this to occur it is essential within the lesson to reduce the anxiety-avoiding behaviours and to help the child to get used to acting effortfully and to tolerate frustration. Students learn that their avoidance behaviours are unnecessary in the lesson because nothing is asked of them that they cannot perform and there is no right or wrong endpoint. They also find that effort generates pleasure and that frustration can be tolerated. This increases what

Waldon calls their 'competence' or ability to use their General Understanding outside the lesson.

Within the lesson, praise, approval or disapproval are never given. The pleasure in performing an action is the only reward. In this environment praise could give the wrong message and confuse the child. The children perform actions for their intrinsic pleasure, and they experience the activity at the level appropriate to their own understanding. They must not become dependent on praise or rewards from the facilitator for two key reasons. Firstly, there is a risk of increasing the potential for anxiety as children try to get praise though a correct performance and become aware of the possibility of failure. Secondly, it is essential that the children become independent and active within the context, and at the level, of their own General Understanding – not the adult's judgement. Children will then be able to produce and respond to variations and move forward spontaneously.

Typically developing children will have performed all the actions which take place in the lesson spontaneously and without assistance and direction from an adult. The atypical child may not. So in the lesson the facilitator causes the child to perform the actions. Until the expectation is understood and is within the child's current level of understanding, the teacher will gently but firmly move the child's arms and hands from behind to perform the required movements or actions. The teacher will ignore any anxiety-avoiding behaviours the child might utilize as an escape mechanism, calmly working on with the child as if the behaviours were not present.

When the instructions are carefully, sensitively, but firmly applied, the child will develop a sense of security in the Waldon Chair,[10] and the avoidance behaviours will gradually cease. The child will slowly become less anxious and finally feel completely secure in the environment. Teachers and parents have described to me their own anxiety as the child resists the early lessons and their sense of relief and accomplishment when the child spontaneously sits down in the Waldon Chair with the anticipation of an effortful and pleasurable lesson about to begin.

Once used to the lesson, children adapt to the position, happily engrossed in the performance of the activities, and for the most part they ignore the facilitator behind or at their side. This is exactly what is needed – the teacher becomes a neutral part of the environment. The lesson is therefore sometimes named the 'asocial lesson' to emphasize the importance of the position and attitude of the facilitators. They stand or sit behind or to one side and have an asocial attitude – neither criticizing nor praising, by voice, gesture or expression. The children will have no expectation of being able to influence the facilitator and will focus all their concentration on the lesson activities.

The aim of the lesson is not to 'teach' anything, but rather to encourage/enable the child to play/learn more effectively by him- or herself during the rest of the day. Many parents and teachers find the asocial atmosphere of the lesson very difficult. It is natural to want to shower praise on the under-responsive child for any sign of improvement or development. It is unnatural and counter-intuitive not to praise when the child does 'well'. However, the lesson is for an intensive period of about one hour, ideally repeated every day. It has its own rules outside of common practice or normal behaviour. That is what makes it special. Both teacher and child grow to understand that this is an environment where conventional rules of behaviour do not apply.

Of course the parent can praise the child outside the lesson; of course the parent must show love and approval. The receipt of love has been shown to positively affect the shape of the brain (Gerhardt, 2004); and there is plenty of time outside the lesson for love and praise and for the important social relationship and bonding between parent and child.

Learning through self-directed activity

Waldon emphasizes that against a background of stability and emotional security, babies and children develop in ways which are physiologically driven and that for significant amounts of their time their play and movements do not need to be acknowledged by the adults around them. He sees this as a mechanism which prevents early interruptions to infant learning.

The Waldon Lesson

A mother's-eye view

It was the morning of Dr Geoffrey Waldon's recent visit to Oxford. In total silence, in an atmosphere of tension that mounted until it was almost palpable, a roomful of adults sat watching as a small boy tried to build an elaborate construction out of blocks. He was attempting to match a model that had been built by Dr Waldon, about one hour into a demonstration of the asocial lesson. The structure kept collapsing on him, and each time he calmly and patiently started again, reworking previous strategies and exploring new possibilities. The tension came entirely from the adult audience. As became clear in the discussion which followed, many (perhaps most), of us were having to stifle a strong desire to intervene and help the child complete the task. To see him trying and failing repeatedly was almost intolerable. But the child, Dan, was oblivious to the atmosphere, completely absorbed in his manipulation of the blocks. His interest seemed to be held by the nature of the activity itself, and he evinced no frustration at his repeated 'failure' to achieve a likeness of the model. The contrast between the adults' and the child's view of the situation was stark and revealing.[11]

I was there because as Dan's parent I was interested in finding out more about Waldon's approach. I had watched Dan 'work' as he puts it once before with Richard Brooks at the Oxford Resource Unit, where he is a pupil. I had also attended a series of evening workshops organized by

Richard on the Waldon Approach, and so my observation of this particular session was informed by some prior knowledge of the principles that lay behind it. I was already persuaded of the value of the approach, but I was unprepared for the impact this session had on me. I say 'impact' advisedly – for it captures the shock of the transition from knowledge to (partial), understanding.

In the earlier part of the session, Dr Waldon was deliberately setting tasks for Dan which exposed and demonstrated his underlying problems. Dan was not entirely relaxed – he played to the audience, became distracted, occasionally he became alienated from the task at hand, and he exhibited a desire to escape through handicap behaviour. It was quite painful, but also fascinating for me to watch this; as a parent it is all too easy to be encouraged by your child's progress (Dan had made great strides since joining the Unit), and to fail to pay attention in a systematic way to problem areas. As Dr Waldon worked with Dan those areas became impossible to ignore. It was glaringly obvious that he had great difficulty in transferring his attention from one area of space to another, that his body does not yet function as an integrated whole and that his perception of the space around him is correspondingly fragmented. These are things which I knew in an intuitive, unstructured way, but was now being forced to pay attention to. My admiration for the asocial lesson as a *diagnostic* tool grew apace, but so did my dismay at the enormity of the problem that Dan still faced in the struggle to make sense of the world. At this stage I found myself thinking: 'okay, this method can pinpoint the problem, but can it really do anything to ameliorate it?'

The episode with the bricks convinced me that it could. Dan, under 'normal' circumstances is a highly anxious child who seeks reassurance from the repetition of familiar, restricted sets of actions and who usually has great difficulty in exploring the world through play. Yet here he was, anxiety set aside, relaxed, absorbed in an activity for its own sake. With great skill and patience, an environment had been structured for him which was allowing him, simply, to play. He was now in a position to amass essential experience which he would never have gained unaided. Our desire, as adults, to step in and 'help' was understandable – but misplaced. It merely showed that we were still having difficulty in absorbing, or perhaps accepting, the underlying principles of the Waldon Approach. Dan did not need our help just then. Encapsulated in the asocial lesson, he was doing just fine on his own.

The early activities – banging

If a child has failed to make the basic movements which a typical infant makes spontaneously these need to be introduced early on in the Waldon Lesson. Banging encompasses many of the arm movements which are fundamental to the development of understanding, including the use of the hand and arm as a single unit operating on the environment. It is the precursor of important carrier movements which in turn are crucial to the development of continuant behaviour.

In the lesson, variation is important and as the child becomes more comfortable more variations are introduced. In the early stage the action will be close to the body, in front and not very high, because the child might resist an unfamiliar position and become anxious. Later, bigger bangs at a further distance can be used and the amount of space is extended to the space away from the child; the space above the child; on the chair, the floor, under the table, to the right and to the left. Crossing over the body, which many children find difficult, is very important for bodily integration.

Lessons very often start with banging and this is a good way to relieve tension and to relax children. As they get more accustomed to the actions and the noise, it can get quite vigorous. The rhythms are changed so that it is never monotonous. Banging can be done on a variety of surfaces – the table, a drum, a cushion and as always in every possible direction.

When young children are banging they do not bang flexibly with a series of pivots as an adult does but they use their arms and hands more stiffly. We want to help bigger children to do the same things that they would typically have learnt as a small child, but for whatever reason have failed to so do. So where it is apparent that the infant stage has been missed because the hand/arm movements are poorly coordinated and there is perhaps not sufficient effortful limb activity being employed, we need to have those large students behave as if they were younger and have their arms and hands working together in a stiffer manner.

Scraping

Scraping is also developmentally important and while banging is usually an away from the body movement, scraping is a multi-directional movement. Unlike banging it involves sustained contact between the hand or held tool and surfaces. Once a tool is used, scraping incidentally encourages an adaptive grasp in order to maintain contact, and results in the production of a great variety of movement traces, vibrational, auditory and visual. In the lesson children will scrape things into containers or push them off the table into boxes to increase their range of movement. There will, as always, be alternate hand use including movements across the midline. Scraping, like banging, starts with paddle-type movements and develops into a fully articulated activity. It can start as a simple hand scrape and develop with tools and different types of objects. Scraping through a tray of pine cones will be different from scraping through a tray of bricks, or beanbags or corrugated iron.

Once the student's grasp is more adaptive and sustained, scraping can be developed into stirring, brushing, digging, scooping, raking and pushing, using a great variety of tools. It later develops into mark making and drawing.

Picking up and putting in

Picking up and putting in is the characteristic activity of the continuant phase of development, during which children become secure in their ability to repeat a movement in a particular direction relative to themselves and to the environment. The continuant phase leads to an increasing interest in the traces of movements in the environment, particularly in different ways of arranging objects, and this in turn leads on to the learning-how-to-learn-tools.

The Waldon Lesson aims to recapitulate the normal sequence of development of continuant behaviour and the increasing space in which the child can operate.

Movements of objects from place to place become more automatic and develop their own rhythm. Children pick an object up, move some distance either with their arms over the table or, as their understanding develops, with the whole body around the room, and then place the object in the position indicated by the facilitator. Then the whole process is repeated with variations over and over again. Appropriate objects are used as tools for children to produce patterns of movement and, as Waldon and others have hypothesized, all early learning is derived from movement (Waldon, 1980; Stern, 2010: 20).

The precursors of the learning-how-to-learn-tools

By the beginning of the third year, through their activity in banging, scraping and placing, together with the acquisition of continuant behaviour, typically developing children will have acquired the following precursors which represent the emergent stage of the learning-how-to-learn-tools. They learn to do an activity deliberately after it starts to arise incidentally from continuant behaviour. Children apply each tool, or each way of organizing experience, in an increasingly refined and systematic manner.

Separating (the precursor of sorting), is the bringing together of objects which are similar to each other. The teacher will have prepared a box of disparate articles – perhaps four each of buttons, corks, pencils, marbles, cars and animals. There will be a separate container for each category of items. The student, guided or assisted by the teacher whenever necessary, separates each category into one of the containers. It might start with two perceptually distinct sets (Figure 5.1) fir cones on the left, bricks on the right, requiring large movement to either side of the trunk. The student comes to notice the distinct categories and begins to anticipate and to participate more actively. Sets may also be functionally distinct – for example rings can be put on a stem but bricks are difficult to put on a stem and have to go somewhere else. At this stage the emphasis is on large bilateral rhythmic movement. Later there may be more sets in more areas of space.

Pairing (the precursor of matching), is the process by which through a process of elimination of differences, with few pairs available, students are prompted to bring them together within a rhythmical series of movements. This is repeated until the students begin to notice and anticipate the pair, at

Figure 5.1   Separating using two small H-Boards.

which time they take over the finding part of the activity. Once this level of engagement is attained the space might be gradually increased so that the students may be wandering round the room looking for something. At this stage students have to bear something in mind. As with all progression within the Waldon Lesson, motivation has to be built up through the effortful practice of the earlier activities to become available for activities which are less familiar.

Sequencing, defined as 'the placing of things in order'[12] (the precursor of seriation which is defined as 'the action or result of arranging items in a sequence according to prescribed criteria'),[13] is the process of putting things or doing things in a rationally discernible order. This may be done in a multitude of different ways, perhaps with differently sized bricks or containers. It emerges and follows on from continuant behaviour. Sequencing, or rhythmical arrangement of objects or of perceptual experiences in space or time, is therefore dependent on continuant activity and on the space structuring which precedes it. An example of sequencing often used in the Waldon Lesson uses two wooden boats, one of which contains ten men (Figure 5.2). The child can be prompted and assisted by the facilitator until he understands and becomes able to extrapolate and continue independently as he moves the men one at a time, using alternately his left and right hand, to fill the empty boat. As the student develops different patterns will be used, such as one man, one space, one man, one space; and then ever more complex patterns will be introduced.

Practice in continuant behaviour, sequencing and later on in seriation will be included in all lessons. It leads to students' recognition of their own patterns of behaviour and eventually to the extrapolation of the behaviour of others.

Piling (the precursor of brick building), simply involves putting things on top of other things. It is vigorous and clumsy and has lots of accidents and no discernible endpoint. Gradually this gives way to more stable and deliberate construction. It is a type of basic sequencing which, as objects start to become more interesting, and the carrier movements more automatic, leads to more active attempts to place things on top of other things and hence to discoveries about what works and what doesn't.

Scribbling (the precursor of drawing and use of tools), is the process of making undifferentiated marks on a surface. A child will hold an object in apposition to a surface for a prolonged period of time and pushes, pulls, makes circular movements, in fact all the sort of arm and hand movements previously associated with banging and scraping, but now holding an object. Things in apposition tend to leave traces. A facilitator may start with simple scribbles and might develop over time to geometric shapes – circles, squares, triangles – whilst the child may be encouraged to make similar marks. These marks and traces are the beginnings of graphic productions, or drawing.

All of these precursors will be within the capability of typically developing 27-month-old children and will have been learnt by them through self-directed experimentation and play. It is of critical importance for children with difficulties that they are all practised in the Waldon Lesson and that continued and spontaneous practice is encouraged, by careful placing of objects in the play area, during the rest of the children's day so that they can continue to play and to learn on their own.

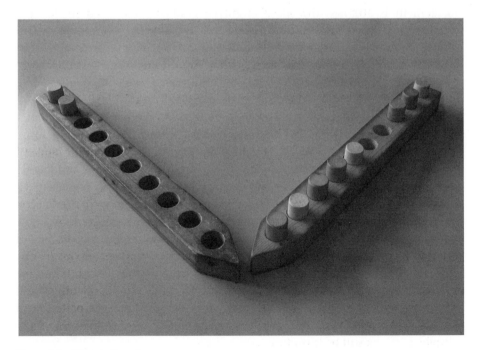

Figure 5.2 'Men in Boats'.

Used in many different ways to develop sequencing and seriation using alternating hands. They were made by Escor Toys, now sadly out of business. They are now available at www.autismand understanding.com

The learning-how-to-learn-tools

With the precursor activities absorbed, typical children are ready to assimilate, on their own, the experiences derived from the use of the more advanced learning-how-to-learn-tools Their developing General Understanding leads them on to the developmental steps which Waldon calls the learning-how-to-learn-tools, which provide a framework for understanding both typical and atypical development. The learning-how-to-learn-tools grow spontaneously from activity. The child practises the activity, accidentally generates variation, starts to notice the new variant as it happens more often, and then deliberately reproduces it. Through their self-directed exploration of these tools children further develop their General Understanding and it is on this firm foundation that the remainder of their lifetime learning will be based. The lesson is designed to help atypical children absorb all of these tools as far as their potential will allow.

Sorting (which follows on from separating), is the process of putting things together in groups according to what they have in common. Similarities are registered so that sorting becomes the basis of classification and categorization. It is the process by which we group experiences and develop collections of things such as stamps or Chinese snuff bottles. Sorting is a straightforward development of separating and differs in the complexity of the attributes which the items to be sorted have in common. In playing sorting games the facilitator may have the containers in different parts of the room, at different levels, even hidden in cupboards or up ladders so that the child expends effort in finding the appropriate container – pre-seeded with one or two of the appropriate category or class of object being sorted. Remember, the more effort that is expended, the more fun is the activity, and the more fun there is, the more motivation is engendered.

As true sorting develops the student has to make decisions about which things go together and eventually how many sets are needed. Watching Mary Jo give Edward a lesson (see Chapter 7), he had a pile of disparate objects and she had a cupboard full of different containers. Each time Edward decided on a new sorting category he had to rummage in the cupboard for an appropriate container thus maximizing his independence in establishing categories – true sorting rather than separating, where objects were being allocated to a fixed number of containers.

Matching (which follows on from pairing), is the process of eliminating things which are different in order to find things which are the same as something else. Pairing can continue up to a fairly advanced level of perceptual discrimination as objects become less and less identical and it develops into true matching via the use of increased space, abstraction, consideration of multiple features and redundancy – an excess of similar possibilities – which forces both more effortful scanning and a sequential ordering of more and less likely matches, so that the eventual match is the best available rather than the only one. Matching and pairing are often carried out with the use of an H-Board (Figure 5.3).

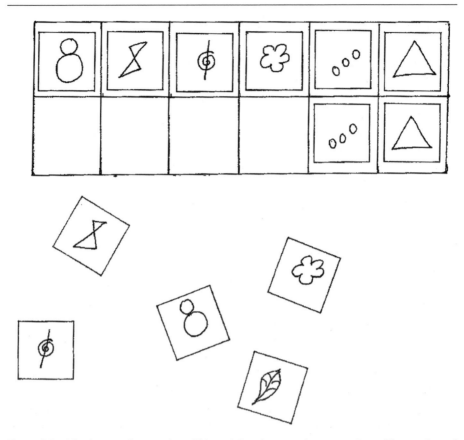

Figure 5.3   Matching cards on a short H-board. Simple monochrome outlines. The number of redundant cards and the space which needs to be searched can both be increased as the student becomes more comfortable with the level of matching involved.

Cards become more and more abstract as the card becomes a line drawing, then a pictogram and finally a symbol. All these progressions may take months or even years of patient work, very gently extending the child's comfort zone but without inducing anxiety. Whilst matching, children begin to notice differences in form, size, orientation, colour, number, etc. They will recognize one-to-one correspondence and be able to separate out items of different correspondence. Matching increases the number of things which are paired – there may be 10 kinds of animals, from photographs, to models, to different textures, etc. all kept in one group, whilst non-matching items are discarded or placed to one side.

Sorting and matching are reciprocal and largely functionally inseparable, but, counter-intuitively, matching is about noticing differences and sorting is about finding similarities. Matching is the process which helps us to find something specific we need. Sorting is how we organize incoming information and allows us to recognize the need for a new category, or combination of categories, of which an item may be part. Sorting is open ended because new categories or sub-categories can emerge at any time. Developmentally, sorting comes before matching so it will usually be introduced at an earlier stage.

Seriation follows on from sequencing and is at the heart of Waldon's theory. He refers to it as 'pervading'; that is, spread through or into every part of his theory. It is from seriation that we learn to extrapolate and predict. Waldon writes: 'seriation is the basis of inferential thinking, the origin of deductive reasoning' (1980). The development leads from 'motivation' (in the Waldon sense of the word), through rhythm to continuant behaviour, then via sequencing, to seriation, which is the lynchpin of the learning-how-to-learn-tools.

There is a prescribed sequence for almost all constructive activities, such as getting dressed or going to the toilet, or delivering the post or playing a team game or cooking. Poor memory of such sequences and disorientation or confusion during them implies lack of familiarity with and lack of understanding of the component parts of the patterns and connections within them. But without an understanding of sequencing daily tasks can take forever. Pamela remarked to a friend that helping Robert to get himself dressed could take all morning.[14]

It is interesting that two psychoanalysts at their first meeting managed to say, almost simultaneously, 'the difficulty for the autistic child is in sequencing'.[15] This difficulty is at the centre of the Waldon Lesson.

Intersectional Sorting

The advanced student will be introduced to Intersectional Sorting which is a type of sorting game, played on a 12×12 H-Board (Figure 5.4), which requires looking at a card, then looking first at a vertical and then at a horizontal key and then deducing

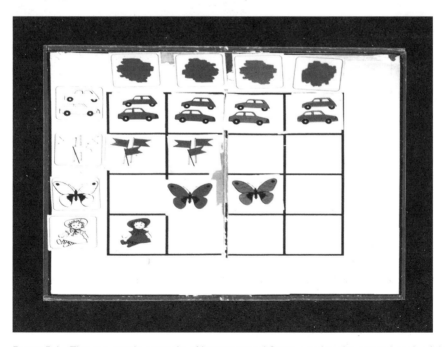

Figure 5.4 This is a simple example of Intersectional Sorting and in the original, each of the blobs on the top line and the various objects are in different colours.

the square in which the card belongs. This helps to develop the ability to consider multiple and variable criteria referring to two (or more) axes. In Intersectional Sorting, seriation, sorting and inferential thinking all come together.

Brick building (which follows on from piling), promotes the understanding of three-dimensional relationships and of necessary, but sometimes hidden, supports. It involves the discovery of direction and distance, of relative position and functional relationships. It leads to the ability to recognize, follow and interpret the changes of position, translocation, reorientation, deformation, which are the basic components of behaviour, both of materials and people.

Figure 5.5   Brick building at the Autism Base, St Nicholas School, Oxford.

Brick building has thus both a practical importance and an abstract application. In a practical way it enables understanding of how things are put together. In an abstract way it is an important basis of deductive thought, in calculating that: 'If I do this then that will probably happen'. Most importantly, Geoffrey Waldon suggested that brick building is the tool that develops understanding of the behaviour not just of inanimate materials, but also of human behaviour in terms of movement in space.

Typically, in a Waldon Lesson, the facilitator will build a model and with a second group of bricks the student will build a lookalike, copying the facilitator, movement by movement (Figure 5.5). As the students gain understanding from the movements they themselves have made, the complexity of the structure will increase and eventually students will be able to copy or construct more complex models without support. To successfully recreate the model, from further apart, requires a fuller understanding of its structure because the students need to create a picture in his mind before physically reproducing the three-dimensional original.

Drawing (which follows on from scribbling), is a particular form of tool use which leads to the understanding of two-dimensional space. It is important because human beings make two-dimensional marks such as writing on paper or drawing in the sand and we have to be able to read and write them. In the lesson this is a natural development from scribbling.

Coding is essential for conventional language and is the process by which one thing can be allowed to stand for another. In Morse three dots are code for the letter S. Coding is based on the capacity for simple association but can only develop when the other learning-how-to-learn-tools are in place and interconnecting. It does not have a specific precursor but derives from the overarching pattern of development of General Understanding (Figure 5.6).

In terms of early speech, simple association can be seen to operate from a pre-continuant stage. For example, a 12-month-old baby may well associate several word sounds with people, objects or events. However, it is not until development occurs within the other learning-how-to-learn-tools that coding can start to be used systematically to fix or clarify notions. This is because true coding requires flexible sorting and matching. A practical example of coding is the acquisition of new words, where the child has to hold a word in mind, even in the absence of the object or activity, while also discovering its scope of reference.

Thus pairing games are initially played on the basis of perceptual similarities, but once the student understands that all objects must have a match, it becomes possible for the match to become more conceptual – to involve objects which have few perceptual similarities but have a related conventional function and may share a name. So two very different objects may both be called 'ball' and be related by being the least unlike of a set of pairs of objects.

Expressive language or speech

Expressive language or speech generally lags behind receptive speech or comprehension. In their anxiety for the child to match conventional milestones parents may be anxious about their child not talking and it can be hard for them to accept that without understanding of receptive speech any expressive language is likely to be unintelligible and often echolalic. Pamela and I thought that if only Robert could speak all his problems would be resolved. Waldon continually counselled us to wait until his General Understanding had reached the appropriate level.

Moving outdoors

Once the activities in the lesson have been well established and the student is secure in the Waldon Chair, it is both fun and valuable to use the outdoors as a large workshop. Here you can extend children's range of movements by using a climbing frame. Start with small apparatus and have them walk round the

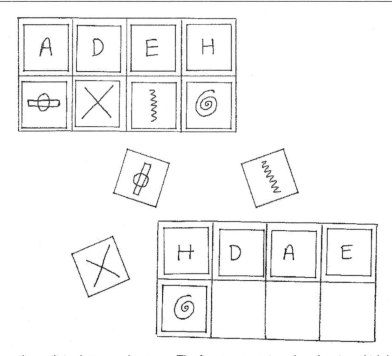

Simple coding utilizing letters and patterns. The first tray contains a key showing which letter goes with which pattern. The student refers to the key when placing the pattern cards on the second tray. Usually done on longer H-board.

Coding using pictograms and words. The first tray contains a key showing which word 'goes with' which pictogram. The student refers to the key when placing the words on the second tray. Usually done on longer H-board.

Figure 5.6

garden without touching the grass. Use tables, chairs, stepping stones, small ladders, wooden boxes – whatever is at hand. Keep it at a low level and as their confidence increases introduce more challenging arrangements. Intersectional sorting can be fun with coded children (one a duck and one a teacup) coming together on squares. At Bishopswood School (see Chapters 6 and 8) these activities are called 'Walking Waldon'.

There is no upper age limit for using the Waldon Approach. The work of the Leeds Waldon Group exemplified by the story of Michael in Chapter 8 clearly demonstrates this. But the earlier the lessons are started the greater the possibility of progress. It is increasingly recognized that early intervention is extremely important, especially in reducing the impact of the avoidance and self-delighting behaviours (Lytel, 2008). Waldon was as helpful with 'hot housed' and stressed Manchester Grammar School students[16] as with those with cerebral palsy or with remote children.

Parents and teachers who would like more structured and detailed information on the lessons are recommended to read *Every Child Can Learn* (Stroh et al., 2008). The authors of that book very successfully used this approach to help many children.[17] The book also includes an instructive DVD.

6

Centres Influenced by Geoffrey Waldon

'I don't know what you are doing but whatever it is it works' (Teacher in Leeds)[1]

In Waldon's lifetime several centres worked with children and young adults following his approach. In this chapter many of the teachers who learnt directly from Waldon, visited his centre, attended his workshops or learnt from others and became passionate about his ideas speak about their experiences. This section concludes with a study carried out in Iceland on the use of the Waldon Approach within a school setting.

The Leeds Waldon Centre

A group of teachers first came together in an adult education service at Meanwood Park Hospital and from 1984 began to use the Waldon Approach with hospital residents of all ages (18 to 70), and all kinds of learning difficulties. After a number of years the hospital closed, the patients were transferred into care in the community and the Waldon work continued in different locations, as part of the same adult education service.[2]

A Leeds Waldon Centre was also established where students were seen privately. This ran from 1989 until 1995. Three of these teachers continue to give Waldon Lessons – two in Leeds and one in London.

Marilyn: I was asked if I would be interested in setting up a pilot adult education project at Meanwood Park Hospital.[3] I knew Eileen and Terry socially at the time and slowly a number of us became involved there. Eileen had worked in special schools previously, as had I, and other people came from other avenues of education. We ran small groups of four or five which was essentially what I had been wanting, but the people had tremendous difficulties because they had been institutionalized over long periods and a number had no speech. Eileen had experience with special care people. We were addressing physical needs but again it seemed to me that we were not addressing their learning needs.

Eileen attended a course at the Leeds Poly where she had seen a video of Geoffrey Waldon, and she had said: 'Why don't we have a look at what he's doing and see if we can have him come over?', and that is how the link with Geoffrey occurred. It was a wonderfully exciting time where as soon as you heard Geoffrey talking and saw him working with people – it felt like a sea change. It took a long time to fully understand what he was doing, but instantly you could see the engagement of the person, the attention span, the focusing that was going on in these lessons. It was what we really wanted – for someone to be engaged with the world, with what they were doing. It was a genuine connection and that was the remarkable thing that we saw as we began to work with people, following the Waldon way.

Mostly my experience over the years has been with people with quite severe learning disabilities; it is mostly authentic contact with the world that is missing and that is what we wanted to redress. We watched Geoffrey facilitating that connectedness and slowly we tried the ideas out ourselves. Our residents were bigger than most of the people that Geoffrey saw; we did see him dealing with people who were older but they were also more able than our group. So we had to scale up everything that he did for it to make sense for our people. He came to visit and to do some assessments for us in Leeds. It was an exciting time then; developing materials and everything. We went over to Manchester for seminars and study groups regularly and to watch him work and used to discuss a great deal amongst ourselves.

Eileen: As a group we continued for such a long time because we were a group of like-minded people who were willing to explore his ideas, and who were less than satisfied with the conventional teaching methods.

Ann: I came across Geoffrey in 1984 when I was working at Meanwood with adults with very severe and complex learning difficulties and a lot of challenging behaviours and I just found what he was doing really intriguing. It seemed to me to contrast greatly with what other people were doing. Previously I had worked alongside various people using different methods and although everyone was very well intentioned and staff might be very busy, pupils commonly were very passive. Geoffrey's approach was just so different. He was bringing about a lot of activity in other people; they were getting on with things for an hour at a time, which was just absolutely incredible. I was very struck by that and by how he managed to bring it about.

Waldon in mainstream school

Ann: What is so striking about the ideas is that they do apply to everyone and it was really exciting to use it in an ordinary classroom. The children loved it; they were instantly engaged and it produced results. I was supply teaching, and the class teacher I was supporting was very struck by how the children were progressing. She said to me: 'I don't know what you are doing but whatever it is it works.'

Pat: It does seem very odd to people – they don't understand what is going on because it is so different and extremely hard to explain.

On one level it seems so very simple and people see the simplicity without understanding the complex thinking behind the activities. There is so much breadth and depth there that the richness is not easily digested by the casual, even if interested, observer.

Eileen: Resistance does not only come from an inability to grasp the ideas; it is a deeper rooted resistance which comes from people's self image. We like to think of ourselves as nice caring people, and this is one of the reasons that we are involved in the work we do; but ingrained in that is the idea of encouragement and praise and we don't want to admit that this too often fosters dependence. The child often works just to please you and in turn you reward it with praise and approval. And because we ourselves need praise and approval it is very hard to use the asocial approach without actually altering yourself.

Pat: A typically developing child is not disadvantaged by this praise because he needs to feel valued; he is highly motivated and naturally spends much of his time developing his General Understanding. But for a child who has special needs, all that praise impedes the development of General Understanding and creates a dependency. Conventional training teaches one to be more interactive when what is really needed is less interaction or interaction in a specialized asocial way, allowing the technical task, rather than the relationship with the teacher, to be the centre of attention.

The fundamental concepts are General Understanding and Particular Understanding, motivation, learning through movement, the asocial lesson, the learning-how-to-learn-tools. If you can get those things across – people can develop their own lessons.

Ann: We are keeping the physical materials in good shape so that they can be disseminated to people as they want or need them. Also we are able to help if people want advice. We can answer parents' questions and then hope that parents take it on themselves.

Eileen: The children we saw tended to be very early developmentally due to conditions such as cerebral palsy. They were severely challenged physically. I took my own daughter to Geoffrey when she was about seven, because some things that were going on at the time were having a bad impact on her. So I thought that going to Geoff might help steady her up – she had a lack of self confidence, felt that she could not do things, and of course working with Geoffrey confidence was a never an issue.

She has recently said that it had affected her in a positive manner. She used to get quite thrilled – look what we did today – because she was at the level where you could do all kinds of different things and she was quite captivated with the lessons.

Pat: I am thinking of Ian who was remote or autistic. When we first had him at Meanwood he could not put his hand on anything; he reacted as though the things he touched were red hot. I was his teacher and I used to struggle not to laugh when I attended his case conferences. At one, his carers spoke of him eating a tennis racquet. I asked why they did not take it away from him and they responded that he had chosen to do it! But even starting work with him as an adult – from when we took him to when he had to leave because the hospital closed – there was incredible increase in his repertoire of behaviours. It just shows that Waldon works and how he could learn!

Terry: The two things that I heard said by care staff most commonly at Meanwood, after we had been teaching their residents, was that some of them became much better at using their hands, so they could feed themselves or pick up cups. But then there was a nuisance element – now they could press down handles and open doors. Initially they would be surprised it opened because they had never opened a door before and now they pressed this thing and it opened this door to freedom. So that was very obvious to the staff.

Less immediately obvious was that their walking became much better. They became able to walk across grass which is very uneven and much harder to cross than walking on a path. For the first time these residents were walking on grass with a degree of confidence. And they could walk up and down stairs using the banister when previously they would just stand at the top or the bottom of a staircase and freeze. We were doing with them what Geoffrey had taught us to do, and in particular alternating the two sides of the body was obviously affecting their feet, and the weight bearing through the feet. That contributed to their being able to balance better when they walked. It was quite impressive.

Pat: Walking is a big, obvious thing that you are cued in to looking at; but they could be doing all kinds of subtle things, arranging things in their room, and moving objects around that the staff would not necessarily have noticed. So that was very encouraging – real everyday progress. The more astute staff members would notice that they could do more for themselves and were more independent. Before they had their Waldon Lessons they would just sit there passively after their dinner and now sometimes they would pick something up or take it to a sink or do something else which had a positive impact on the life of the house.

Ann: Attribution is difficult. Very often we were required to supply some kind of proof that our students were improving. And for us it was a very easy thing to do because we could see lots and lots of changes happening over a period of time. Those things might seem small, but to us they would be very significant. But others with no Waldon background could not always grasp how it came from what we were doing. You would come across care staff who said that since a resident had been doing Waldon Lessons they were so much better. They might be quite vague about it but just have this general sense that this person seemed to be in some way different. But we could actually specify and say why they could now do this, this and this. So we could get very excited because over two, three and four years you could really see a remarkable difference.

Walter: Working with these young people did you find in concert with the improvements in their abilities and comprehension, that there was also a reduction in their self-handicapping behaviours?

Terry: Yes – the two things go together and people do notice if difficult behaviours are reducing, certainly those behaviours which are difficult for other people to manage. Quite often the situation eased; the person became calmer and more comfortable with themselves and less agitated in their behaviours. As their understanding grew it was mainly positive in that they could do things they could not earlier have done, but there is also a negative aspect as they became adaptive and resourceful in finding undesirable short cuts.

Eileen: There was no parental support in the situation we were working in. Those people were very extreme and had been institutionalized for years before we had got to them and they were having one or, at the most, two lessons a week. The parents were not involved in supporting it because of the type of institution they were in. It is amazing that we got any kind of results at all. It just shows how good Waldon is.

Terry: Institutional life is a two-edged sword. The bad part is that there are unfortunate pressures on the residents to conform in certain ways. The good side is that a lot of the time they were left to their own devices for whole stretches of the day, so they had a lot of undeveloped potential. When patients moved out into the community, their behaviour became more problematic; in terms of their Fundamental Learning this was, because they were subject to pressures that they were not subject to in the institution and they were required to do things that they could not possibly do.

What Geoffrey did was to confront us with the videos and invite us to observe, which now we could do very readily, although at the time it was alien and we did not know what we were looking at. Then he had to tell us what we should be looking for and guide us through the process until we could actually see the movements which before we had just been gaping at with our more adult way of looking at things and we could not see what was really going on.

Geoffrey explained that it all starts from the sensory receptors, and we sat there not understanding, so he explained to us very patiently what sensory receptors are and what they do and how the nervous system is such a vital part of the body's functioning. He took us through that painstakingly in the initial session and we realized that it was up to us to educate ourselves. Once we had some familiarity with the terms and were thinking outside categories like brain and body, and realized that there was much more to it than that, we could to an extent educate ourselves and catch up on some of the scientific literacy that we now needed.

With arts degrees we were very lacking in those areas. So he threw us in at the deep end but helped us to swim. That made us realize that if we were going to follow this up we had to put a lot of work into it. We began to realize that the Waldon Theory itself is multifaceted and the only way to understand it was through the effort we put into the understanding of it.

Ann: Geoffrey was so generous with the time he gave us and his patience was just remarkable. The way that he approached things was interesting because he did not just sit and talk; he provided thinking exercises to help us along. After he had given a child a lesson, he could then spend up to an hour talking to the parents. He did it as if he had all the time in the world for those people, although they were one of perhaps five or six sets of parents he was going to see that day. Very often he would be saying the same sorts of things in slightly different ways.

Walter: It is interesting to hear you talk because you obviously had a broad experience with a lot of children. I just had a very narrow experience watching him teach one child and being emotionally involved in it as well, being my own son. So it is really interesting to hear what you say. When we asked the questions and got the explanations, the explanations themselves were difficult to understand because we did not have any theoretical background for it at all. We would say why are you doing this and get the answer which was sometimes even more complicating for us. And at that stage there was nothing written to read.

Ann: It must have been daunting. We had a reason to learn because we were already engaged in a certain educational process so what he was saying was making sense to us. We just had to find some way of understanding it conceptually and it was helpful doing it as a group because we supported each other.

Meaning from movement

Terry: Maxine Sheets-Johnstone is the person whose ideas seem to be the closest to Geoffrey's. She is a Professor of Philosophy and was a Professor of Dance before that, but the books she writes are written more as if by a biologist – she has studied biology to an advanced level – so from all of these different aspects she has an enormous appreciation of the relevance of movement in everyday life. She highlights meaning from movement in the same way that Geoffrey did. We think in movement. We cannot help but think in movement because everything we learn and everything we understand comes from physical movement and this is reflected in everything we do and in how we express ourselves.

She gave an example: tutoring in an elementary school she came across a 12-year-old boy who had been diagnosed as dyslexic and was asked by the parents if she might help. So she looked at how the boy wrote, how he moved in writing his name, for example, and devised a programme from there. She got large rolls of newsprint, unrolled them, and pinned them on a wall. She gave the boy some chalk, and had him draw continuous spirals, large, substantive ones across the roll of paper pinned to the wall, going first in one direction, then in reverse. She had him do the same with angular marks such as 'v's', and so on. When she spoke to us about this we were enthralled because it was exactly what Geoffrey used to do – using something that you had to put a lot of effort into; pressing hard in order to make a mark and stretching, so it was enormous use of space and a highly motivating activity – the child had to use so much effort on this.

Marilyn: Over the years I have worked with a range of people, including people with severe psychiatric difficulties. I have used the principles in different ways with different groupings and they remain valid because they apply to all of us. I don't officially do Waldon in my local authority work any more but I do use all the principles and it remains a massively effective tool for me when I am working with people with challenging behaviour.

I use the principles and whenever I can work one to one I implement as much of the Waldon Approach as possible. And in groups, whether it is a PE or an art class I still try and deliver it in a way that is fostering bodily integration and helping to increase focus and concentration – General Understanding rather than Particular Understanding. It is the flow of engagement and attention which is usually lacking in people with learning difficulties and which doesn't get addressed by conventional educational inputs. What Geoffrey gave me an angle on was looking at that continuity of involvement and engagement, and the physical, whole body, focus.

There were surprising things like how putting things further away makes it easier for people to manage a flow in activity because it engages them more fully. It's just a lovely thing, watching students trying to do things; they are trying to bring things close to make it easier for themselves and you suggest to support staff to 'put it further away and that will help'. And you can see the staff looking at you and thinking: 'What?' But it works.

Walter: I saw this on Pennyhooks Farm where they bring in about 15 autistic young adults to work on the farm and they do all sorts of farm jobs and one of the jobs they do is taking wood from the woodpile, putting it in a wheelbarrow and taking it to where it is needed. So they put the wheelbarrows quite a distance away from the wood. Well there is one young man there who always takes the wheelbarrow and puts it really close. He cannot understand why they place it so far away. And they gradually move it further and further and further away. You can understand why!

Marilyn: Yes – even if it is an art project where they are basically cutting out and gluing – you need a large space where they have to go and fetch something and go somewhere else to place it. Their whole body becomes involved in the activity and you can make a clear demarcation of all the different processes.

I work with two students on a private basis and have carers and parents who are very supportive of the work. Both have challenging behaviour so their home environments are particularly appreciative of the impact of the work we have done with them. They have funding coming through which their carers or parents have organized for them. There is a specialist autism service in Leeds which has been supportive over the years of the work we have done with them. Student nurses and new staff come to observe sessions to see what the Waldon work is, and seem to have high regard for it and for its value. They take on the principles of a low-key emotional atmosphere, principles which are now accepted within a lot of autistic communities because of sensory overload issues, but at the time for them it was new and it was really the Waldon people in that setting who had introduced that.

Working as a Waldon facilitator you observe people in a careful way and you can properly see what they are doing with their bodies and where they are looking and so can facilitate fundamental processes like the simple switching of attention from place to place. This is a simple process in one way yet crucial to learning. But it is so hard for a lot of people who, because of anxiety and over-demand, tend to be fixated and are physically and experientially limited.

These observations are made possible through the 'asocial' approach of the facilitator. A Waldon practitioner makes no judgement upon a student and is willing not to get anything back socially from a student. That is crucial. It is like a conduit of trust that is established and you can explore and tune things so finely to the individual need because you have this intervention that students feel safe with.

So many people want to develop a relationship and need EMOTIONAL feedback from students and that is quite contrary to the way that Geoffrey would work. It is a demanding thing for staff who are there because they want to be 'caring'. And a massively important thing that Geoffrey introduced was the importance of reaching and grasping and how critical that was in terms of communication and the development of pointing. A lot of people with autism have difficulty with pointing and it all comes from reaching. He so carefully integrated the pointing finger when he was using the matching boards and the intersection boards, and made use of the pointer as a self organizer. Later on it was used to make choices and to specify things. It is such an effective tool.

Something else we worked with a lot at Meanwood was the development of the use of tools to facilitate people's engagement with the world; the use of tools to develop grasping, introducing obstacles, making things more awkward and difficult as a way of encouraging more manual dexterity; so that when they were out in the world and having to do something, that was facilitated by their earlier interactions in the lessons.

And just playing transferring games apparently for the games' sake but in fact to develop continuant activity; students can sense that they are learning, at an appropriate level, and they totally enjoy it. People look on and may say 'it is a bit repetitive' or it is a 'bit boring'; but that is from an outsider's view. From a student's inner point of view they seem to be totally delighted.

Breakthroughs for people with challenging behaviour

Marilyn: I have used the Waldon Approach with people with challenging behaviour more than with any other group and the breakthroughs have been so evident, because for the first time they are being challenged at the correct level of their understanding. They can feel themselves not to be under any pressure and their 'problem' behaviours just seem to fall away.

Terry: Inside the Leeds Waldon Centre we displayed a notice with these words which Geoffrey Waldon had given to us. And it was against this background that my colleagues and I began to look at the specific area of formal education, and the even narrower subject matter of education for people with learning difficulties. This is important because the more someone can come to appreciate the breadth and scope of Waldon's philosophy, the better they can understand the specific educational applications of his ideas.

THE INTERESTS OF THIS CENTRE ARE:

- First: in how experience is created and becomes understanding, and how this understanding develops and determines the forms and directions of our behaviours
- Second: in the interpretation of human behaviours and attitudes in the light of these ideas
- Third: in the exploitation of the ideas in guiding educational practices
- Fourth: in the application of these ideas in facilitating the growth and adjustment of understanding in anomalously developing and distressed children, and in redressing distortions in this growth.

In just these few dozen words Geoffrey outlined his amazingly ambitious project: to investigate human understanding and behaviour and to explain the mechanisms of learning, and the processes of development, that make human beings the unique species that we are. His underlying interest was in the phenomenon of survival – how do organisms learn to adapt to, and to modify, their environment so that they can continue to live and reproduce, and so on? He looked at humans as a special case of an organism that is particularly adaptive because of its extremely unspecialized nature, which is a function of its unspecialized – or general – understanding.

Simple as that.

The Oxfordshire Service for Autism

I would like to dedicate this section to Sheila Coates. Sheila introduced the Waldon Approach at the Chinnor Primary School in Oxfordshire and together with Richard Brooks was instrumental in having it accepted by the Oxfordshire Service for Autism. Today it is used in special schools across the county and one, Bishopswood Special School near Henley on Thames, had three 'Waldon Rooms' specially designed and equipped in their newly built primary department. Sheila was of enormous help to me in the preparation of the technical chapters but sadly she died in late 2010 before seeing the book completed.

Sheila Coates

I was a teacher in Oxfordshire for 10 years or so before I came across Geoffrey's work and this was via Richard Brooks. We had set up Resource Bases in Oxfordshire which were partly therapeutic and partly educational, but on the mainstream school campus, and we were catering for about 20 or 30 children. I am a teacher and became a teacher working primarily with children on the autistic spectrum.[4]

The children I first came across who had autism would most likely have been categorized as severely emotionally disturbed or maladjusted and the local psychiatrist, Dr Mercy Heatley, felt that for the child with autism the provision offered in Oxfordshire was totally inappropriate and there was a very clear need for something specific for these individuals. This was very illuminating of her in the early 1970s and quite pioneering. In her own indomitable way she refused to sign the standard educational forms which would allocate these young people to a special school and set about finding an alternative way of educating them.

The route which she initially took was home tutoring, which was also unsatisfactory, and I became one of the early home tutors. I used to bring this young child home to my house and tried to 'educate' him. He was a young boy who already showed signs of hypolexia – being able to read the road signs, labels on food tins and things like that but could not really hold a proper conversation. He had some very unusual and scared behaviour and it was quite by accident that I managed to hook up with another local psychologist.

We were lucky enough to talk to the local primary school headmaster who said: 'You really cannot work at home with these children for hours on end. You must have a base to come in to. So come into school, bring the young people with you and I will talk to my staff and as long as you are there all the time you can select whatever is going on in the school that seems appropriate. Have a go. We will give you books, pens, pencils, paper and all the rest of it and if things get too much then disappear for a while'.

Geoffrey Manser was an amazing, enlightened man who was headmaster of Chinnor Primary School. There were three of us who started in Chinnor. There were three children in the locality who had similar difficulties. We now know that is not particularly unusual, but it seemed unusual at the time, so we began to take them into class. We were able to talk to the other children and the staff so that they were completely unfazed by the behaviour of these youngsters. One boy that I particularly looked after would dive under the desk as a kind of private retreat, would curl up for a while and show many other little incidents with that kind of outward manifestation of his anxiety, timidity and autism that we began to work through.

Almost at the same time we were introduced to Professor Nikolaas Tinbergen, FRS. He was a zoologist who was awarded a Nobel Prize for his work on herring gulls, which seems a long way from autism; but the kind of, what he described as 'anxiety dominated motivational conflict behaviour' which he was looking at in terms of being defensive behaviours, some children with autism also have.[5, 6]

We all tend to become anxious and underperform under duress. Professor Tinbergen noticed that the herring gulls he studied displayed behaviour similar to many children with autism. He became interested in the approach adapted by Geoffrey Waldon which 'ameliorated outward symptoms of Autism' (Tinbergen and Tinbergen, 1983: 180–4). As children began to work under asocial conditions their anxiety diminished. The condition of the asocial lesson mirrored many of the behaviours used in Tinbergen's advice on the non-intrusive therapeutic approach when working with children who have autism.

Professor Tinbergen taught in Oxford, became very interested in what we were doing and gave us some of his Nobel Prize money so that we could set up a real building on the site of the school. Instead of having to bring the children back to our own houses when they became tired, anxious or upset we could just take them into the schoolroom that we had on site and we could work with them in reducing their anxiety.

This is where we got to know Frances Tustin because she was very interested, through our psychiatrist, in how we were using this idea of observing the youngster very closely and as soon as we observed signs that the activity or the relationships in the classroom were breaking down we were able to give the youngster the opportunity to come away from that situation and come in to a quiet space, where we began to introduce alternatives such as music therapy, art therapy, some psychotherapy and drama for those who were ready to tolerate small groups of two or three.

So we began to get this mix and match of what I call pedagogy – the academic learning (for three hours or whatever), and the therapeutic side trying to understand what motivated the child, what got in the way of their learning, and why they became very stuck and repetitive.

It was about this time that Richard [Brooks] joined the staff. He kept asking: 'Have you come across Geoffrey Waldon's work yet?' He had been introduced to it before going to Greece where he found the asocial approach extremely fruitful in overcoming his language communication problem!

So Richard said: 'Have you heard about Waldon' and I said: 'No' and he went on to explain it a little. So I then went up to Manchester as part of my study leave, spent some time with Geoffrey and spent several days just seeing and watching the different clients that he had and working through the different levels of development and understanding. Some of them were quite sophisticated by then and doing intersectional sorting and seriational assembly. I was completely bowled over and went back to Richard and said: 'Yes – I see what you mean. I think we should see if we can introduce it at Chinnor'.

So we did. We managed to put on some workshops and to persuade Geoffrey to come to Oxford at the time with part of the team from Meanwood Hospital in Leeds, who were already working with the 'Approach'. He gave us some workshops working with our children and with our staff in situ in the classroom on an ordinary working day and a seminar at the weekend. Little by little we managed to interest quite a substantial number of the special schools in Oxfordshire and the neighbouring counties.

Geoffrey's work has helped enormously in two ways. Firstly, from the teacher's point of view, was the absolutely crucial understanding of the difference between mental age and chronological age. The developmental age is so exponential, and it is vital that it is not missed; but how easy it is for teachers to miss it because we are not trained for it and know hardly anything about it.

Behavioural difficulties are caused by lack of General Understanding

Secondly, that part of development that Geoffrey always described as being within the child's own motivation – the Fundamental Understanding – is absolutely crucial and if as teachers we try to rush or gloss over it then we create enormous pitfalls for later learning and understanding and create huge tension in the child. So many of the difficulties children experience in the classroom that lead to negative and anti-social behaviour or lack of motivation, are based on lack of General Understanding – the learning-how-to-learn-tools [which have been discussed in Chapter 5] are a prerequisite to all other learning. If they are not securely in place, the later development of the child will be impeded.

Waldon was so amazing because he gave us a platform to go back to the fundamentals which I had never had the opportunity to experience in my entire training and teaching career. It was new to me, so clear yet quite hard to replicate as a teacher. On the other hand the benefit was just so obvious – glaringly obvious. The second thing was to be able to couch the observation and understand it in terms of a child's developmental behaviour so that when one needed to introduce anything that was therapeutic it was much easier to know how to pitch it – how to offer it to a child at a level that he could utilize. The meshing of the two approaches, learning-how-to-learn and psychotherapy, was very helpful and latterly some of the youngsters who have made progress and who have been able to reflect on their experience with us, have been able to give us some good feedback on how it felt for them. How they had tensions from not being able to understand the process and suddenly the penny dropped because they had the opportunity to explore things in a different way, without constant adult intervention, especially ill understood praise for the outcome rather than for the process.

The asocial lesson

Geoffrey Waldon devised the asocial lesson for working with children. During the period of the lesson his aim was to replicate the conditions as naturally as possible, where the child is behaving as if functionally alone. (Like the young child playing in its room alone, while Mum is in the kitchen, but keeping an ear open.) The 'play' undertaken is explicitly not to teach or interact, to praise, or to point out right or wrong outcomes. It is to encourage the child to engage in the process of developing and using the learning-how-to-learn-tools. For instance, the play might be to allocate to sets three objects where at some point the child has to make a decision about something that doesn't quite fit either a group of spherical objects for the kitchen, random objects for the kitchen, or a group of objects for the bathroom. The appearance of choice invites extrapolation and reasoning and in the asocial lesson the outcome is not important. The process is where the learning is taking place. It is the choice and behaviour of the child during the process which informs the understanding. Boundaries are important and the adult (facilitator), is just there to support the process.

Parents often found the asocial lessons very difficult and it took them a while to get used to the concept. I remember working with one child, the child was co-operative but quite bemused. He just looked over his shoulder and said in a very loud voice: 'SHE IS NOT TALKING TO ME'. But once one had established that state, the conditions of the asocial lesson as Geoffrey described them, the child usually became comfortable and forgot about the adult presence.

Today it is not the class teachers that one has to convince, but the executive and managerial layer who are often looking at cumulative targets as the outcome rather than the developmental gaps which precede it. There are the building blocks which have to be used in order to comprehend the underlying principles. The national curriculum applies even to special needs children here in the UK. It is quite restrictive and is taught in steps which boil it down in a very unsatisfactory way which does not really make any sense to many children.

I recently observed in a special school a classroom of mixed diagnosis, some Down's children, some with autism, some just very intellectually challenged and saw them doing what would be a 'science lesson'. The topic would be the same as any topic in a mainstream school. It was concerned with the different features and properties of materials – there was a tin, a piece of wood, a piece of cork, etc. But these children who could neither read nor write had to have some semblance of recording so they had their worksheet and scissors and were doing a cut and paste and they had to scribble on it.

A young Down's child was absolutely fascinated with her chair and some paper. Her worksheet was in the middle of the table where she could not quite reach it so she jogged her chair towards the table so that she could reach the piece of paper, whereupon she very neatly tore it into strips. As soon as she started to do that the staff came along and moved her back so she couldn't quite reach it again, and as soon as they moved off to another child she moved her seat forward and went to pick up the piece of paper to continue tearing it into strips. And I thought that this is just an example of the mismatch between what the curriculum is trying to demand and the developmental level of this young person. She needed to be working in Geoffrey's terms for the best part of her day. She was really motivated by the whole idea of scrunching paper and tearing it and was operating at the level of six to nine months old. She should be very active in her environment, exploring the materials with staff recording their observations and she should certainly not be trying to learn science!

Regular sessions to learn the underlying reasons behind the activities

It was just wonderful sometimes to see some of the older children, usually boys, who really adored it, got stuck into the banging and scraping play and when you had a good session with them and they got into the idea that it was OK to really bang and make a noise they would stretch and reach, explore sound and the quality of objects and it was so exciting to watch them doing that. We found that by having regular workshop lessons with Geoffrey and the team – sometimes we would go up to Manchester and sometimes Geoffrey would come down to Oxfordshire – we could keep on top of and abreast of some of the things we were doing, and not let them slide into mere rote activities. It was important to understand the underlying reason behind the activities.

We were trying really to understand where each child needed to move to next, how to create interest and extend the scope of the activities without making it just an activity for its own sake. At the same time we were thinking what a child might next be doing for itself.

We helped a lot of children a good deal. When I was doing outreach work in Oxfordshire, I used to go around to other schools and observe children who were considered to be on the autistic spectrum and give the staff some ideas. I noticed that a huge gap always seemed to be in the teachers' capacity to really understand what Waldon called seriation. Children could sort and match quite readily, but the concept of being able to work out an extended pattern in whatever form presented, was problematic. If the child could not master this then they would need a huge amount of work at that level in order to get them through all those things, like being able to dress and undress in the right order, being able to follow an organized timetable, being able to know what time of day it is or what lesson – all those things are contingent on being able to understand a continuant pattern and many of them were stuck at that stage. Yet they were being required to work at higher-level tasks. It was often not understood that the 'learning tool' of seriation was not securely understood.

So Chinnor continued to enrol children, mainly on the autistic spectrum, including many Asperger's youngsters who are chaotic, very verbal, and quite bright, intellectually able at the things which interested them, but in terms of their capacity to extend and develop ideas, missing out great chunks of what Geoffrey would call Fundamental Understanding. So the Chinnor day might include an hour or so of the asocial lesson and some solitary play. They then would have some opportunities to go into the main school and participate in lessons with the other children.

The parents are also encouraged to do some work but they find it quite difficult. They have a different relationship with the child and most would be happy to be thinking about how the child could help load washing machines, put the socks in a pile, all the trousers in a pile. They got the idea of putting out appropriate toys and observing the child get on and play on his own without over-direction.

Chinnor was perhaps the first place where the Waldon Approach was adopted in a school situation. It was replicated in Oxfordshire but I think that several things happened which lessened the opportunity. One was the introduction of the national curriculum to children with special needs – that they should be treated like everybody else, experiencing a watered down curriculum. That limited the opportunities to justify wholeheartedly that the hour or so a day of asocial learning had its rightful place in the programme. And without people like those who were on my team at the time really being in school and up front and supporting the process at every stage and fighting for the principle it was much harder for the teachers to keep going with it.

Waldon's view of primary and secondary impediments

The primary impediment is a physical or emotional state, original to the child at birth, such as cerebral palsy, which impairs a person's ability to gather and use information from their environment. The secondary impediment is the effect of the first or primary impediment, on the subsequent development of the child. Self-protecting behaviours are produced in order to cope with this situation, which then tend to become the major obstacles to continued learning and development.

At Chinnor we now have a therapy team which is a marvellous development. I struggled for years to convince people to follow Frances Tustin's role. She was one of the first people I think to call educational therapy an educational tool. If you are not beginning to understand yourself emotionally then you cannot learn in the same way. If you cannot motivate yourself and pick things up and move them from place to place you can't learn either.

The Service for Autism has several centres. The therapy team combines music therapy, art therapy, psychotherapy, movement and dance therapy and occasionally some drama. The different specialist therapists work together as a discipline and talk with the school staff and look at the profiles and behaviours and hence the needs of the autistic children. They then decide which therapeutic intervention might be the most fruitful or the most helpful and one of those therapists will take that youngster on for a time. The Waldon Approach is outside the therapy side – part of the pedagogical or teaching side following Geoffrey's ideas.

Frances Tustin was very impressed with Waldon's work. She said: 'He was one of the first people she had come across who understood what learning was about' (personal communication with Sheila Coates, 22 October, 2009).

Jenny Wager

I am head teacher of Bishopswood Special School which is located on the site of three mainstream school sites to promote inclusion at each stage: nursery, primary and secondary. I had not heard of Waldon before I came to the school about eight years ago, I had worked in a couple of other special schools, and it was mentioned in the information about Bishopswood. It sounded interesting and since I have been here I have been very much converted to the practical use which can be made of Waldon.[7]

Waldon has been well established at the school since it was first introduced about 30 years ago and there are still some staff here who went to the original training which came through the Autism Service in Oxford. We still have links with and ongoing training from that Autism Service, particularly with helping new staff learn how to use it, but now we rely mainly on our experienced staff to carry that forward. We have set up a system where we looked at the range of competencies we would like teachers and support staff to develop in leading Waldon sessions, and our support staff, who do quite a lot of the Waldon sessions with students, are also recognized for their skills and would be able to say that they have been trained and can use Waldon and carry it out elsewhere if they move.

This year we have had quite a few new staff members so we have had our autism outreach advisor come in to talk about Geoffrey Waldon and how he developed the learning-how-to-learn-tools and the concept of General Understanding to make staff aware of where it has come from. She then gives general examples of what to do and when and how to do it. We follow that training session up with meetings of class teams or departments where our experienced teachers work with newer staff to work out for individual children what their current Waldon menus would be; where they are and what sequence of activities to use and how to progress these. We then review those and ensure staff have the skills to assess what the next steps should be and how to modify things according to the child's response. They learn when, where and how to introduce some prompting; to be sure that they can understand the different reactions which might arise and recognize their competencies in doing those things. So at the end of it they can say with some clarity what they are able to do in using the Waldon Approach.

The first Waldon session I observed after coming to this school was a pupil, probably about seven years old, severely autistic who was quite distressed and could not cope with what was going on. He was quietly taken into a Waldon Room where Waldon activities were going to happen. This building is new and was planned with that in mind. I observed what was happening through the window into the Waldon Room and within five minutes he was a changed child. He was calmed; he was engaged with the activities and came out of the room in a much more receptive state. Through the session he was going through familiar activities and they were being extended and he made some progress in what he was doing. I was just so impressed in the way that it matched him and his abilities and so obviously helped him.

This school has taken the approach that Waldon is not just for autistic children; there is a range of other children that can be helped through the structure it provides and the focus it gives to children and it leads in so nicely to some of the other early learning systems we use. It is a very effective approach.

So we have kept the emphasis on training new people as they have come into the school, and use it for those children for whom we feel it would be appropriate. It is not routine for every pupil. We are very selective and the approach has been adapted in some cases to suit individual children. We use it for any child who needs a very finely tuned, structured approach, and children who find it hard to concentrate on tasks and who are easily distracted. The asocial approach, the absence of other distractions, is just ideal for these children. Some children can cope in a classroom and focus on what you want them to do and others simply cannot. It is not only about moving into a quiet space; it is about the teacher working from behind and allowing them to focus in an asocial manner on the materials and the learning-how-to-learn-tools.

Some children don't settle to it straight away. They find it quite difficult because it is the adult who is directing everything; the movement of their hands, what they are looking at, what they are handling, and the younger children can be resistant to that. But usually it is a short lived resistance and I think that the repetition of the movement is actually quite soothing; it is rhythmic and that seems to be calming. Then they go with the flow of what the adult has commenced and get into it. I think having the rhythmic repetition is inherent to their acceptance.

Children can start at the Bishopswood nursery at age two. Not all do, some come at three. Carol, who is our nursery teacher, spends half her week supporting children in mainstream placements in their local pre-schools. She can sometimes begin to introduce some elements of the Waldon Approach with those children. Some of those children might subsequently come to this school anyway. Most of the children who come to our nursery class stay there until they are five or six, then they can stay on this site (the Primary School) up to the age of 11, and then they move to our Senior Department to the age of 18.

Sue Saville

I was a primary school teacher in Abingdon and Oxford for 10 years. When I returned to work after the birth of my daughter I became a supply teacher in a local school and it was there that I met my first child on the autistic spectrum. He was a wonderful cartoonist but found it difficult to socialize and had a strong obsession for spotting cars with headlight wipers. I knew fairly little about autism but received some excellent advice from Sheila Coates from the Autism Advisory Service. Another boy with a diagnosis was enrolled in the school and I began to work with him also. When he was nine he transferred to the Autism Resource Base, at St Nicholas School and I was appointed as a teacher to support him.[8]

One of the teachers in the base introduced us to the Waldon Approach and through visits and workshops run by Geoffrey, the method was adopted and staff began to incorporate the ideas into their everyday work.

I have talked about the Autism Resource Base at St Nicholas School in Oxford. The Service for Autism in the county has bases in Oxford, Chinnor and Thame attached to primary and secondary schools. The Special Educational Needs Support Service (SENSS) embraces the hearing impaired service, visually impaired, speech and language and the PD service. The children can be referred to us at pre-school age and begin school at rising five. Also we have referrals from children in mainstream who are having difficulties. We have a capacity for 13 children at the base at St Nicholas and we are full at the present time.

We aim for inclusion at St Nicholas. A number of our children attend mainstream classes accompanied by a teaching assistant from the base. The children are very well accepted by the host school and there is a good under-standing of autism by children and staff. When the children leave this base they transfer to a base at Cherwell school, a secondary comprehensive nearby. The base is run along the same lines as St Nicholas. Where possible pupils attend mainstream classes with an assistant and return to the base for selected activities. The pupils transfer to Cherwell upper base at 15 and can stay on until they are 18. On leaving some pupils are accepted for college placements.

In later years the intake of pupils changed somewhat. Children with diagnoses of Asperger's syndrome were referred to us and as they were more able to follow the National Curriculum and integrate into mainstream classes, we did not use the Waldon Approach as frequently as before.

In Oxfordshire the approach is used in several special schools and as an advisory teacher I make regular visits. A colleague and I have run workshops for the staff groups – we explain the learning-how-to-learn-tools, give demon-strations and encourage the staff to explore the equipment, matching, sorting and sequencing equipment. The schools have invested in: 'Every Child Can Learn' and found it most useful. We had an Inset Day in the Autism Resource Base last month and showed the DVD to the staff. They especially liked seeing the progress made by the children featured. Our staff examined all the Waldon cards and placing equipment and then worked with each other. It was an extremely useful session. The interest has been rekindled somewhat. The younger group of children take part in a weekly group placing session and the older group enjoy intersectional sorting every Friday.

In the past we ran workshops for parents where they made sorting and matching cards for us. They had some wonderful ideas and we still use some of these cards today – they must be at least 15 years old.

High Wick Psychiatric Hospital for Children

Dr George Stroh, Psychiatrist in Charge of this hospital, met Dr Geoffrey Waldon through Frances Tustin in the mid-1970s. They started to work together and Stroh introduced the Waldon Approach, which at High Wick was called Functional Learning, in the school attached to the hospital. In the late 1970s Alan Proctor became the Head Teacher at the school and was involved in developing and extending the use of Functional Learning in the classroom. Unfortunately both Geoffrey Waldon and George Stroh died before any of their collaborative work had been published. The hospital closed when many specialist units and other psychiatric units were being closed throughout the UK and patients were officially transferred to 'Care in the Community'. Katrin Stroh, a developmental therapist, and Alan Proctor continued to work with children and they, together with Thelma Robinson, have written a book which contains a wealth of information on Functional Learning (Stroh et al., 2008). Dr Chris Holland became Psychiatrist in Charge in 1978 after Dr Stroh's death and remained there until High Wick closed.

Alan Proctor

I am a teacher of emotionally disturbed children, counsellor and developmental therapist. What appealed to me about the Waldon Approach was that it followed normal development. You were never asking the child to do anything that any other child would not, under normal circumstances, do. Which meant two things: you can go right back to the very beginning of naturally exploring things the infant can reach, and so do picking up, putting in – all that sort of thing which children do on their own. The only thing which was different was what Geoffrey would call 'starting to get the wheel going'; giving it a push so that effort started to run and hopefully would continue to turn on its own. And that was the only difference, apart from systematizing those activities so that the child spent a lot of time with doing the placing. Geoffrey was also very keen to emphasize that the reward for what you were doing was intrinsic to the activity. In other words the joy of placing was placing. There were no rewards, no smiles, no praise; nothing was on offer that was not connected with placing.[9]

A simple example is the game of golf. What is golf but placing made more difficult! The holes are placed far apart; and the ball is placed in the hole by hitting it with a stick. It is placing. And it is done for pleasure. The infinite pleasure that adults derive from playing golf or that children get from their placing activities and the variety you can introduce within that is enormous.[9]

You can and need to be creative. I did not understand when I went for my interview with George Stroh why he said to me: 'The reason we would like you, Mr Proctor, is because of your design training'. When I started working with Functional Learning[10] at High Wick Hospital, I realized that there were basic activities which needed to be developed. A creative mind is needed to ask: 'In how many different ways can children put things into other things and take them out?' That is what children typically do.

The longitudinal studies at High Wick filmed babies from birth. It is fantastic the way you found children finding different ways of putting things in. One example was a child scrunching up paper and shoving it into a jar. The joy of that was that the child could actually see that the sheet of paper in its original state would not go in the jar so he transformed it by scrunching it up. Then having got it in how was he going to get it out? And there you got the tool use that Geoffrey did in banging and scraping. The child got the spoon and pulled it out. This was invaluable in looking at typical children doing the same things that we were doing with our children but that they would not have done without our prompting.

It seemed to us at High Wick that the link between the use of the learning-how-to-learn-tools as Geoffrey called them – the banging, the placing, the pairing, the matching and the sorting – and the child's emotional development was absolutely crucial in helping the child to relax.

Geoffrey talked about self-handicapping behaviour, those defensive avoidance mechanisms children adopt. It is very powerful in therapeutic terms just to get a child to sit at a table and to drop those, because its fear has actually been removed. The child is saying: 'I no longer need to protect myself'. He is then given a developmentally useful activity with no expectation of success or fear of failure. You have taken away the fear and you have added the pleasure and hence the motivation derived from performing an effortful activity. That is therapeutically enormous.

The meeting of George Stroh and Geoffrey Waldon was the coming together of two quite extraordinary men. Spending time with Geoffrey was always an extraordinary experience. But High Wick was a psychiatric hospital for children. It had research. It had children who were residential and in those days that meant that they were residential for 365 days a year. There were resident care workers and this changed something. Whereas you, Walter, would take your child to Geoffrey and your wife would work at home with him; at High Wick, Functional Learning ruled the day totally and completely. The child care workers were trained to be a part of the Functional Learning system which was put into practice from the moment the child got up. Could the child dress? How could the child dress? And so on. They also worked in the classrooms.

It is interesting that you, Walter, realized that you needed some psychological input from somebody like Frances Tustin. That is not always so but at High Wick we were able to offer that therapy as well; not with all the children but it was decided which children would benefit from it.

At High Wick our children were all physically capable but with emotional problems, and Functional Learning was bound up with their emotional development. As they worked through Functional Learning emotional issues would sometimes come up. I remember one little lad who had been abused. We would start Functional Learning and he would start screaming and shouting. I would just keep a hand on his shoulder, no restraint, I just kept contact, and he would continue to scream and he would stop just for a brief second and say: 'Don't leave me Proctor' and then carry on screaming. Eventually he would calm down and the lesson could start.

So within Functional Learning you might go down a path which was pure therapy. In private practice sometimes I was mixing Functional Learning with therapy. As one little boy said: 'I come to see Mr Proctor not just to learn but to talk about the way I feel'. Now that was a beautiful way of describing it. He is a young man (Larry in Chapter 8), who is just going to university to work with young people who have disabilities. He is already on a government group looking at this and he could see that as a child both of those things were going on in the work we had done.

And that is what happened at High Wick. George Stroh, as Psychiatrist in Charge, would select which children would benefit from therapy adjunctive to their Functional Learning.

As an adult in a children's residential setting, it was important to create strong boundaries within yourself. A child could see me attached to a family group – perhaps in the morning to get them out of bed. That same child would see me at a mealtime feeding them; then as their teacher and later as their therapist. It is unique that as one person you could have all those quite different roles with any one particular child. Geoffrey used to say that as long as you knew which gear you were in the child would engage.

How the children used therapy varied enormously. One child knew I was there for a certain set time. He never came on time for therapy sessions but would arrive 10 minutes before the end. He would say: 'You are here Proctor', I would say: 'Yes, and I have been here since whatever time it was, say 9 o'clock and I shall be leaving at 10'. He took from it that that was special and that therefore he was of value.

For other children who had very little language it was more difficult. We would use the learning-how-to-learn-tools and we used sign language to help them towards language. If we had a child with very few words we would have to use some sign language in therapy and we used drawing.

Functional Learning is an essential foundation for therapy

It is an important point that we were not saying that Functional Learning is everything. It is an absolutely essential foundation without which these children could not have used the adjunctive therapy. Therapy is highly complex and to engage in it a child does need some ability at symbolic language at however basic a level.

One of the joys of working with children is that they will let you know if you have got something wrong! When a child screams you interpret what that is about. You do not say: 'Oh you are making a noise. You're a naughty child. Go away till you stop'. You do say to a child: 'I understand you are frightened. I understand you are finding this difficult. Therefore I will stay with you'. This is all without speech. The child understands that; or feels that; or feels it through the supporting hand. When you see a foot twitch or whatever physical indication lets you know that you are pushing this child you drop the level of activity and you can see the child relax. I think that is pure therapy and pure Waldon. You are taking the anxiety away and bringing the person back to the point at which they feel they can actually cope.

The activity is maintained at a level which does not put pressure on the child but children vary from day to day in what they can do. They have their good days, they have their bad days. And though I know that Johnny could do that yesterday he may have had a bad night for all that I know. Our child care workers had a routine when they brought a child into the classroom. They would stand with the child and say to the teacher: 'Johnny had a bad night last night'. So the child knows the thing has been communicated and the teacher knows that last night was not very good and would try to tailor whatever he was going to do with that child at an appropriate level.

High Wick was split into three different school groups, not chronologically but at the level at which the children could cope emotionally and thus in line with their level of General Understanding. So we had pre-nursery, nursery and school. I had worked in all three groups.

At the end of my first year at the school, when the previous headmaster left, George Stroh asked me to take over the school group for the following year, saying: 'I want you to see whether Functional Learning will lead the children on into normal education. I want you to work purely on Functional Learning terms. If you cannot move the children into normal education then we have got something wrong and we will have to sit back and rethink the whole thing'.

I had the summer holidays to reorganize the classroom in Functional Learning terms. Each child had his own desk; there was no carpet on the floor, all equipment was behind the children and in front it was neutral but relevant to what they were going to do.

Why don't I find it difficult now?

It was extraordinary. At the end of the first term I brought my first lot of results and observations and Dr Stroh said to me then: 'Mr Proctor – I was expecting results at the end of a year not a term'. He realized that he was asking something big and he supported me all the way through. But I have to say he was so excited with those early results. Just one short simple example of what had happened. I was doing times tables which is as near to normal education as one could possibly get and one little boy said to me: 'What is going on? I used to find this difficult. Why don't I find it difficult now?' I thought that was absolutely wonderful.

Years later this boy took a cycle ride with three or four of his pals, rode to the gates of High Wick and said: 'This is where I went to school'. What he was saying was: 'This is what changed my life. It made easy what I found in normal school difficult – all the problems had gone'. This was a lad who was incredibly disruptive at normal school, and impossible to control. He had language but everything he tried he found difficult so he would play up in classes. He was never violent but would interfere with other children and it was absolutely impossible for a teacher to control him in a normal classroom.

He came straight into school group at about age nine. I decided that most of these children had gone through banging, scraping and the use of tools and had reached the point where they could hold a pencil and make a mark. So I devised some means of doing worksheets in Functional Learning. Some of the children were hostile to this. There was no way that they were going to have worksheets, so I did not impose that on them. But I sat at a desk at the front of the class and made the worksheets and the children could see that I was doing it for them – starting with a simple pencil manipulation of a football or aeroplane or whatever.

I sat this one boy at the front and he would crane his neck to see what I was doing. He would see some of the other children taking notice and saying: 'Mr Proctor – can you do me a so and so for tomorrow morning?' 'Yes, I can do that'. He began to notice that other children were having pleasure from this so he began to join in. It seemed to me that when the children came into the classroom I needed to convey to them in some way that I had thought about them and cared for them while being away from them. So that when they came into the classroom they would have on their desk 10 worksheets. I had not at that point worked out the amount of work I would have to do! Eight children, ten worksheets each equals 80 worksheets a day! Each child would have his own worksheets depending on his interests and set at the level of his General Understanding.

It was a short Functional Learning lesson with 10 sheets of paper and with the expectation that they would work on their own. This was one of the things that I was developing that George Stroh did not know anything about but I would take to him and say: 'This is what I was talking about – the unique creativity in Functional Learning. This is what I have done, and this is the result'. Once we had a schools inspector who came in as these eight children were sitting quietly doing their worksheets with no adult help. There were adults around if they had wanted them. You could have heard a pin drop. The inspector said: 'I don't see why these children are in this special place'. I said: 'If you really want me to show you I can show you in five seconds flat'!

We had gained something enormous to have these children, residents in a psychiatric hospital for children, sitting at a desk, working on their own with pencil and paper – and having pleasure and no fear.

I also did some outreach work in Hertfordshire. I remember one lad who was very mentally disabled and when I went to the school he did nothing but lay on the bed. I spoke with the parents and offered to work with the child just to be able to pick up and place. You have to understand that sometimes there are limits to what you can do. They said that their doctor had advised that if he had too much movement it may shorten his life, but after thinking about it they asked me to work with him. They came back later and said: 'We don't know if it has shortened his life but wanted you to know the enormous amount of pleasure we have had. He plays in the bath. He comes round the supermarket with us and puts things in the trolley – we have never had that sort of relationship with our son before'.

I was once doing some external training sessions. I was asked to teach a teenage girl how to apply make-up. I agreed and went into a session with the girl. I was watched in utter amazement because we had got a bucket on the table, a pile of stuff on the floor and she and I were picking it up and putting it in the bucket. People said: 'What on earth are you doing? We asked you to teach this girl to do make-up'. And I said: 'Have you thought about the process of putting on make-up? Where are you going to start?'

Work at the developmental not the chronological age

This girl may have been 14 but she had not learnt the basics of putting in and placing. So I said: 'Unless I can get her to pick up things and put them into the bucket and make the effort to do that; and then move her on so that the placing becomes more and more accurate, and she can put a peg into a narrow board. Now – you want her to put make-up on. She is looking in a mirror which is difficult enough for most of us and without basic placing skills, how do you think she is going to put on mascara or lipstick? You have got to start with simple picking up and placing and then continu-ant behaviour and to be effortful'. They half got the point, but continued: 'She is 14'. 'Yes' I said: 'but look at her face. She and I have been doing this together; we have had great fun together. She loved it. You have to accept, and children do sense this, your utter respect for them as a person at their developmental and not at their chronological age'.

That means that at 14 although typical girls would be doing something, she may actually not be able to do it. We say simply that you can do this, so this is what we will do together. That goes for all of us. We have all reached a certain level and we say: 'I can do that, but don't ask me to do so and so because I don't know how to do that really'.

One of the things I teach care workers is that their body language must say to the child: 'This is an interesting thing that you can do'. Don't look at placing as if it is boring. Watch yourself when you go shopping in the super-market. You take an item off the shelf, you place it in the trolley, you walk up and down the aisles, you go to the cash desk, you put it onto a conveyor, you take it off and place it into a bag that you place into a trolley. You go to your car and you take the bags out of the trolley and place them in the boot of your car. You go home and take the objects out of the car, carry them into the kitchen and place them on a table and then place them in various cupboards. All placing and picking up and putting in.

George Stroh and Geoffrey Waldon both very much valued and respected each other, but were very different men as personalities. One of the huge differences is that Geoffrey was working in isolation. He was a brilliant man, absolutely brilliant, and his world focused around his theories of General Understanding and these highly intellectual papers that he wrote that people have great difficulty understanding. His argument was that the responsibility is on the learner not on the teacher. You had to put more effort into it.

In contrast, George Stroh was in a psychodynamic institution. He was Freudian – can you get more difference in the settings they were in? Stroh in an institution that is also research oriented, was connected to the Health Authority and to the Tavistock, and is travelling to the various seminars and meetings around the world where he was giving papers. This was a totally different world from Geoffrey's world. George Stroh is moving in the world and is rubbing shoulders with the child psychiatrists of the age; George Stroh is very much into understanding feelings and emotions – I don't think that Geoffrey ever got hold of that completely. He was into learning and although he would not dismiss feelings, and I am not saying that he did, he was not into it in the same way that you can imagine a Freudian institution was. What George Stroh did was to very remarkably pull together Geoffrey's philosophy of child development and the Freudian emotional development. He merged and knitted those two together.

George Stroh died before any papers or talks on Functional Learning were prepared by him and that is what Katrin put together in the book. There is very little published on Functional Learning and I know that is a great sadness to many. The great sadness was that George Stroh died and then we had the death of Geoffrey Waldon. We were in a position at High Wick to start publishing the results of Geoffrey's work or what we were calling Functional Learning but that never ever got done.

Katrin Stroh, Thelma Robinson and I got together to write a book, because we are the three people from High Wick who were still in contact with each other, in the last few years.

We wrote this book from a technical point of view, BUT so that any parent who wanted to, could pick it up and read what to do and how to do it. Our book provides the parent with the joy of having something practical to do with their child, at whatever stage that child is at, and the possibility of establishing a relationship with your child which comes from doing things together. It can transform relationships within the family. Siblings also can find – and this is something that needs to be looked at – that they have something they could do with their sibling, which can be as important as the parent having something to do with their child.

Staying with Geoffrey for a weekend was an experience because his mind was on other things. On one occasion we went to see a nursery school and he got extraordinarily angry. We were looking at pictures that teachers had put up on the wall and most of the pictures were double mounted. I suppose most teachers do that to make the pictures look good. One little girl had made a picture and she had been crying and there were tears she had created on silver paper and Geoffrey said: 'We prettify something that was painful and we are not looking at the reality'.

It seems to me that what Functional Learning does is to look at the reality. I recognize that the crying of the child is pain and therefore I am not going to walk away from this child's pain. I am going to stay with it. You so often see a child for the first time and the child screams and the parents expect you to hand the child back to them and say come back later when you can control your child. But you stay with the child. And you wonder whether the parent is going to allow me to stay with him. And then one of two things happens. Either the parent says: 'You are forcing this child against his will. Stop it. I remove my child'. There is nothing you can do about that. Or the parent says: 'You are the first person who has ever stayed with the child whilst he is screaming' and they stay with it and suddenly perhaps the screaming stops and the child settles. If it is a very small child perhaps it is on your knee and the child moves back towards me and you realize that you have gone through its pain by staying with it. I believe that a true relationship is one where you stay with somebody when they are in pain and screaming; if you don't stay with them then you are not a true friend. And that is what Functional Learning has enabled me to do with children by realizing that the screaming is a manifestation of fear. As the little boy said: 'Don't leave me Proctor – stay with me. I don't want you to go'. If you go then what message are you giving? And of course Geoffrey would always stay with a distressed child.

So the interpretation of what is going on is critical. If your interpretation is that the child is complaining because your actions are cruel or because you are doing something against the child's will then I think your interpretation is incorrect. I say to parents: 'The fact that you have brought your child to me says to the child that you have understood that the child is saying that he needs help. You are saying to the child we recognize that what you need is a bit beyond us so we are going to someone who will help us understand what you want. But we have understood that you are telling us something. You are not being naughty, you are telling us something. If as a parent you don't respond to that in the early stages what option has the child got but to seek more and more intrusive things to do as a way of saying: "Will you please listen to me? I will scream louder, or spread faeces all over the place" – the child actually has not got many options. It has got food, or what it expels from its body or its mouth to tell you that something is wrong and the longer you leave it the more unpleasant it is going to get. You have to stay with that and you cannot walk away'.

The Waldon concepts of General Understanding and Cultural Particular Understanding were important because that actually made a good distinction between where you can give rewards and where you never give rewards. There is no value for the child in shaking hands or whatever it is apart from being able to fit within that cultural group. Therefore I have to reward in a cultural way: 'Good boy' or 'Yes, Auntie Maud will like that' and separating those two kinds of learning was vital for understanding why you don't reward in the Functional Learning or in the use of the learning-how-to-learn-tools.

Geoffrey used this term the asocial lesson. This was a difficult phrase which was often misunderstood. You are standing behind the child so the child is not having you as a stimulus. You have no sensory input and the child just feels your hands helping him. You have no facial expressions and that is why the child can absolutely focus on what is going on. At the beginning the child may be facing a blank wall but later on the child can take more and more sensory stimulus but in a way that it does not over-intrude into a child's vision.

Obviously that gradually changes and it is interesting when you take Functional Learning things and do them outside. You can do something like intersectional sorting outside on a big area and chalk out your board on the ground and have objects and a group of kids and play intersectional sorting with them. It is fun to do and it is interesting because they have not got the security of a desk, they are outside with everything that is going on around outside, the movement of the trees, all the things in the garden, and that is one of the things I used to do with the school group kids. We used to go out and do Functional Learning outside. And that is fascinating to do and good for the confidence of the children to wait their turn; so they sequence; to scan a big area, do the intersectional sorting and come back and join the queue.

It is intersectional sorting at its most simple. So I have got various objects at this side like a cup, a ruler and all sorts of different things across the top. I present the child with two objects and say find the square that those go in. What I have done, which is what you always do is, when you increase the environment in which the child is working you have to lower the level of that activity. Whether that is making them use a pencil or whatever it is and moving them outside, I could not use the level I might have used if they were inside at a desk, because some of this intersectional sorting gets quite complicated, I just kept developing it because it was such fun and the kids just loved it. And it is good problem-solving stuff. But to take it outside I had to reduce it to its most simple form. And they were able to adapt to it.

I was asking the children to wait in a line, to take turns, to work as a group, and the same with the sorting, when we did sorting as a group four children, each with piles of stuff, four trays, four sets, and one starts off putting something there, two does something else, number three thinks I don't think they go like that and moves them and you think: 'How are they going to cope?' Are they going to produce language that says: 'Why did you do that?' 'Well I thought …' and can they actually sort this out? And you can take the sorting into all sorts of really fascinating things and a lot of group work and the thing about group work is that you can mix levels. If your friend is doing sorting and the other person is only at the placing level you can get them to bring objects and give them to others so they do their bit while the other person is sorting, they are only placing. That was interesting getting groups of children actually working together and we did a lot both in the nursery and the school groups.

Basically there is no difference between the Waldon Approach and Functional Learning. If you were watching any of us at High Wick doing a lesson it would be no different to watching Geoffrey. But at High Wick there was more of a conscious psychodynamic dimension. We were more geared into seeing how the emotional maturity was developing. That in my opinion is one area of difference.

Excerpt from a letter by Chris Holland to colleagues and friends, dated December 1982 after 18 months of work and learning as Psychiatrist-in-Charge at High Wick Hospital

The thing that most pre-occupies me is that High Wick had been working away for over 20 years and then got an enormous impetus from a chap called Geoffrey Waldon, who had also been working away on his own for 20 years at the same problems; children with severe difficulties in development such that they have no language (or no useful language), and a very poor capacity to organize themselves, including very primitive relationships; these things all getting mixed up together.

A reliable environment can help such a kid who has further troubles from his family's inevitable reactions to his/her underlying problem; but for the real unscrambling you have to go back, much further than doctors or teachers find easy, to re-lay the foundation for learning.

So High Wick with its psychoanalytic background, but struggling with what didn't work especially in words, found inspiration and understanding from a fellow student of the 'nearly-impossible-to-help-with-our-present-knowledge' children. Geoffrey Waldon was a neuro-physiologist before becoming a doctor cum neurologist cum educator cum psychologist cum philosopher cum genius (breath for disbelief and to discover what this paragraph was all about before the eulogy).

Well the team at High Wick near St Albans and Geoffrey Waldon in Manchester work with this method or approach to kids (or adults), whose development has become almost completely bogged down or snarled up.

The system for working with all these individuals has so many applications that I quite often think that I should give up all other forms of work to spend all my time and energy helping to develop, understand and promote this Waldon Approach as it was called by Geoffrey Waldon or Functional Learning as it was called by George Stroh at High Wick.

This system enables the expert or relative expert both to diagnose the problems in practical terms and to prescribe in great detail what to do, not only in a treatment room, but in a classroom, playroom or bathroom. It not only helps the professionals and parents to learn what is wrong, as well as what is right, but turns from assessment into practice and so helps the child to do its own learning better. Furthermore as all development depends on learning to understand the world and one's own body and mind better – so learning is the title.

'UNDERSTANDING understanding' is how Geoffrey Waldon describes his approach, as that is what he is most interested in: how does physiological, proprioceptive and cognitive understanding of anything or of everything develop? He does not talk very much about emotions but I remember well one conversation I had with him, for its atmosphere; as he could have been expounding Winnicott on early development, but without really realizing it. [11]

He's very Piagetian in ways, but looking and working at much finer detail; and so coming to understand development as it goes along normally as well as some of the disasters it can encounter along the way. The Waldon Approach is the result of 30 years of his work whilst moving from neuro-physiology through medicine, at the same time studying about fifteen thousand children.

What I can't possibly describe in this long overdue letter is how it all works; but the system could be as influential as Froebel or Montessori or even more so, especially in special education, with implications for normal schooling, again especially for the 15 per cent of children in normal schools with 'special needs': of course that means learning problems whatever their origin.

Both a psychology and a methodology

What I cannot always hold on to is that an approach which includes a philosophy of education, a psychology of education and a psychology of learning is not only a psychology of development but a methodology which enables the experienced worker to move from autistic or remote children (or adults), to those who are deaf, blind, physically handicapped or non verbal, as well as over pressurized 'hot house', 'normal' children, let alone the mentally handicapped, the hyperactive or the traumatized.

Furthermore, at High Wick the most experienced staff could move very easily into a play therapy or informal psychotherapy with kids who the psychotherapist would be afraid of working with. As long as the professional knows which gear they are in, as Geoffrey would say, the child would follow. As one normally very confused child would ask just to check: 'Is this learning today or playing?' And the simple clear answer from the child care worker sorted that out and the very disturbed child relaxed into the session, be it play therapy or Functional Learning ...

Excerpt from letter from Chris Holland to Geoffrey Waldon dated 16 September 1986

Dear Geoffrey,

I found it hard to believe that two years had passed since the previous symposium. I found it again very heartening to hear from others struggling with difficult problems and often against, or amidst, what feels like a sea of incomprehension.

What you are I am sure aware of, but may also forget is that so many aspects of your practice – quite apart from though in parallel with your theories – are years ahead of most professionals. Your completely open attitude to 'the clients' – most atypical of most doctors, lawyers, etc. sharing your knowledge, expecting the family to watch the work, writing reports for 'the clients' – viewing the family as partners in the work.

All of these things are being hesitantly moved towards by many professionals and held up as good practice – and probably viewed by yourself as 'common sense'!

We often find at High Wick that things the senior staff have come to view as 'obvious' and 'common sense' are quite new to colleagues and to junior staff recruits. My mother often said that 'common sense is not very common'!

When you have worked something through over years and years it is hard to imagine how others don't see it.

I think this can apply to an awareness of the amazing complexity and sophistication of the central nervous system from before birth onwards. For so many people who are quite well informed in other ways the head is a mysterious box which mostly does what you want and has inside some switches to translate what you want into action. The whole brain being imagined as an orange sized walnut! I think the simplicity of view contributes to the puzzlement when things go wrong and a simple view of remediation.

Best wishes

Chris

Using the approach beyond Britain

Slovenia

'This tiny country welcomed Functional Learning with great interest and open mindedness'. (Personal email communication from Katrin Stroh, 9 April 2011). Through international conferences attended by Katrin Stroh, special needs teachers, speech therapists and psychologists in Slovenia developed an interest in Functional Learning. The approach has become widespread in Slovenia and this section briefly reviews their activities. Their training consisted of workshops and seminars lasting a week and spread out over 10 years. They were eager to practise with the children. After every visit Katrin wrote extensive notes and reports to help them to keep up with their practice and progress. These papers were the foundation of the book *Every Child Can Learn* (Stroh et al., 2008).

Dr Breda Sustersic, Developmental Paediatrician, Domzale

There are 20 districts in Slovenia each with a secondary reference developmental centre headed by a developmental paediatrician with a team of Neuro-Developmental Treatment (NDT) therapists. I am the developmental paediatrician of the region Domzale and Kamnik. Developmental departments are located at health centres or at regional hospitals.[12]

When babies are born in Slovenia, they are seen by a general paediatrician, who takes care of the routine check-ups regarding weight, nutrition, vaccinations, illness, etc. and in the case of suspected developmental problems they are referred to the developmental paediatrician who will perform further tests and neurological examination. Further diagnostic tests can be carried out at the tertiary centre at the Children's Hospital in Ljubljana if necessary.

All children are routinely developmentally screened by the Denver II test. If necessary psycho-diagnostic test BSID II or BSID III (Bayley's test) is used to detect motor and mental problems at a very early stage. Usually the first referral would be for NDT to ensure that all typical developmental movements, which are fundamental to the child's global and cognitive development, are facilitated and exercised. Beyond that at three and at five years of age all children have physical and psychological tests where any problems can also be identified and when necessary children are sent to a developmental centre.

When children with speech delay are referred at the secondary level, the parents are given a comprehensive questionnaire to complete, which asks questions about use of gesture, ability to make sounds, number of words used and level of understanding, motor skills and level of affect. Further speech and language examination and/or tests are done by speech therapists.

Each secondary unit also works closely with the kindergartens and schools which the children attend. There is a specialized centre for children with autistic spectrum disorder at University Medical Centre Ljubljana. They are not trained in Functional Learning but use other methods, although Functional Learning is used in the Institution for the Deaf Children in Ljubljana, which also includes many children with the autistic spectrum problems.[13]

Functional Learning in Slovenia is used by speech therapists, special needs teachers and psychologists and many of these are well trained in the approach and incorporate it into their daily practice.

Anamarija Filipiè Dolnièar, Speech Therapist and Instructor for Functional Learning, Domzale

I met Katrin Stroh at the Inclusive and Supportive Education Congress (ISEC) in 1995. She presented a poster on Functional Learning together with a video. I was also presenting at the conference and Katrin invited us to see the tape and explained the theory of Functional Learning. We purchased the tape, presented it to other schools in Slovenia and started to use some of the ideas. A year later we invited Katrin to give a seminar in Slovenia for eight speech therapists and special needs teachers in the Ljubljana School for Deaf Children where I worked.[14]

We began to use Functional Learning more extensively and Katrin returned about two years later and gave another seminar for another eight speech therapists and special needs teachers. Since then I have visited her many times in England. When we had questions we were able to correspond with Katrin about them. This process of mutual visits and questioning continued over several years.

Two hundred Slovenian professionals trained in Functional Learning

Later we started to present our own seminars in Slovenia with Katrin's help and support. Katrin visited Slovenia again with Alan Proctor to train other professionals and parents and over the past 15 years we have trained over 200 professionals in Functional Learning. Some of these experts spread ideas about Functional Learning among others through their own work. So Functional Learning is widely spread in Slovenia with various experts, each adapting it to their own method of working.

All children can benefit in different ways

I have been using Functional Learning for over 15 years and use these ideas with all children, even with those who have only articulation problems. The learning tools – placing, pairing, sorting, matching, sequencing, drawing, brick building – are basic and can be used with any child according to the type of their developmental delay, cognition, understanding and learning capability. Children with better cognition have more demanding activities using sorting and matching cards of differing complexities and other materials. Children with a low level of understanding start with very basic activities. I believe that all children can benefit in different ways from this approach.

Functional Learning combines with other programmes and approaches

Over the years many new approaches have been developed and each expert uses what he believes in. Functional Learning can be easily combined with other programmes and approaches.

During 15 years I have used Functional Learning with many children, and all of them have benefited from it. I made various changes according to my own ideas and bearing in mind that all children learn at their own pace. With family support and cooperation all children improve through the therapy sessions. We know that children cross culturally can use the same learning tools, which are mental tools to develop communication, cognition and language in an emotionally safe environment. Following the typical pattern of child development, using the learning tools and taking account of the child's emotional state, we can help any child with developmental delay to develop their understanding and to begin to overcome some of the problems of everyday life.

Irena Roblek and Anuška Kovač, Special Education Teachers, Special Education Centre Janez Levec, Jarše, Ljubljana

The Janez Levec Centre is the largest special education centre in Slovenia and is funded by the Ministry of Education and Sport, the City of Ljubljana, The Health Insurance Institute of Slovenia, The Ministry of Labour, Family and Social Affairs and private sponsors and donors.[15]

Tutoring and educational programmes

The centre offers three officially recognized educational programmes, additional expert assistance through special adaptation of the regular education programmes and a social security programme of guidance, care and employment under special conditions. These programmes, alongside the individual education plans designed especially for every individual pupil, aim to approach the pupil's learning abilities. The success of pupils in achieving their goals leads to an improved self-image and helps make the transition into independent life and work more successful.

A special education programme is intended for children with moderate or severe mental disabilities. It has no prescribed levels of acquired knowledge and the final goal is set individually for each pupil. We lay great stress on improving the pupils' ability to adapt and their working skills. Pupils generally take part in this programme between the ages of six and 18, although they are presented with the option of continuing the programme for three more years. We offer this programme at both our elementary schools (Levstikov trg and Dečkova ulica), as well as in our educational departments in Jarše.

Specialized mobile teachers offer special educational support in mainstream elementary schools. This support is generally offered to special needs pupils with specific learning disabilities.

Functional Learning has as its main goal to help pupils 'learn for life' and it is intended for pupils with severe mental disabilities and undeveloped speech. It is one of many programmes including elements of the Montessori method, activities with animals, psychological counselling and physiotherapy which we offer in Jarše. Selected children will receive weekly Functional Learning sessions over the period of three to four years when they are in our department.

Icelandic teachers learn the approach

Safamyrarskoli, Iceland

Jiri Berger first met Geoffrey Waldon in the early 1980s when he was an Honorary Research Fellow at the Hester Adrian Research Centre at the University of Manchester. A native of Bohemia, he instigated a study in Iceland, the following is an extract from his report, *The Waldon Approach to Educating Developmentally Backward Children* (1985).[16]

Introduction

When some eight years ago, I first listened to Dr Waldon outline some of his theoretical ideas during a public talk, I was immediately struck by their freshness as well as their conceptual coherence and elegance. Moreover, they appeared to offer valid and novel answers to many of the questions and practical problems with which the field of special education and mental handicap has been struggling for many years and with only limited success.

Later, through many hours of discussions and observations of Dr Waldon's practical work with developmentally backward children my first favourable impressions were further reinforced. I became firmly convinced that here lay a rich and extremely valuable resource for the whole field of special education.

Nevertheless doubts arose in my mind about the wider applicability of the Waldon Approach. In particular, its uncompromising emphasis on the theoretical underpinnings of education, the deliberate omission of prescriptive step-by-step guidelines for everyday teaching practice, and the methods which in many ways seem to contradict conventional wisdom and practices, could pose considerable obstacles to its acceptance and application by the wider professional community.

I was fortunate to receive a one year research grant from the Icelandic Science Foundation which enabled me to begin a short term feasibility study aimed at answering at least some of these questions.

Discussion

The present study demonstrated quite conclusively that it is feasible to introduce the Waldon Approach into a school for educationally retarded pupils and within a reasonable period of time enable teachers to apply it in their everyday work. The results indicate, moreover, that this can have beneficial effects both on the pupils and on the teachers themselves. In the following discussion, these effects will be considered in the light of the quantitative results as well as more subjective experiences and insights derived during the course of the study. It should be emphasised, however, that the enthusiastic and open minded co-operation of the school and the teachers was a necessary pre-requisite for any such benefits to be realised.

Effects on the pupils from an established pre-intervention baseline

These can be classified in terms of effects on the pupils' understanding (here referring primarily to various forms of cognitive and fine motor competence), and on their general behaviour during teaching sessions. Although these two aspects are not unrelated, they will first be considered separately and the links between them later. The pupils were tested twice three months apart to establish a pre-intervention baseline, and the intervention itself lasted only three months.

The changes in pupils' understanding, measured by means of standardised developmental scales, were quite remarkable. The group's mean increase in developmental age between the second pre-intervention baseline and the end of the intervention period was six months. Given that the intervention lasted only three months this increase represents a rate of progress twice that expected for an average non-retarded child. Even when allowing for the great individual differences in the pupils' improvements (i.e. range from .2 to 25 months developmental age), the median increase of 4 months still indicates a highly significant increase over the whole group.

The fact that no increases in developmental levels were found between the two baseline assessments, which were separated also by about three chronological months, indicates that the above improvements were primarily due to the use of the Waldon Approach during the intervention period. In addition to the double baseline control procedure, the amount of individual teaching and the teachers remained constant throughout the whole duration of the study. Consequently the test performance gains seem to reflect genuine intervention effects.

It should be noted that the gains are seen as somewhat of a bonus since they were not really expected in view of the relatively short duration of the intervention period. Moreover any gains in General Understanding facilitated through such an intervention would not necessarily be expected to reflect immediately in the pupils' criteria performance on standardised test items. The fact that this in fact seemed to happen strengthens the case for the use of the Waldon Approach.

The general behavioural effects of the intervention were assessed by means of direct observational ratings of the pupils' behaviour during lessons and subjective ratings by the teachers.

Between the pre-intervention ratings of a regular individual lesson and a rating of a Waldon a-social lesson near the end of the intervention stage, a significant overall decrease in problem behaviours was found; with most significant changes being recorded for visual avoidance, stereotyped behaviours, mannerisms and self stimulation. There was a mean group improvement in six out of the seven behaviour problems categories used in the recordings. Overall, this represents a mean drop of over 30% per pupil, the frequency of problem behaviours being reduced from almost half of the recorded intervals (49%), to less than one fifth (18.6%).

Also a corresponding and highly significant mean increase of 36% in the pupils' 'on-task effortful concentration' was found between the recordings of the regular and the a-social lessons. This increased on average from 50% of the recorded intervals to almost 90%.

These findings which are not particularly robust due to methodological limitations (all the ratings were performed by the author and the data were based on only one regular and one asocial lesson per pupil) were corroborated by the results of the teachers' subjective ratings.

The most significant improvements in terms of the number of pupils showing a positive change were found in the teachers' ratings of pupils' compliance, visual attention to tasks, interest in teaching activities and a decrease in behavioural problems. This corresponds closely to the author's observational findings. There were however great individual variations in the teachers' ratings of individual pupils, and on two of the 12 scales less than half of the pupils showed an improvement. For example only five pupils were rated as improved in their independence of teacher's help (five scored no change), or in the amount of constructive activity (three no change). Thus, an analysis of the scales in terms of the magnitude of rated improvements only, was also carried out in order to assess the strength of the intervention effects on those pupils who did show at least some degree of positive change in behaviour.

The greatest mean improvement was found for the pupils' constructive activity, the second greatest was for the decrease in behavioural problems and the third for their co-operation during lessons.

These findings indicate that while the Waldon Approach appears to have been highly effective in improving the pupils' behaviour during lessons, these effects were not equally strong for all the pupils or for all the different aspects of their behaviour.

The significant increases in attention, effort and concentration and the corresponding decreases in problem behaviours are, of course, in line with the Waldon theory of handicap and retardation. This postulates that such behaviours as escape, visual avoidance, or stereotypes are all defensive strategies designed to protect a pupil from excessive demands on his understanding and performance. By minimising these demands during the course of an asocial lesson such defensive behaviours should automatically diminish.

Another implication of the Waldon theory is that a close relationship exists between understanding and effort/concentration, any increase in one augmenting the other. It would thus be expected, that as the pupils' understanding increased, their effort/concentration should increase too. It is, however, difficult to test this hypothesis directly by means of the available data, since both the normative test measures and the behavioural ratings are too global and non-specific. The theoretical prediction refers more to particular kinds of activities/understanding, rather than to a general competence as measured by normative tests.

Nevertheless, the positive significant correlation between the improvements in the pupils' test performance and their teachers' behavioural ratings indicate that a link between gains in understanding and in improvements in attention, interest and effort does exist.

It is certainly also true that improved attention and effort in appropriate activities will enhance the pupil's experience and learning, and will thus most likely lead to a growth of understanding. The above correlation could thus be equally attributed to this process.

The positive significant correlations found between the pupils' effort/concentration already before the intervention started and their gains on the normative tests do indeed suggest that a positive behavioural 'set' will maximise the developmental benefits derived from the asocial lessons.

Effects on the teachers – sceptical at first

The observational ratings of the teachers' behaviour during regular and 'asocial lessons' revealed several important changes. Probably the most significant was the drop to zero levels both in their use of extrinsic rewards and in talking during the a-social lessons. This indicates that they all followed the Waldon conduct guidelines very conscientiously. Moreover, and somewhat against expectations, most teachers did not find this 'unusual' way of behaving particularly difficult or unnatural once they began using it themselves. This contrasts with their initial misgivings and scepticism, as expressed during the theoretical phase of the course.

Equally important these results demonstrate that effective teaching can be carried out by relying entirely on intrinsic (specific) reinforcement derived by the pupils directly from the activities they engage in. The test performance gains suggest that indeed this represents a more effective learning paradigm, and that as such it may be generally preferable to the behaviour modification approach with its heavy and systematic use of extrinsic reinforcement.

It is also worth noting that the test performance improvements occurred despite the fact that the activities during asocial lessons bore no direct similarity to the majority of the test items. Consequently, the so-called 'coaching' effect cannot account for these gains. Rather they would seem to reflect an effective generalisation and application of learning and understanding.

It would also appear from some of the results that for the more difficult and backward of the pupils, the use of direct physical guidance was a highly effective way of facilitating concentration, and effort, and a decrease in problem behaviours. By contrast little such guidance was needed with more able pupils, who responded well to a mere presentation of appropriate teaching materials.

The effect which the use of the Waldon Approach had on the teachers was also assessed through their own responses to a structured questionnaire. These were very positive with regard to their feelings of increased competence, understanding and work satisfaction, as well as their expressed desire to learn more about the Waldon Approach. It is worth noting that they were not afraid to be critical and that they did on occasions give more negative responses, particularly in their course evaluations. The main areas of criticism related to their lack of understanding and coverage of behavioural problems, and the design and selection of teaching materials. It is felt that any future course of this kind must deal more effectively and devote more time to these highly practical issues.

Postscript

I visited Jiri Berger in Iceland in August 2011 and recorded the following comments from him:

The study was done in a special school for the most retarded children with combined mental handicaps, sometimes combined with physical handicaps. It was very encouraging because when I started I could see that the teachers were really at a loss to find things for the children to do and specially things that they were prepared to do by themselves.

It was a revolutionary discovery for the teachers to find that they did not have to do everything with the children and sit with them all the time. The children started to work very independently ... Initially they started on a one-to-one basis but after a while some of them, not all, were able to work independently and it was those who were enrolled in the classroom study. The teachers adopted the approach quite quickly because they saw that it worked. When you watch the tapes some of the children do not seem to have many difficulties but when we first started to work with them they looked very different.

At the Hester Adrian Centre I was doing a research study on the interreaction between mothers and their Down's syndrome babies. It was very social – completely the other end of the scale from Waldon. I met Waldon really by chance and became interested in his work and visited regularly to observe and have discussions with him.

After I moved to Iceland I designed the research study on the Waldon Approach. The school was mixed with autism, cerebral palsy, mental retardation and Down's syndrome children. Waldon is general and works with all the children. There is no reason why not also with Down's....

As Geoffrey enphasized, movement is a very important basis for cognitive development, so if children are limited in their movements either physically or by motivation it is more difficult for them to develop well intellectually.

7

Case Studies of Children on the Autistic Spectrum

'He won't eat unless I am up a ladder outside the house!' (G.Waldon)

However interesting and convincing the foregoing may be, a case study of one (the author's son Robert), is unlikely to persuade many of the validity of Geoffrey Waldon's philosophy of child development or of the efficacy of the Waldon Approach. This chapter adds a number of case stories of students who have had Waldon Lessons from many of the teachers in the centres discussed in Chapter 6. These are told through the voices of one or both parents or facilitators and sometimes through the voice of the student talking about his own experiences and how the approach has transformed his life. Some parents have wished to use real names and others have asked for anonymity. I have made this clear in each case.

Case studies in the UK

Edward (assumed name)

Father

Edward was born in 2000 and it was a difficult birth – a forceps delivery. He was in the birth canal for a long time. They were going to do a caesarean but his sister had exactly the same events with no ill effect, so you might speculate. But Geoffrey didn't indulge in that kind of speculation, he liked to deal with what was and what was presented. I started to notice that Edward did not move as much as Christine had moved, in terms of generating movement; and as he got to his first health check, at three or six months they had a slight concern, not particularly about his movement but about the fact he seemed inattentive to sound. He was not displaying functional deafness or anything like that but was not turning his head towards sounds. That started to ring alarm bells to me. I would like to say that I leapt into action immediately and sought a diagnosis but like any good parent there was a long state of denial when I thought it would all be fine.[1]

The first way Edward's difficulties manifested themselves was in his expressive speech. He was quite a silent child and when he did speak it was babble and it was fairly late babble and there seemed to be no movement from babble to organized words. There were certain pet words that we recognized as a sort of attempt to communicate but that started to worry me more. He would make eye contact and he laughed and he would sing. It became more noticeable between 18–24 months that his attention lacked the intensity which you would normally associate with a child of that age. Certainly it lacked his sister's intensity. His activity would be intermittent, dictated by large movements rather than small and he was starting to make flapping actions with his fingers; a sort of self-delighting behaviour was starting to emerge.

As he started to walk and move around that would be quite regularly punctuated by – I want to say absences but there is no epilepsy involved – but that is what it looked like. To use a Geoffrey analogy it is like a radio with not a great tuning mechanism. The signal dips and you can almost feel it – it was almost a physical force; you could feel the energy and the force disappearing.

I can remember very clearly when we were on the beach on the Isle of Wight and there were some children of Edward's age and I was watching Edward and I noticed that he was isolated and that he made no attempt to make any social overtures. He was doing a strange little turning circle dance, looking at his fingers against the sunlight. I remember thinking well I'm going to have to bite the bullet here and I said to my partner Jane: 'I have got something to say to you and I need to say it but you are not going to like it' (she thought I was going to say I was going to leave her), 'I think Edward has some problems. By the look of his behaviour, and I have been reading a little about it – don't be alarmed – I would describe his behaviours as autistic in kind'. So she thanked me for telling her and was relieved that we were not going to break up and glad I had raised the question because she had also noticed that he wasn't interacting in the same way as our daughter had with other children.

Because of people's understanding or misunderstanding of what being on the autistic spectrum is – because he was making eye contact and because he was displaying a sense of humour and so on – people were immediately dismissive of that diagnosis.

But after that conversation we moved pretty quickly. The health visitor was concerned that he wasn't hitting the mark for speech development, but for me there was a much greater concern – that he wasn't generating enough activity. But both our babies were huge, although his muscle tone seemed low for the activity required. I noticed that I could pull things from his grasp quite easily at a stage where you could virtually pick a baby up by a pencil and it would not release a grip. I was a friend of Mary Jo (Mary Jo Middleton, a Waldon and Special Needs Teacher), and had even been to a lecture by Waldon when we were all living in Leeds and had got to know him a little.

Mary Jo was always talking about child development and Geoffrey Waldon and how amazing his approach was. So I asked her to start working with Edward and she encouraged me also to start working with him myself. I think Mary Jo started seeing him when he was three and I found out that in order to get him additional help at school a statement of special needs was necessary before he started. What I didn't want was for him to start school at five and not get a statement until he was seven. It was important to start early.

Simultaneously we went privately to see a speech therapist and Edward was as hyper as I have ever seen him; he was running about flapping his arms; she couldn't get him to sit down and she said: 'Well he's autistic isn't he?' And then: 'I don't know how you cope'. And two things happened there – apart from the fact that my suspicion had been reinforced rather badly at that stage, it was also quite a wakeup call seeing it through a stranger's eyes and I could suddenly see these behaviours that I was already grown accustomed to were quite strange and already causing problems both socially and in his learning.

Meanwhile we started doing Waldon Lessons with Edward. It was an immense relief – it felt like exactly the right thing to be doing. From the moment I started I can remember what I did. I used threading balls and he was passing them onto a stick and putting them into a bucket. Not only did he not resist, he was absolutely taken with it and taken at being directed – even when it was crossing over with his arms.

The resistance came later. We did banging, which was quite amusing. He could not believe he was getting away with raking, scooping, threading, putting in, taking out and posting. And then I remember saying to Jane: 'The strange thing about this is if you come in, and Edward's attempts are doing wonderfully well, the last thing I want you to say is well done. I repeat I don't want you to say well done'. But sometimes she just could not resist. Giving the lessons took an immense amount of pressure off me because I knew instinctively that it was best for Edward.

Also a part of the genius of the Waldon Approach is taking the sting out of the need for speech. The need for speech is gone. One of the cornerstones of the difficulty had been removed. The anxiety which I transmitted when trying to communicate with Edward was completely gone. It was very liberating and heartening and immensely moving.

I was giving Edward about three lessons a week and there was never any doubt in my mind that we wanted him to go to mainstream school unless his problems got so bad that socially it would be inappropriate for him and for the other children. So he went to Lincoln nursery. I was of the mind that if he was having a nice time there and they were being kind to him I couldn't go in and beat them over the head with 'do this, do that'. I was in a very privileged position. Mary Jo was involved and he was having his Waldon Lessons taken care of. I met Geoffrey again when he came down once to see Mary Jo and I remember him saying that it is not meant to be all day, it is meant to be a short but very intensive part of the day.

At this stage we had been to the paediatrician twice and because by now Edward was talking, inevitably the focus was on his speech – drifting away from the fundamental problem as Geoffrey had explained it. It seems ironic that the assessment of children with language difficulties is conducted through the spoken word. Mary Jo explained to me that muscle tone is incredibly important in speech sounds because if you are not getting sufficient feedback from the facial muscles and your throat, which cause speech sounds, then you don't know what it is you have to do to repeat a speech sound that you have attained. And again that just fell into place.

It was interesting with Edward. He was late, very late controlling his bowels, he was late controlling his bladder, and that would all fit in with muscle tone and being underpowered and of course as he got bigger the problems were compounded by growing expectations.

Every time we visited the paediatrician she would do the same tests which I suppose is reasonable because you have to have something to measure against, and I was sitting there like every parent, willing Edward to perform at some level that might be seen as some sort of achievement. I remember there were two tests in particular that were agony. One was building a tunnel through which you had to push a train of four bricks and I could see that his pincer grasp just wasn't sufficient to be able to achieve the balance. So he started to improvise and push pencils through the tunnel hoping that would satisfy her. Then she showed him a huge picture of a harbour with ships and sailing boats and ducks and seagulls full of interest and visual stimulation. There was this unearthly silence and she asked: 'What can you see?' And there was a tiny house on the headland and he pointed at the house and said: 'A door'. And she said: 'Anything else?' And he said: 'Aaah', pointed again and said: 'Another door'!

At that stage he was not making coherent sentences but was still babbling. He was babbling in rhythm. I recognized the rhythm of the babble – it was from *Toy Story* the movie, and at one stage she said: 'Edward – what is it you are trying to say to me?' And he put his face close to hers and said: 'You really are a strange little man' (quote from the movie). She took this seriously as though it was something she could work with but for Edward it was self-handicapping behaviour. He was putting some distance between them – he could see himself at a disadvantage so he threw a speech from Disney at her. There is a lot of that with Edward.

It is quite interesting how the word 'autism' came up. It seemed to me that she was trying to get me to say it and if I acknowledged the problem then it would be easier for her to say it. I don't know if doctors are trained in 'softening the blow'. So I said: 'I have been looking at his behaviour and those kinds of behaviours could conceivably be interpreted as autistic in its widest sense'. I volunteered that and she immediately wrote 'autistic spectrum disorder' on the form!

I neither mind nor don't mind this diagnosis. I would say, in Waldon terms, there is a lack of affect, but if you are going to come up with a diagnosis which is useful to Edward then I would say it is a motivational problem; slightly low muscle tone compounded by various behaviours and it is those secondary defensive behaviours, rather than the primary condition, which place him on the autistic spectrum. So there it was and I am sure that on the gauges they use that was correct.

The advantage of the diagnosis was that it opened doors in respect of help even if the help was not always appropriate. It started the process towards getting a 'statement'. We lobbied the council. Edward is an August baby so he would be the youngest in his class, just as Christine was, so we started to campaign with the council that he could start school technically out of his school year. He was born three days before the end of August, if he had been born three days later on the first of September he would start school a year later. So I said that as he was developmentally young anyway and on top of that had these difficulties, it made no sense for him to be starting school at four.

The council was very resistant. We played good cop/bad cop. Jane was saying: 'We are really grateful that you are doing so much to help Edward'. I would ring the next day; and they would say that the research shows that a child should be educated with its peer group. I said that statistically he would be with his peer group because actually if the cut-off point is September and he is August then statistically there is six months either side. And then they would say: 'Yes, but' and I would always say: 'Can you tell me what the research is? Can you give me references for the papers you've read?' There are reports which show nothing of the sort. There are plenty of reports which show that it is very harmful for August born boys who are developing normally to start school so young. The school itself was supportive all the way so that by sleight of hand almost, we had his entry delayed by a year.

He was now going to speech therapy. Speech therapy people were always lovely. The good speech therapists have a good grasp of the theory of language but it is quite easy to practise it badly with a very shaky grasp of theory. You do not necessarily stimulate coherent speech by talking to someone. You can't transmit understanding by speech to a child who already has speech and language difficulties.

At four years Edward had consistently failed to hit any of the significant milestones – by any measure this child had special needs. So he finally got his 'statement' which gave so many hours per week with a teaching assist-ant and then an extra hour and a half with a teacher. We converted that to another three hours with a teaching assistant because that would give more consistency. As we already knew the school from our daughter being there, we knew that the teaching assistants were very experienced and had done this kind of thing before. One was Gail who has been fantastically receptive to what we perceived Edward's needs were, and she was fantasti-cally inventive in her own right. She did stuff that I had never heard of but which seemed to me entirely complementary to anything that Geoffrey would do with a child.

Edward is now in his fifth year at the school. Prior to that he spent 18 months in the nursery where his socialization was very much on his terms. One day he was completely social and the next day not so. That was rather a confusing state of affairs for the children who wanted to play with him but, as most children are, they were completely accepting of Edward's idiosyncrasies. But he was often left alone in the playground and is perfectly happy with this. Another helper worked with Edward – just setting up games that he played with other children and which he enjoyed. But initiating that is beyond him and not where his first inclination would be anyway.

He still has a big problem with gender and pronouns and can easily call a boy 'she'. He has a problem retaining names so he says 'he', 'it', all of which can almost be designed to alienate potential friends. As he gets older it is a particularly unfortunate kind of slippage.

Edward's happiness, his capacity for happiness, his temperament, is remarkably level and jolly and his inclination is to be funny (another great way of deflecting demands of course), and in that respect that is less of a worry. Whenever I get most pessimistic about him I think well actually the ability to be happy, the ability to create a happy feel around you is probably one of the great gifts.

The great dock in Edward's life is his Saturday morning session with Mary Jo. She is an amazing teacher. She has trained teachers; she has understood and debated the Waldon theories over the years; she is also a physiotherapist, and if I was going to invent somebody to help Edward it would be Mary Jo.

The school recently made him do a Scholarship Aptitude Test (SAT report). For all your Waldon training, parent's perspective, happiness and all that, there is this nagging feeling that everyone else measures achievement in certain ways. There is a grading chart and Edward's grade is interpreted in the bottom one and a half percentile of his mean group. And every grade subject is the same. It is where he compares with his peers. I remember saying to Jane: 'Not exactly scholarship stuff'. So there have been a couple of low points, but I have to say on the whole his experience of school has been good. He has made remarkable progress in the last six to nine months.

He is nine now. At every stage at which Edward has struggled, the great thing for me is that I had learnt Geoffrey's theory and could see where things fit in. It is obvious that where he is having problems sustaining a series, his capacity for seriation is not fully established therefore his capacity for extrapolation isn't established. Therefore when reading a story, the notion of narrative still kind of eludes him even though he will read a story from beginning to end. But then you can see that Geoffrey's theory helped. The very beginning of seriation is 'men in boats' and I can see how men in boats and moving them in patterns would help somebody's reading. It just takes so much of the angst away from it.

I like the story that Geoffrey used to tell about how a child with this sort of behaviour can dictate the entire emotional temperature of the house and how in order to accommodate the child, almost anything will seem normal to the parent. Geoffrey told the story about how he told some parents: 'I think what you need is to institute rules, no matter how arbitrary they feel, just so you are imposing your plan on his, for some of the day. Meal times might be good'. 'Well' they said, 'we can't really do that'. 'What is the problem?' asked Geoffrey. 'I am always up a ladder outside. He won't eat unless I am up a ladder outside the house!' And this had been absorbed into the family's 'normal' fabric. And you know exactly how you get there. I always tell that to Jane about rituals. We had a ritual of opening and closing car doors and I think it stopped because we stopped trying to address it. Somehow it was allowed to slip away because our anxiety was no longer reinforcing it.

Mother

We realized very early on that we needed to get some early support for Edward and for that we needed to get some sort of diagnosis and we had a bit of speech therapy and at about three we started the sessions with Mary Jo.[2]

We always talked about Waldon quite a lot and I was really quite curious about this man. Mary Jo loved him and it sounds as though he was an extraordinary man. There was never a definite moment – we must do this. We came to it quite slowly when he was about three, when there were some behavioural problems. It was perhaps developmental which was late for Edward. He was quite a big chap by three or four and he was often running off and getting very angry and having really bad tantrums and we did see health visitors about it.

I can remember once going for a walk in Barnes and realizing that I needed help, perhaps a lot more than Edward. He had a bike and he abandoned the bike and ran off and I remember thinking do I go for the bike or for Edward. It was all quite safe. He was looking at me and I think I picked him up once or twice and he ran off again and I was thinking that I don't know what to do. I can't really lift him. I was feeling out of control. I remember him looking at me and I remember thinking how frightening it must be for a child when they sense that their parent can't be the parent and doesn't know what to do.

It was soon after that we started to put some structures in. We had not been great disciplinarians and we now started to impose rules about what he could or could not do. We put some boundaries down and his behavioural problems passed quite quickly after that. We felt that perhaps that was what he needed at the time.

Often parents do not realize that the child has moved on a stage and they have to adapt as well. They might get cross with you and you realize that they have grown up a bit and you need to adapt to that. I had not experienced that with Christine and I remember feeling quite out of my depth – quite alarmed. I had not had any knowledge of autism before and emotions are my business and I can make that link and that connection, but I find it quite hard to understand what is going on inside Edward quite a lot of the time.

There seems to be a real emotional component within Waldon, a real grounding. My experience of Edward coming back from or having had a Waldon Lesson is this grounding, and confidence, and earlier when he was struggling with speech it gave him easier access to speech. There was a real liberation from doing something which appears to be very simple work with Mary Jo. It has really given him a huge amount. This morning he sat there for two hours and he is only just 10. It is quite a thing I think. He never complains about it all he is just completely absorbed in the work.

It is a beautiful thing to see Mary Jo work with him, almost like an orchestral conductor, it is really moving to watch. I would love to see it more because there is something so moving about it. I am really grateful to Mary Jo. She has put such an enormous amount of time into working with Edward.

He has been having lessons with her for six or seven years. There is a teacher who lives near here and she only sees him in passing and she said to me: 'You know with children like Edward it is like one of those old televisions with an aerial on top; if you get the aerial just right they can learn and get on with life but slightly wrong and they are out of focus'. I feel that when he is doing Waldon he is completely focused. He very rarely drifts off. It has given him a really solid foundation within himself and I would say that there is an emotional component within that as well because I imagine that it would be very easy for a boy like Edward to give up; to be angry and to act out rage – because it isn't fair; and I imagine, although he never complains, that there must be times at school where he feels quite far down the pecking order.

Edward is doing well. He still has days where he gets things muddled up. We always describe it as if English is his second language. He is fluent but does struggle and get things the wrong way round sometimes. It feels like my French, but it is much better than my French! I think my aspiration for him, and it is very interesting to hear about your son, is for him to have that willingness to engage in a relationship with someone outside the family.

Peter (real name)

Peter's parents, Derek and Christine (real names)

Peter was the youngest of our four children.[3] Having had three children already we had some direct experience of child development, as well as what we had picked up from general reading. Peter was a lovely looking child with curly blond hair and a quiet, easy baby to manage. He came away with first prize in a Butlin's baby competition! At about 18 months he had a severe case of chicken pox and then German measles; after which he became more difficult to handle because he was resistant to being touched and nursed. It was at about this time that we sensed that he was not developing in the way the other children had developed by that age. He did not appear to respond to our conversation and voices and showed little or no interest in people. He was far more concerned with examining inanimate objects and things that he could fiddle with than with his immediate family and other people around him.

Our first thought was deafness. We spoke to our GP and he recommended us to the audiology department at Manchester University which is where we first met Dr Geoffrey Waldon. He established that there was no impairment of hearing but that Peter did display behavioural problems which he outlined in a letter the following day, 2 April 1968.

In that letter Dr Waldon referred to Peter as a generally under-responsive or primary autistic child. Peter showed confusion about the location of sound sources and, except when clearly distressed: 'ignored his mother completely, coming passively to anyone holding out an invitational hand and was willingly led out of the room without evidence of concern or even a glance towards his mother'.

After a further meeting three weeks later, Dr Waldon wrote to us and outlined his assessment of Peter in terms of his lack of emotional response and communication problems. He said that he would treat Peter's condition as a behavioural and educational problem and that he would arrange to see Peter at monthly intervals to advise us and encourage our efforts. He reassured us, that: 'whilst no one at this stage knows how well Peter will progress, he would appear to have a very considerable potential and should make continuing advancement'. This lifted our pessimism and gave us hope in the face of increasing behavioural problems and the gloomy predictions about autism that were beginning to enter the public domain. He also referred Peter to a paediatric neurologist to: 'ensure that no serious or remedial pathological process may be overlooked'. The neurologist gave us the all-clear in this respect, although he did give us the impression that there was little that could be done for children such as Peter.

We took Peter to Dr Waldon at regular intervals for the next two to three years until Peter reached the normal age for primary school entry. These sessions took an hour or more and we, Peter's parents, remained for the whole session in order to observe Peter's progress and become familiarized with the process and techniques that Dr Waldon employed. We were impressed, not only by the time which he devoted to each session but by his gentle and devoted patience. A procedure was established which followed a regular pattern, the purpose of which was to teach Peter to understand and respond to language which is essential for social develop-ment. Dr Waldon's approach was to give a verbal instruction to Peter but to help Peter perform it in such a manner that regular repetition of words and actions gradually enabled Peter to associate the words with the actions. The first and simplest one was: 'Bring up the chair (to the table) Peter'. Initially Dr Waldon did this himself, then they did it together and ultimately Peter would bring the chair to the table when told to do so. Dr Waldon had made a range of simple models and toys which could be put together and taken apart – such as a wooden lorry with screw on wheels, or a boat with little men in it. These were quite ingenious constructions and Peter, who was adept at such activities, would become absorbed in the actions whilst gradually assimilating the language that went with them. We recall two key principles at the heart of Dr Waldon's approach. One was the importance of associating and identifying language with actions and movement; the other was to 'suppress language and encourage understanding'. Peter never attempted to speak during these early sessions. Although it is obvious to parents that a child understands language well before developing its use in speech it was a common misconception that repetition or echolalia was a welcome sign of progress.

These 'lessons' given by Dr Waldon were as much for the parents as for the child and we were given instructions to spend an hour each day following the 'Waldon routine'. Peter's mother was largely responsible for this and it became her dedicated task for the next two to three years. The whole process, of lessons with Dr Waldon and the ongoing daily routine at home, required patience and persistence. The lessons involved banging and scraping, moving bricks around, screwing and unscrewing, various hand and arm movements. The physical experience is crucial in helping a child to get meaning from the world. There were particular hurdles that took time to overcome, such as the words *behind, before, in front of*. Peter's mother recalls crawling under the kitchen table, pushing things through and using the appropriate words. Things that other children naturally and without effort drew from their environment had to be deliberately taught and all this took time. One of the biggest steps in understanding language concerned questions. This proved to be a considerable hurdle because the understanding of and response to a question involves a complex brain process. Initially any question put to Peter was simply repeated and it took a long time to achieve the understanding and response that other children had no problem with.

Peter was possibly the first, but certainly one of the earliest, autistic children with whom Dr Waldon tried out his ideas about child development, particularly in the realm of language acquisition. We had several discussions with him about his theory and method. What he was sure about was that his methods worked. What we are sure about is that had we not met Dr Waldon, Peter's problems would have become more and more intractable and he would not be the person he is now.

Although Dr Waldon used the term 'autism' in his early assessment of Peter he insisted that labels could be misleading and unhelpful. Consequently we have avoided its use as far as possible and Peter today prefers to use the term 'aspergic' to describe some of his ongoing problems. Whatever the label, there are characteristic patterns of behaviour that are associated with these conditions, most of which Peter exhibited to some degree and which had a profound effect on our family life and which at times tested us to the limit. A couple of examples are disruptive behaviour at meal times and persistent head-banging after he had been put to bed.

In those early days the outlook for children such as Peter was very bleak. It was Dr Waldon who gave us hope and who helped us to do something about it. Our main hope and aim then was that we could help Peter develop so that he could live a normal, independent social life and not become in any way institutionalized. Whilst recognizing and attempting to deal with Peter's problems, from very early on our philosophy was as far as possible to treat Peter as a normal child doing normal things with others. Consequently we were firm in our view that he should, as far as possible, go through normal educational channels and not go to a special school. When he was approaching early school age he was interviewed by an educational psychologist.

Peter showed no interest in her questions and busied himself under the table fiddling with her shoelaces. She was unable to score him on her IQ chart and consequently put him down for an ESN (Educationally Sub-normal) school. Her conclusion was that he was not yet ready for learning and should spend more time in play, which was the policy of such schools. In our view such a step would have been disastrous because if nothing broke into his repetitive play pattern he would make little progress. He needed intervention and we thought that he would stand a much better chance by attending a normal local school and going through a learning process along with his peers.

Fortunately we knew the headmaster of a good local primary school and he offered to take Peter into his admission class, which had a very good young teacher, for a trial period to see how he got on. From that point he never looked back in terms of his schooling. For some time he would only understand instructions on a one-to-one basis because he did not respond to general instructions given to the whole class. Much of his early development was one to one. As he made advances in his ability to understand and use language he was able to take instructions and communicate as part of a wider group. But he found that difficult and at times, quite stressful.

He was also distressed by noise and would put his hands to his ears to shut out confused and noisy sounds. This acute sensitivity to sound is often accompanied by a perfect sense of pitch in music. This became evident when at school the music teacher was astonished by Peter's ability to pick out and identify notes and chords simply through hearing. He was subsequently auditioned at Chetham's School of Music in Manchester and offered a place in the school even though they were aware that he had some educational problems. Unfortunately Manchester Education Committee, which was strongly anti private education at the time, refused to fund him so he remained in the state system. Whether or not Chetham's would have been right for him, we do not know, but we felt a bit sore about the fact that the local authority refused to acknowledge Peter's problems and would not pay the fees which, at the time, we could not afford.

Another aspect of Peter's schooling was a sort of low level bullying. This has persisted throughout his life, in one form or another. It took the form of social bullying rather than anything physical. Peter was fairly stoical about this and treated it as a way of life that he just had to get on with and maybe we, his parents, were more upset about this than Peter was. Certainly, in later life when he spent some years in independent lodgings, living on benefit in Leicester, with some pretty unsympathetic people, he was ill used and exploited.

Returning to our efforts, under Dr Waldon's guidance, to help Peter develop an understanding and use of language, we felt that he had achieved so much and was coping well with school that he could go forward on his own. With hindsight we wonder if this was mistaken because we had not taken Peter's emotional development into account. We all have to develop emotionally, in the way in which we relate to other people in terms of what is called 'empathy' but this is a particular problem for autistic or aspergic people such as Peter. This inability to read other people's faces, to look them in the eye, to interpret their reactions and emotions, or to use a technical term, to have a 'theory of mind', is accompanied by a difficulty in displaying and expressing such emotions. As he has grown older, Peter has worked incredibly hard on this. He has a lovely smile and sense of humour and can be remarkably perceptive about people but he still finds it difficult to cope, in some social settings, with other people, particularly for any length of time. In no way can he cope with the competitive pressures of the rat-race in the modern workplace. The solitariness that was characteristic of his early years is manifested today in his need to be alone when he feels uneasy in a social setting.

With regard to employment, Peter has always said that he would like a job. He has always had an interest in mechanical things and after obtaining a Higher National qualification in mechanical engineering he found work in a hospital bio-engineering department. This did not last long because the people he worked with showed him little respect or understanding. At the age of 27, he was accepted by Brighton University to finish a degree in mechanical engineering but this did not lead to further employment. Despite his lack of success in obtaining employment he has continued to do voluntary work for Oxfam and in a local museum. His worthy achievements within those groups are often ignored or not noticed because of the more forceful manner of self-presentation that comes naturally to others. What bothers him is that if he is with a group of people he cannot find a way of getting them to take notice of him. His comment is that he can do a job but cannot get on with the other people. He took himself off on a course run by the Autistic Society some years ago which was concerned with enabling people to get back to work. He persuaded the government employment agency to pay for it but he did not learn anything new. When he came back they tried him in a job but the person supervising him had little or no understanding of his situation and nothing came of it. That disillusioned him somewhat, but he did try.

It is significant that despite problems with early language development he has become astute and articulate, particularly in writing and commenting on his personal development. He has written a lot about his experiences, some of it quite detailed and meticulous in what he refers to as his autobiography. He is continually revising it and wants it to be ever more accurate. This aspect of self-understanding is important to Peter and in that respect he is more astute than many who don't relate their past to their present situation. He is now in his forties, living in his own house, managing his own affairs more competently and economically than many. Although he enjoys social occasions, particularly with our wider family, he does need to withdraw and keep his own company and work at his own pace, unstressed by others.

Returning to Dr Waldon and his theory and practice with regard to problems in child development we have no doubt that he made the crucial contribution to the remarkable progress that Peter made in those early years which has given him a quality of life which would otherwise have been denied him. In this sense we would say that Geoffrey Waldon saved Peter's life, as indeed he saved ours. People who have not had to deal with these problems of child development find this difficult to understand. There is a subtle, but crucial, relationship between experience and understanding in so many aspects of human behaviour, which brings us back to the very subject of this book. We hope that what we have written will be an encouragement to others who find themselves in a similar situation and that they too may find the same support and expertise that we found with Geoffrey Waldon.

A conversation with Peter

Walter: What memories do you have of growing up?[4]

Peter: Up and until I was about five they are patchy. I remember when I was five years old realizing that I was in this world and everything from then onwards was continuous. I remember I was in the kitchen and there were some other children around and there was a party going on or something. At that point, I was still trying to make sense of the world, but it was all part of the learning process. I did not have much idea of the use of numbers at that stage. I knew I was five, but thought everyone else including my parents were older – but only a few years older. I remember at one stage telling people my father was six! I was definitely talking by then.

Walter: I am going to ask you to do something strange. You said that from the age of five your life was continuous and you can remember everything so let's pretend that we are at the cinema watching a film of your life. Can you talk me through it?

Peter: I remember outside our back door there was what would now be a very old-fashioned type of black pram, one of big chrome wheels, chrome base probably, that kind of pram; mum says I was about two at the time. I remember when seeing early photographs, being reminded of things like the clothes that my parents and my sister wore, and the surroundings. I have snapshots in my mind of insignificant things like being wheeled around for ages in a buggy, by a friend of ours, and being pushed into our back garden from the front along the side of the house – there were no fences or gates at that time. It was bonfire night, though I did not know this until we got there, I still recognized it. I must only have been perhaps about three at the time. I remember getting lost on the beach when we were on holiday and being upset until Mum reappeared. In the meantime, I was carried along the beach by a woman, which was better than being alone, but not the same as mum.

Some things I found obvious but because I did not show my emotions, other people did not realize that I knew what was going on, or that I understood. I did not realize that I had to show an outward display of emotion. At school, someone would explain something to me and if I did understand, it was difficult for them to know that I had.

Walter: Did you have difficulty understanding things at school?

Peter: I was not very good at understanding things on the spot. When there were things on the blackboard I just made sure that I got everything down in my notes and then would go home at night and try to understand everything then. But I think sometimes the idea was to try to understand it at once but I could not do that. I was too anxious making sure that I had got everything written down.

Walter: And were you able to make sense of it in the evening when you looked at your notes?

Peter: It depends how good the notes were – sometimes; we were given homework and that was the idea anyway. I had older brothers, mum and dad as well, so I would pick their brains when I got stuck. I am quite slow to get things, but when I do, I remember them. Other people can be quick to understand in the classroom, but then they forget it again quite soon. My English teacher said to me that everything you learn is recorded in the brain but the difficulty is in getting it out. I know this because depending where I am, what I am doing or even what mood I am in, different things keep popping out that may have happened 20 or even 30 years ago. You think 'Ah yes!' as though it happened yesterday. I sometimes write these things down. I don't know if it is usual to have an interest or obsession in recording the past in this way, but I find it quite interesting to do that.

Walter: I think that happens to a lot of people. You are somewhere and something triggers off a memory and you recall an incident from the past. That is quite usual.

Peter: But sometimes it can go deeper. I might think of something funny which happened some time ago, even say 25 years ago, and really get the giggles, but it is impossible to explain if anyone is around at the time, so I tend to suppress it. It is completely out of sync with what is going on at the time. When I am with other people my mind does tend to wander and drift; they may all start laughing at something or get something to do with something currently going on, and I have not really noticed.

Walter: How was it at school? Did you make friends?

Peter: It was a mixed experience really. Obviously there were problems. Everybody has problems at school but if you are aspergic or autistic the problems are much more evident. I seemed to make friends with people of a similar intellectual nature. There was a group of people who always did quite well, a group of people who were quite rebellious, a gang if you like, and another group was neither here nor there. That was the boys. Then there were the girls. I never quite understood the groups of the girls as their group distinctions were more subtle.

Walter: Which group were you part of?

Peter: I was in the one which did well academically. I did well on the whole, sometimes average; I was never very good at sports. I was fit and healthy but in terms of participating in sports I was not very good apparently. I did not realize this until I got a report card on which everything was alright apart from the sports which surprised me, because I was no shirk I thought, and even occasionally did well.

But I remember trying to get into basketball, the class were organized to play (the boys). I just didn't like it, couldn't make it work, and anyway I was small for my age then. I was useless at football too – just wasn't interested. At primary school, I was just hanging around the goalposts for ages chatting to my friend about our hobbies whilst others were far away at the other end of the field, each trying to get the ball. Actually, not everyone was into it anyway, the 'rebellious' group tended to fare well in the sports side of things.

Walter: Robert hated sports. Like you he was very fit, very strong, but he hated sports because he hated competition. He hated to lose because it made him feel bad; but he hated to win because he worried that that would make other people feel bad.

Peter: I know what you mean. I know sometimes when there are competitions at parties. For example, someone suggests 'Let's put the boys against the girls!' I hate that for exactly the same reason. I don't want the boys to win because it means beating the girls, and I don't want the boys to lose, because it means the girls have won. It is exactly the same thing.

Walter: Was there bullying at school?

Peter: It was more pestering really. There was not anything too physical. It was more a humiliating kind of bullying – stealing my bag and messing around with it, or pinching stuff from my desk, or tripping me up. It was the rough and tumble of school life. What got to me was the mindlessness of it all, the futility of it, and how some people just found things funny which had very little or no value. It was unimaginative and repetitive. They were not being clever, but doing things out of boredom, or just because they could. When you get groups of people together and they have nothing else to do these things happen. Gang incidents and even conflicts between gangs from other schools have always been there since schools existed.

But I always felt the teachers were on my side. Some people have had really bad experiences with teachers but that has never really happened to me. What probably helped was that my mother's job was in organizing teacher training, hence at parents' evenings they both knew what they were talking about.

Walter: Tell me about your love of music.

Peter: When I went to school there was music involved; my family were musical. At home I took an interest in the piano and at school I played other instruments. It was all classical. That was all I knew.

I was also in the school choir, except in reality my voice was too quiet to be of any use – just a drawl. I didn't enjoy it really, it was just a task.

But then my brother introduced me to the 'Top Twenty' on the radio when I was 11 and that was it. There was no going back. That was the kind of music for me. This was 1977 at the time of say Manhattan Transfer, Abba and cheesy stuff like David Soul and the Brotherhood of Man! They were all in the charts then too along with quality stuff by Elkie Brooks, even David Bowie and Stevie Wonder (I didn't know it was them until later), Donna Summer, The Jacksons, The Electric Light Orchestra, Hot Chocolate and also all those one-offs. I enjoyed listening to them and it made me feel really good hearing this variety of tunes. The names of the acts and the songs were interesting too. It was a kind of therapy if you like. And by the way, yes I had heard of Punk Rock, what 1977 is usually remembered for.

Walter: Is that when you stopped playing the violin?

Peter: No. it was difficult to stop as I felt there was pressure to carry on playing the violin and the piano because I had perfect pitch. A few years back in the seventies, it was found that I had perfect pitch and people thought, even expected that I would be the next Mozart or something. It is quite common with people like me that others think I'm a savant at something I am not very good at, not interested in, or cannot do, like being good at chess for example. People who are good at chess usually recognize people's faces well, which I cannot do. I actually wanted to be a recording engineer and producer in pop music and although I have never actually become one as such, I have been very interested in the people who do.

Walter: What stopped you from becoming one?

Peter: Well at the time, this was the eighties remember, all you could get was vocational qualifications to get a job in industry and there were not really any courses to become a recording or sound engineer. It's easy now, but then they were difficult to come across, highly expensive and unknown. Also, I was less knowledgeable about finding information about such things, plus there was no internet as such, requesting information was tedious, doing it blindly through the post. I was studying engineering at the polytechnic then. I did alright but really just went through the motions of it as it wasn't really what I wanted to do for the rest of my life. Not 'just engineering' or to be seen as one.

Walter: Have you thought about going back to college and doing a course now in sound engineering?

Peter: I did make various attempts but decided it was not really for me because – it is for a similar reason that I did not go into bicycle repairing as a trade. Another example is that I've repaired washing machines for people free of charge without acknowledgements (except from my mum). People expect things to work and to be done, they don't care how hard it is or how clever you are and you could be at the receiving end of some people who are never satisfied, unappreciative of the work and costs involved, and the extra care, time and trouble I take to do things, to get them right which won't be noticed but would be if I hadn't done them. I have heard plenty of stories of bands recording albums and what goes on and am glad that I did not get too involved in it.

Walter: What you are saying is that you don't like to have too much pressure placed upon you?

Peter: It is not so much the pressure; I found that in the workplace in general, the job description looks one thing on paper but in reality, it isn't. The working world is not like being at school, there is no protection for you. People can bully you, be nasty to you or shout and blame you as much as they like and there is nothing to stop that, whereas at school there are always teachers or the head to control things. I did not realize that at the time of my first 'real' job. I assumed that getting a job was a natural progression. I did not realize that work could make you so unhappy. What is the point of selling my soul and my life for this, to be treated like this I thought? It's a world I don't want to be part of.

Walter: Where are you living now and how do you spend your days?

Peter: I am living in the outskirts, and am always busy. I have more to do than I can manage. I do voluntary work in a charity shop and have been there longer than I thought I would be. Although it is on the whole OK I do have to deal with customers as well which can be a bit stressful at times. They come in and think they can run the shop better than you! It has its pluses and minuses but the thing is it reminds me what the working world is like. I could not do this every day – I cannot even do it for an eight-hour stretch. It's not that I dislike working, but even without the actual work tasks involved, just being there for me can be overwhelmingly exasperating.

The work related problems I have do seem unique. People do have jobs, but the problems they have are different. Perhaps I am just being over sensitive or perhaps my standards are too high, but in most jobs there are a lot of underhand things going on – fiddling, lying, deceit and bodging. You know how in newspapers they are always putting things under the spotlight, making anything they want to seem corrupt? Well it's exactly like that in any place I have worked at, but for real. There are always dodgy things going on. You can never do a job with honesty it seems. The working world is a strange place.

Walter: How is your social life at home?

Peter: It is limited, but I do like being on my own – but not too much. I find socializing quite a chore to be honest, something that I have to make myself do. I feel great that I have actually done it and been brave enough to go out to meet with an organization or go to a meeting or something. But I also find that I am never able to commit myself to anything there, or people think that I couldn't do it anyway. I don't look forward to social events and also I can't do it for very long – only for about an hour or two and the rest of it is just like surviving until it is time to go home. It does mentally wear me out.

Walter: This is all very familiar to me – Robert forcing himself to go out and putting himself in a stressful situation where he is uncomfortable. But you feel that you need to do that?

Peter: I like being with people, the same as everybody else does, but if they don't understand me, or I am not doing things the way other people are, it frustrates me. I wonder what is holding me back or what have I done, or not done. It is not dissimilar to problems that other people have with some people that they are either a bit showy, a bit shouty, and are always talking – the ones that always get the mentions in newsletters. But they are the ones that have the least need to be, because they have a high enough opinion of themselves already.

Walter: It is often the case that the showy, shouty ones are doing it because they are insecure and make a noise because they have a need to be noticed.

Peter: Yes, that is true. I have known that for a long time and you can see the insecurity in there.

Walter: Are you quite good at understanding people's feelings and are you able to judge character well?

Peter: I am sensitive to some feelings and others I miss the point. Some aspects exceptionally well, other aspects not at all. If I meet somebody, later I can joke about stereotypical aspects of their personality, and am usually right, but I am useless at remembering names. Even being introduced to just one person with a name – it is soon gone as my short-term memory isn't good anyway, and is disastrous in social situations. I am too busy thinking about the options of what to do or say next to remember the name. But my long-term memory is very good. I remember things that other people would have or should have forgotten. I can still be upset by thinking of what somebody said say five, 10 or 20 years ago, which I can't do anything about.

Walter: Have you had any girlfriends?

Peter: No, not really. I remember the first time 'noticing' a girl when I was about ten and a half and she was in the same class. I fancied her but thought I was a bit young for going out with a girl, and looked forward to doing that when I was at secondary school. It did not happen, it was all this 'waiting' until I was 'old enough', then … well there never seemed to be a right time. And then I did not have a clue what to do or how to go about it anyway, I assumed I'd find out automatically as other people seemed to do it.

In the seventies, it was a bit of a dirty subject in a way and easy for people to make jokes about interest in the opposite sex, 'Phwoor!' and all that. I wanted a girlfriend, but looking back it is probably as well that I did not have one as I never seemed to be ready for all the stuff that one has to deal with when having one. But then a few years later, I find myself in the same situation. It is a difficult one when you are interested in a girl but have absolutely no idea what to say to her. I don't know her, know nothing about her, and have nothing in common. And try as I might, I can't really find out anything either. I also don't like people watching me and when I am attracted to girls who are around, I cannot behave normally … I find it impossible to be myself.

I remember the story of Mowgli in the Jungle Book, when he sees a girl for the first time. Near the end of the film version, he goes loopy and uses acrobatics as in joyfully leaping about to express his emotions. He has been with animals all of his life and then sees a young girl in a human village. Sometimes, I feel a bit like that, and if I actually did that, I'd be left wide open for people to make fun of me.

Things like falling in love, finding people attractive, leading on from that, I can think about relationships that other people form and then marriage and children. In almost all circumstances I've come across, although it sounds fantastic and heaven like, I have learnt that really it isn't like that at all. It is a bit of a conflict within me, so I keep on observing and developing my thoughts about the subject.

Walter: I have been collecting a number of stories about children who were autistic and quite severely autistic and who had Waldon Lessons and who have developed really well to be able to lead independent productive lives. I think your story will be inspiring to others as well. So thank you very much.

Peter: All that is just the tip of the iceberg really. I have written quite a lot of notes about these things over the past few years which have helped me to understand more as to why certain things have happened to other people but have not happened to me. It helps to clarify and explain things. I am still working on this and it might be one of those things that I will never be able to finish but when you get to beyond four decades of your life you get better at dealing with certain problems, but as you get older, your opportunities recede. I know that there are some things I will just have to put up with now rather than thinking I can somehow fix them, or I'll get better, or they'll go away.

At the moment I feel that I am not quite a complete person; I have blanks here and there. Sometimes I just cannot see things coming or happening in the way that other people can and that is where I get caught out. It as if I am living in a two-dimensional world and I can see everything on a plane and then things come from above and below me and catch me out because I don't see them coming. This is particularly to do with other people and planning ahead. You have signals coming at you from all directions. It is knowing how to take things on, whether to lead off things or to stop things or divert things or how to control things by taking the initiative. I can't do that, my attempts usually end up being done blind.

I can end up saying yes to everything simply to get involved without any confrontation, only to find that I can't physically commit myself any more, to the point where I am forced to say: 'No. Stop'! Often they don't realize or notice and then think I am being rude when I do. That's why I don't like to commit myself to anything in an organization. If I end up in charge of something it feels as though I have committed myself for the rest of my life. Then I'm afraid that if I don't want to do it any more no one will take my place.

Derek: Can I ask you a question? You have spoken a lot about your past, and I suppose we all do that to try to discover how we got to where we are. How do you see your future?

Peter: I'm a bit shocked actually. When you are in school it was like: 'What do you want to do when you grow up?' Then at college it was to go out get a job, find a girlfriend, get married and have children. I really did think all that at the time. But it never really happened although it happened for everybody else. I thought that was a mixed blessing because if I had gone through all that life might have been absolute hell; but having not gone through that I feel as though I have copped out of it. I am so afraid of responsibilities that I don't want to commit to anything; but then in retrospect, who knows? I might have met the right people.

Derek: You are still talking about the past, Pete, what do you think about the future?

Peter: That was the future – but now for the future I am more concerned about my health and looking after myself. I don't really have any plans for the future, which I don't believe is a good thing, I'm just being honest. Life changes, you know, and that's why I find it impossible for now to make any plans for the future. I don't seem to have any control over it however hard I try, and whatever it is I try to do. But I can look after my health and get my memories out there like I'm doing now. I have a different vision of the future from what I did 20 years ago. Now I expect more of the same, but back in 1990, I really believed I and the world were changing and moving on. We were.

Walter: If there were one thing in your life you would want to have changed, what would that be?

Peter: To have the missing piece of my brain back. I don't feel quite complete, as if there is this void in the brain. Mostly it is alright but then sometimes, a message cannot register. There is a black hole there and I am not seeing things or missing things. I am not aware of them so do not know that they are there to miss. So, I would wish not to be aspergic but just to be healthy really, and the things that make me stand out and draw attention to me and at the other extreme not to occur. But I know that is not going to happen – and it could be a lot worse.

Dan (assumed name)

Father (parents have real names)[5]

Waldon's theories made great sense to us both at the practical level and in terms of the theory that underpinned them. Frances is a linguistic anthropologist and I am an anthropologist of art and material culture, both of us also have a reasonable understanding of biological anthropology and theories of human evolution and human development. Waldon's breadth of intellectual engagement was exceptional, but he was also a very practical theorist who developed simple ways of applying and testing his ideas. His objectivity was one of his great strengths, there was no dogmatism, no imposition of a particular ideology or theory to the exclusion of others.

Our son Dan was diagnosed early on as being on the autistic spectrum, but was never classified as having some specific condition such as Asperger's syndrome. He had suffered from temporal lobe epilepsy from the age of around eight months with often severe seizures. He was on high doses of anti-convulsive drugs that we believed were delaying his development. He was never particularly withdrawn though he was often disengaged from the world around him, his language development was delayed, he had many obsessional traits, he would have uncontrolled temper tantrums, his movement often appeared uncoordinated, he would often behave inappro-priately and had difficulty in grasping the world as a whole – he found it difficult to follow narratives beyond 'Where is Spot?'

We lived in Australia then and were very depressed about the kind of support we were able to get either for his epilepsy or for his 'autism'. My parents lived outside Oxford and my mother told us of the Park Hospital's reputation for treating childhood epilepsy and also informed us of the Chinnor Unit. So I applied for a job at Oxford University and we moved! Dan was enrolled in the Chinnor Unit but we also were given the go-ahead by the Park to take him off the anti-convulsive drugs (Frances and I had carefully monitored his treatment and concluded that there was no relation-ship between the drug therapy and his epileptic seizures!). They did warn us that his seizures would become so severe that we would soon be back. But they were supportive. However with the withdrawal from the drugs the seizures stopped and he has not had one subsequently.

The Chinnor unit was a marvellous environment for Dan. It enabled children to gradually integrate (as they were able to) within the school as a whole and provided helpers in the classroom in addition to specific additional support and therapies. Dan was early on able to take part in football in the playground. Football was one context in which Dan did not appear to be physically clumsy and where he seemed to develop a strong sense of the game as a whole. However, in other areas Dan continued to be very delayed in his development and obsessional. He classified foods accord-ing to their colours, he would play the same simple game over and over again, he could not write stories (though he had a strong sense of the grammaticality of sentences and he was always a good speller). When he did read it was usually the football statistics in the newspapers, for which he had an uncanny recall.

I think it is fair to say that Dan's encounter with Waldon and the Waldon method applied by Richard Brooks was transforming. Learning how to learn made great sense in Dan's case. Because of the epilepsy and its treatment Dan had clearly missed out on crucial initial stages of development when the world was blocked out from him. Dan was a very cooperative Waldon student. He seemed to calmly enjoy doing all the exercises with the toys. The environment of assisted asocial learning with the facilitator behind him and the absence of any encouragement, praise or criticism, seemed to work incredibly well. Dan was used in classes when Waldon visited as an example of the method in practice. Following the introduction of the Waldon method Dan began to overcome many of the conceptual problems that he had had. His writing began to improve, and he began to grasp a sense of things existing as wholes rather than parts, he was able to put things together. From then on he began to progress incrementally. Frances remembers writing a short essay about one of these occasions (see page 73). When Dan moved to the Cherwell School at 13 he was able to be based in the school full-time with a helper. A moment in time was reached when Frances and I felt that despite the great benefits of integration he was beginning to suffer more from the stigma of being associated with the Chinnor Unit. He felt that he was being treated as an outsider. We were contemplating moving him out perhaps, reluctantly, to a private school. Reluctantly – because private education could never have provided what Dan had gained though the Chinnor Unit and the state sector.

However instead I applied for a research fellowship back in Canberra in Australia and we returned when he was 16. We felt that by moving back we would move him to an environment where he was free from the way that others had positioned him and could create a new life for himself. Again we were very lucky because the state school we sent him to had an ideology that all children are special needs children in different ways and that atmosphere pervaded the school. In the sixth form children tend to have overcome their adolescent angst and on the whole are more tolerant of difference. There are also structures that enable children to spend a shorter or longer time moving through the programme according to their needs. Dan spent an extra year there and was able to leave with good enough grades to get him into a College of Further Education to undertake a Diploma in Community Recreation, following his lifelong interest in sport – football in particular.

Since then Dan has continued both his career and his education (and he still plays football). Of course there were no jobs in community recreation so he became a childcare worker and is currently training to be a pre-school teacher. He has thrived in that position. He is now a room leader and has just completed a second Diploma in child development. His next plan is to undertake a degree in education part-time at University. He is married and a home owner – the latter years before his parents managed to be! Apart from Waldon, Dan has been very lucky in having always had a strong set of supportive friends and relatives. However there is no question that Waldon and his method enabled a conceptual transformation to occur in Dan's understanding of the world, which may not have happened without his intervention.

Christopher (assumed name)

Mother

Christopher is now 29.[6] We first found out that he had autism when he was two and a half and lived in Didsbury. A colleague of my husband, who lived nearby, mentioned Geoffrey to us when Christopher was about four and he was about five when we started. Geoffrey assessed Christopher and began to give him lessons; and I gave him a lesson each day at home and we even took bricks, pegs and sorting and matching cards with us when we went on holidays. Most days Christopher would have had a lesson from me and at other times of the day I might have encouraged him to pick up bricks and that sort of thing.

At the stage when he first saw Geoffrey he was non-verbal and needed guidance in a lot of ways. He would not have been toilet trained. He was still developing his Fundamental Understanding from the Waldon point of view but from another point of view Christopher has always loved having stories read to him and loved poetry. He was great at doing jigsaws. He was tactile from quite an early age and was able to make his needs known in a non-verbal manner. He was quite passive and was not resistant to change so he would come along with most things that we did, meaning all the normal things that one would do.

We had our second son just before Christopher was two so Christopher did everything with Nicholas and when Nicholas was learning to read at school Christopher sat on the other side of me and was terribly interested. So from a Waldon viewpoint Christopher was at quite an early level of General Understanding and yet he seemed to be quite interested in other things. He probably had islands that were higher but he still needed a lot of prompting in the lessons. I was still guiding him quite a lot in the lesson although he would sort and match on his own.

His motivation was poor. I can remember Geoffrey saying that Christopher was like an old car that needed to be wound up. I used to ask Geoffrey a whole lot of questions and rather than answering he would respond with questions until I found the answer for myself. So I had my lessons as well. All autistic children are different and their different personalities tend to shine through. Christopher was not one who needed fixed routines and who did not like to be touched.

He was physically perfectly fine. We would go on lots of walks and Christopher would have problems negotiating stiles so we did lots of practice with that sort of thing. So he did have problems from a perceptual point of view. He is a great walker now and is at the front of any group he is walking with.

It is hard to know what difference the lessons made to Christopher because I don't know what he would have been like without the lessons. From a parent's point of view it was good to have something positive to do that you felt was helping. It gave something productive for Christopher to do and for me to do with him. He had about two years of lessons with Geoffrey and after he died continued with lessons with Bee Bee Waldon and then with Pat Evans[7] until he was about 12.

Christopher today shares a house with two other chaps with autism and they have support workers round the clock. He walks dogs for three elderly ladies with the support of his support workers. He walks with two walking groups. He still loves his stories and poetry. He likes music and to be with other people so long as he is accepted and the vibes are positive. Not unlike the rest of us. He does not much like waiting. He loves the seaside and the outdoors and has a reasonable quality of life because we have created that for him around the things that he likes to do. It could get better the more he is understood. I would like him to get a wider circle of friends, but it will not be Christopher making those friendships. It will be other people who understand Christopher and accept him for who he is. I would like him to have as many experiences as he can so that he can choose what he wants to do.

He comes home about every third weekend and might pop in with a support worker in between times as well.

We did the Waldon Lessons because we believed in the approach and hoped that they would help Christopher. I wish that we had had the opportunity of having Geoffrey give him lessons for longer. It was good meeting other parents and children at The Place which we set up after Geoffrey died and I also went on a number of the workshops that Geoffrey gave for teachers and some parents in Manchester, Leeds and Oxford. That was good because it helped expand my understanding of the philosophy behind the lessons. Waldon helped me understand Christopher better which clearly benefitted him.

Case studies in Slovenia

Marko (assumed name)

Barbara Šömen, Special Education Teacher, Family Psychotherapist, Instructor for Functional Learning programs, School for Deaf and Hard of Hearing, Ljubljana[8]

Marko was in regular kindergarten before entering the kindergarten here as a part of the Slovenian Ministry of Education project to study a kindergarten group of children with autistic spectrum disorder. At the moment there are six boys of which Marko is one and he came in autumn last year. He is five years old and lives with his parents and older sister. His father works all day until late and his mother until four in the afternoon so that Marko spends a lot of time in the kindergarten and has little Functional Learning at home. It was hard to motivate the parents to get involved but finally they came for a meeting with all the people who work with Marko: occupational therapy, physiotherapy, speech therapy, special education teacher and kindergarten teacher.

We explained the situation to the parents because he is five years old and at the age of six it is obligatory to enter school. We have very little evidence that he will be ready for school. He has progressed well but still needs a lot of support for his sensory integration. He is quite hypotonic with very little of his own body tone, poor tactile sense and problems with the balance mechanism. However, his eye contact has improved and he is more open for social contacts. He has difficulty relating to children of his own age but is better with adults.

We started with simple Functional Learning activities like placing and pairing and now, six months later, he has more flexibility. He uses more objects for matching, performs more activities with drawing, connecting lines from a central point for example, and is getting better at sequencing. He uses effortful behaviour, for example, in taking items out of screw top jars, and sorting them into dishes and then replacing them in the jars, re-screwing the tops and placing them on the tray. We do more and more of this combination of sequencing and sorting with him and it will become progressively more complex as his understanding grows.

He has half an hour on his own with me a week doing Functional Learning and also has a group session doing sensory integration activities with my colleagues (occupational therapist, speech therapist, physiotherapist and special education). All four of us work together for another one and a half hours a week in a special room called a 'snoozle room' where there are many possibilities for using sensual materials, lights and sounds to relax the child. Combining sensorial activities with Functional Learning can give very good results – especially to prepare and relax children before a Functional Learning session. Playing with shaving cream for drawing on the table is part of the same idea to have fun with the children and relax them before a session – especially when we have a visitor which makes everyone a little more tense!

I cannot imagine working without Functional Learning which is an integral part of everything I do with these children. It is basic for me and also my colleagues – especially in speech therapy. The occupational therapist uses some elements of it although she has not had formal training. It makes it easier for us to work in a team. We speak the same 'language' and we use the same activities from different perspectives. It is the basic understanding which helps us to understand the children and to assess them in the different areas of the learning-how-to-learn-tools. It is a very good system for assessment and diagnostic processes.

We have had some good experiences with children who when they came at age six or seven we were not optimistic about.

There is a boy who I have been following for about five years. He has hearing difficulties, and had many problems in settling down and in communication. He has now had five years of work with Functional Learning with a special education specialist and also therapy with a hard of hearing therapist. He has three hours of extra support in his kindergarten and devoted parents who support him very well. His understanding is very good but his speech has not progressed. His communication is still so poor so that even his parents sometimes do not understand what he wants. He will probably enter mainstream school with extra support.

We are starting to use a picture system to combine pictures to make a sentence. He is good in matching and in the use of symbols. His palate has been repaired so that is no longer the problem but his motor and sensory consciousness are still delayed. In the last two years he has been letting us know that he is capable of much more and of telling us what he can do.

It also became apparent to me that he might be on the autistic spectrum because of the special way that he gets in contact. His difficulties may be more deep rooted and they exist in many areas of his development. But with all his problems he has done really well – the best he could – and the parents support him at home with Functional Learning activities that they have seen here.

Kaspar (assumed name)

Anamarija

The first boy I started to see with together with Katrin Stroh was called Kaspar and he really benefited a lot from this work. All the methods I had tried with him earlier had not worked. I had tried 'Body Language' but it made him even worse. So if he threw things on the floor and I threw things to copy him it made him even worse. He just threw even more and tore everything into shreds. Nothing came into his hands but he would destroy it. Using Functional Learning his behaviour started to improve, his under-standing grew. His parents also participated in giving lessons.[9]

Father

Kaspar is now 19 years old. He was handicapped from birth. The moment he came into the world the doctor said that our child was very strange. Even today I can still feel the shock of that. But I discussed it with my wife and we agreed we would give him all the support which we could to raise him.

When he was about five years old his behaviour was described by some doctors as being autistic. At that time in Slovenia there was little knowledge of this condition and professionals did not want to make the diagnosis because they did not know how to deal with these children.

As a baby he was extremely small. It was impossible to find toys for him because his fingers were like matchsticks. You could put seven Kaspars in a child's cot. We do not know the reason why. He was a full-term baby and my wife had a healthy pregnancy with no smoking, drugs or alcohol.

At three years he went to the School for the Deaf where Anamarija was teaching and at about five years old we started with Functional Learning.

Anamarija

I met Katrin [Stroh] and said: 'This is for Kaspar'.

Father

I was doubtful because Kaspar was so small and could not reach all the things which were also too big for his little hands. One problem was that Kaspar does not want to repeat things. He learnt very fast and after he had repeated something five, seven, 10 times he did not want to repeat it again. When he learnt something he wanted to stop doing it and my opinion was not to push him. I was in doubt whether to firmly help him or not.

Now we are where we are. Maybe these things helped him. But he has other problems than just autism. He is medically deaf in one ear; one eye does not open fully – many things that I don't want to remember.

He understands everything we say to him but he is an autist. For example he wants to drive in an ambulance and I am afraid that when he is walking he will suddenly jump on the street, get hit by a car and then will get to travel in an ambulance. He understands a lot of things but the problem is that we do not understand him as well as he understands us.

He now recognizes that he is not like other children at the school he is in. He is in a special group of six children where one is a Down's syndrome child and can speak; but Kaspar cannot speak to him. He knows that something is wrong with him.

I am here as part of my work which is to help him and I am proud that he has taught me a lot of things.

Anamarija knows that I was always in doubt about Functional Learning and perhaps it has helped. Orthodox medicine has not helped so we must find other ways. Also Kaspar was the first in Slovenia for Functional Learning so we had no one else to ask about it. He is happy when we are together and everything goes well. He is a fighter and so I will be a fighter alongside him.

Meeting the Waldon Approach at age 29

Michael (real name)

Parents

Michael was born in 1966 and when he was six weeks or so there did not seem to be much response from him. Labour had been proceeding for 21 hours, under a registrar or some fairly junior doctor, and there was no dilation and it was: 'Let's wait a bit longer'. I went in after the baby was born and Michael was making a noise and it seemed somehow animal-like or primitive to me and I said: 'I don't like that cry. Something is wrong. There is some distress'.[10]

But in that very early period he seemed to us to behave just like a normal baby. He fed alright, he smiled, he was good looking and we just thought we had an A1 baby. The only thing that seemed wrong at about six months was that he was not responding to sound. He had eye contact; he would play with things. The alerting thing was this failure to respond to sound.

At the time the Social Studies department at Nottingham University, had a course of lectures on developmental psychology given by Mary Newsom of the well-known Newsom Report.[11] As one of the highlights towards the end of the series a six-month-old baby was produced and she would demonstrate the skills that baby had, particularly picking up and putting to the mouth, and at six months you would get a reaction to rustling papers behind the ears and things like that.

We offered Michael as a specimen for Dr Newsom to do her thing. Well as we got to six months and were rustling bits of paper, Michael was taking no notice. We had to go to Dr Newsom and say that we have to withdraw Michael as he will not respond to some of the tests you will do. In other words it came to a crunch and we thought that perhaps there was a deafness problem.

We did nothing until the health visitor did her normal hearing check at five and a half months and when he had not responded she said that it was a bit early because they usually do the tests after six months and when she came back and still said that he would probably be alright, it was then that I thought that this was not right and took him to the Children's Hospital who referred us for a hearing test. There was some hearing loss and we had an appointment to take him back for a three- or four-night stay to be fitted up with bilateral hearing aids.

We were then referred to the peripatetic teacher of the deaf, who came to the house, and it was on his instigation that Michael went to the school for the deaf. After half a term there they decided that they could not keep him because he wasn't a normal deaf child and they could not cope with his behaviour. Obviously the rituals were showing through and we actually met a lady five or six years or so ago, who had worked at the school for the deaf, and she said that she was the only one that Michael allowed to put on his coat.

We next took Michael to the Audiology department at Manchester University. It was important to try to pin down what his problem was because if he was deaf then the deaf school should buckle to and solve the problem. But as he was not yet five, so not of compulsory school age, we were left rudderless.

Manchester could not get a response to sound so could not definitively say he could hear, but equally well they did seem to feel from his overall demeanour that the hearing loss was only part of the problem. They advised us to remove the hearing aids so that what sound he was getting would be normal pitch. We felt bad because the aids had made a terrible screeching noise and we thought what have we put this poor lad through with this great big box producing amplified sounds.

Next he was seen by a children's psychiatrist and somehow the issue of whether he could hear or not was sidelined and he was labelled as mentally handicapped. The psychiatrist did not want to know the word 'autism'. So there were two things going on. He was three or four. The school was saying that he was uncontrollable and we could not do anything with him either.

The peripatetic teacher for the deaf realized that he was not getting anywhere and contacted the peripatetic teacher for autistic children, and she came and said that he was typically autistic.

The paediatric psychiatrist would not acknowledge that as the appropriate diagnosis. It was said unofficially in the social services department where I worked that the authority did not want to acknowledge autism. The implication was that extra attention and an educational methodology suited to its needs would need to be provided and they did not have the resources.

We realized from very early on that there was no magic cure and we had decided for Michael that the most he would get out of life would be via the educational process and so we were concerned when he was consigned to a special school for the mentally handicapped. We were relieved however that this peripatetic teacher actually did sessions at the school.

Sister

I also had another, younger, brother. When I was younger it was never an issue that Michael was different. It came up at school a few times because when we used to walk up from the primary school and he would be at the bottom gate, shredding leaves and would giggle when we came in, but Mum and Dad just said that, well, that is how he is. When I became a teenager and had to go out with him I got embarrassed about things but after a while it was just – well here he is.

As we got older my brother and I realized that there would be a responsibility shifted on to us at some point and we started to help Mum and Dad, taking him out sometimes and that was interesting because it did not go particularly well. Although we were brother and sister, I found it quite hard work. My husband is very supportive. But generally Michael is just there; tactile at some point, affectionate at some point. I have had a giggle with him the last few days. He gets on really well with my children. They sit on his knee; I also sometimes sit on his knee and have a laugh with him and stuff like that. We have a Jacuzzi in the back garden and he will come and sit in it and they play around him and he just laps it up really. He did go through a phase of having quite bad temper tantrums and that was difficult. Sometimes he would come into our rooms when we were working, so it was a bit of an interruption but generally I can't really think that it was too bad.

Mother

The autism lady said that she knew a good school that he ought to go to. It was a local school for the mentally handicapped; it had not been open for very long; it was in a little building down a little street, but they were building a purpose-built school which was going to be lovely. So we took Michael to see the head teacher and she said that he could come.

She took to him just like that and she had this class that he could go in and there was a teacher coming up for retirement who would look after Michael. So he went. Really he did not look back. He was just a little under five years old and when it was ready he moved to the purpose-built school and just progressed through it. In each class all the staff all took to him, because he was so amenable. He was just lovely and if he really wanted your attention he would come and look up at you as if to say: 'I am here, you know'.

There was nowhere locally for Michael to go residential and somebody in Social Services, suggested a home in Essex. We were desperate; I was particularly desperate because I seemed to be so ill and just could not take any more. But it was an absolute disaster. It was a privately run home for mentally handicapped people, not especially for autists, and he was most unhappy there.

So he came home and there was a hostel nearer to us with a day centre. He was there during the week and home for weekends and that did not work out too badly at all; but one of the area directors in Social Services saw that we needed more help and had come across Ashlar House in Leeds. So we contacted all the authorities who suggested that we went to see them and Michael went when he 24 and has been there for 20 years. That is now his home.

It was very informal at Ashlar House in the early days. The staff were very caring, and there was this older lady, who took him under her wing and she knew somebody who could help Michael. She had the idea that 'this Waldon thing' would be good for Michael and suggested it to the manager, and that is how it all came about.

Starting Waldon at age 29

It was about five years after he went there that he started the Waldon Lessons and they took several years to make any impact on him; but they persevered and then he started to pick things up. We used to often walk on the Yorkshire Moors and he walked with us, but tended to bring up the rear because that way he knew where you were. He just walked straight – God help you if you got in his way. On this particular day he was just walking along *and he walked around these people.* We could just not believe it. It was quite a thing for him to do that and demonstrated a greater awareness of his surroundings. Waldon exercises show that he has the ability to see a task through with good humour and expertise – something unknown in his earlier years.

Marilyn gives him one lesson a week and has been doing so for about 15 years and the following report gives all the details.

An anecdote: when Michael was working with another student at these Waldon classes and they were taking it in turns to do things, and the other person was a bit slow in doing her bit then he was pulling a face and making a noise, just a grunt, to prompt her to do it. To us that was a very big leap forward.

Report by Jo and Brian Loader (Michael's parents), for Leeds City Council, May 2010

Prior to commencing with the Waldon Method Michael was very difficult to manage and didn't have a very enjoyable life. He had no ability to communicate verbally and very limited signing skills. His existence was dominated by rituals, repetitive activities and the apparent need for set routines. Getting Michael either to engage in or desist from an activity would often cause him acute distress leading to head banging. He became distressed for reasons unfathomable to those around him. He never had any inclination to initiate recreational/educational activity for himself. His manual skills were very poor and his use of tools was tokenistic. Seemingly the Waldon Method was tailor-made to counter these deficits.

Within months of commencing the Waldon sessions we observed on the occasions when we visited and took him out, a change in Michael's demeanour which was more relaxed, more amenable and he adapted himself to alterations we made in the routine of the day. This change was, in our perception, sufficiently dramatic that it could reasonably be ascribed to his Waldon experience, given that other aspects of his daily existence remained the same at this time.

For at least one learner, our son, for whom person to person interaction had always been a fraught business, the 'asocial' or 'emotionally neutral' approach has been an absolute godsend. It in no way inhibits the learner from expressing a sense of self satisfaction with the progress of an activity and sense of achievement when a task is completed. Nor does it preclude a (positive) interaction between two learners who are cooperating in one activity – both of those aspects being well illustrated by recordings and stills of Michael and others in action. [Author's note: these can be viewed on the associated website www.autismandunderstanding.com]

Recent reports, recordings and stills show a progression in Michael's activities and his animated engagement in construction and cooperative exercises.

We think there is evidence of the continuing need for/benefit of a Waldon input in that when this was interrupted 2–3 years ago Michael showed a marked regression in his ability to cope – with some composure being restored when Waldon was re-started.

8

Not Only for Autism – More Case Studies

'Whenever I talk about Geoffrey's lessons I start flinging my arms about in all directions.' (A Waldon mother)

NOT ONLY FOR AUTISM is the strong message of this chapter. The Waldon Approach is for all people with and without difficulties. The philosophy on which it is based is of the need to develop the General Understanding which is fundamental to understanding the world we live in, leads to competent Particular Understanding, and can help all people, regardless of age and circumstance. In this chapter I focus on studies of children with a variety of special needs.

Case studies

A conversation with Larry (and his parents)

Larry: I was born with a brain condition called hydrocephalus which meant that I had to have a shunt introduced and later, when I was about three, I was diagnosed with epilepsy. I have a visual impairment and have very poor peripheral vision. I have one-sided hemiplegia which at best is a weakness down my side and at worst is a paralysis of one side. I have partial epilepsy which is only on the right side and the hemiplegia has a certain degree of effect on that. I have a horizontal and vertical squint which I have now had corrected twice[1].

I still have the shunt, although at various points it needs to be revised. The first revision was in 2007 which is something of a miracle because the surgeon told my parents when I was six months that the shunt would only last four and a half years and in actual fact it lasted 15. That is pretty incredible. The one I have now which is much more technically advanced is said to last 30 years. It sets off airport security scanners but luckily they do not affect its function!

It was quite nice because the surgeon Professor Robert Heywood who did the revision in 2007 just before he retired was the same surgeon who did the original operation in 1991. I was one of the first people in the UK to have a programmable shunt inserted.

As I have got older I have gained a greater understanding of my condition. I am 19 now and even at this relatively young age I have quite a comprehensive understanding of how my needs affect me and in the wider spectrum of things how they affect others.

I was at primary school for maybe one and a half academic years. It was a mainstream school that could not deal with my additional needs, as they stood at the time, so I was moved into a special school which was very good. It was an excellent experience for about one and a half academic years but then I had a teacher who I did not get on with so my parents moved me to another special school.

Walter: What was the problem? Was it your behaviour?

Larry: I was quite behaviourally challenged when I was little.

Walter: Challenged or challenging?

Larry: Both. I do not think it is normal practice to lock a child outside of a classroom in the playground, in all weathers, for basically what boils down to having quite severe special needs.

I started seeing Katrin [Stroh] weekly or fortnightly from April 1999 to April 2000 [aged 9–10]. I did not really know why I was going there. With hindsight I know much more about why I went.

I left the second special school in 1999 when I was about eight and Katrin referred me to Alan [Proctor] in May 2000, age 10. Every Thursday my dad would pick me up from my school – an excellent special school which I would recommend to anyone who has children with additional needs. We would drive up the A10 to the M1 and then along the A5 to Alan's bungalow, called Four Trees because it used to have a palm tree in each corner, but they had all been blown down in a great storm.

Alan saw me privately and he built on the work that Katrin had done. When I was seeing Alan it was more a case of playing battleships and investigative role games while we talked about my feelings.

Walter: Can you remember what you did with Katrin?

Larry: No – but obviously the stuff that I did with her worked. If I had not done that with her and with Alan I would not be as I am today. I would still be having quite severe behavioural difficulties and no way in the world would I be thinking about doing an Occupational Therapy degree. It transformed me as a person.

Then I went to a special secondary school where I was learning the regular curriculum but with extra support. There was normally a teaching assistant in each classroom and I had a Statement of Educational Needs.

After I finished seeing Alan that was the end of that type of therapy. In 2004/5 I started seeing a more conventional counsellor. I had re-integrated into mainstream and was at a small school in the West End. This had been suggested by an educational psychologist as being the best way of getting back into mainstream. I understand that this move was quite a struggle for my parents who had to battle a degree of opposition from the school I was at and the local education authority. For a child with special needs who had been in special school for most of their school career it would have been horrendous going to a large comprehensive.

There were at most 300 students at this new school but I was now faced with the different challenge of having two very macho sports teachers – an ex-army sergeant from the Iraq war, the fifth strongest man in the world, and the fourth strongest lady in the world. It was quite intimidating and it took them the best part of two years to get to grips with me. I was probably the first person in the school's history to have such complex needs and it was a learning experience for the school as well. On the whole the teachers were incredibly supportive towards me.

I have not had a serious fit in nine years but some minor ones at the time of the shunt revision. They stopped when I was seeing Alan, if you think about it, perhaps his influence helped to calm me down emotionally. The one thing that could make you have a fit at that school was that the idea of a small warm-up in sport was doing two laps of cross country and then 60 press-ups in front of the whole class. That was some small warm up!

Walter: So there were no allowances made for your special needs?

Larry: On the face of it – no. It took my peers a while to accept the fact that I had disabilities. But they did set up a special educational needs co-ordinator. I did my GCSEs and now I have just finished a B.Tech. National Diploma in Social Care at a Further Education College. I came up against my demons again when I thought the Head of the Health and Social Care Department said: 'Disabled people have no place as health care workers'. I was outraged by that. Happily for me, he resigned from the college at the end of that term. I was pleased about that and subsequently got a Head of Department who actually pushed me to get the grades that I needed. So now I am just waiting to go to university.

Walter: It seems to me that over the years you have become a pretty keen observer of your educators.

Larry: Yes – with a view to prove them wrong if they come out with an outrageous view. Alan Proctor and Katrin Stroh were the first two people who clearly said to my parents: 'Larry is going to go to university'. This was before I had even been to secondary school. These guys believed in me at a very early age. Goodness knows how they could see that – it remains a mystery but you might be right when you said that they could see an intelligence peeping out from behind all the behaviour.

I am looking forward to university. I will be in a Hall of Residence. It is brilliant because the Halls of Residence are in the same building as the Disability and Welfare office for the whole university.

Walter: Going back to the secondary school, how did you manage with the sport?

Larry: I managed to get the position of goalkeeper. I did not disclose to them that I was visually impaired and I only lasted one match as goalkeeper, because on my first and last match we lost 52–0. I broke the school record for the worst defeat in living memory!

Walter: Have you any brothers or sisters?

Larry: Yes. I am the youngest of three. I have an older brother and an older sister. I get on with them very well. For a while it was terribly noisy. I play the trumpet and was practising regularly while my brother was playing drums in the same house. They were quite angry when Great Ormond Street suggested that I should have a play station to help my hand-eye co-ordination because they were never allowed one. So whenever I got a new game my brother insisted on playing it too.

I met Alex, my French exchange in 2005, through the French teacher at school. Alex is an amazing character because he is French and yet he flies the Union Jack out of his bedroom window, he has God Save the Queen as his ring tone, he supports England in any competitive sport and his favourite meal is fish and chips. So go figure. It doesn't make any sense. I felt quite patriotic as I walked up his drive to see the Union Jack flying out of a window. I went to his family's holiday place on an amazing farm and it was so warm that we all slept on camp beds outside with no covers. We did put up an old Canadian army tent on one side of the field and that was a very good idea because on the third night there was a six-hour thunderstorm. It just bucketed down. The rest of the time it was warm and sunny.

Alex is a year younger than me and is doing his baccalauréat at the moment. Both his younger and his older brother have come over here at different times. The older brother is a pilot and there are lots of parallels. Both families have parents who are both doctors, both have three siblings. It is a really lovely connection. It was very funny when Alex first tried peanut butter – he compared it to the stuff that comes out of the backside of a cow. We go through maybe two or three jars a week.

Walter: Have you had any girlfriends yet?

Larry: One, but it did not last long. She was not quite sure who she wanted to be with so she had to have five at the same time. So it ended quite badly between me and her.

Last year I went sailing from Jersey to Southampton via France. The Jubilee Sailing Trust is an organization that has two tall ships which enable people with additional needs to go sailing. So we went and stopped off in Cherbourg in France. I went 31 foot up the rigging which is quite high. I had a thin rope attached to the harness and that was all that was holding me. At the start we had a safety briefing, we knew nothing about sailing so the first mate gave a talk and fell overboard! I don't know if it was deliberate or not, but we had to heave this 16-stone guy out of the water and he said in a very chagrined way: 'This is not meant to happen'.

I don't think I would have been able to have all the experiences that I have had recently without Katrin and Alan. I would not have been the person I am today without them. It is a huge credit to both of them.

Walter: You have told me of the broad range of Occupational Therapy. Do you know which area you plan to concentrate on?

Larry: I don't know which area I will specialize in but I am thinking primarily of paediatric upper body, because this is the area in which

I have had the most difficulty. For example, a few years ago I would not have been able to pick up a piece of paper like I am doing now. It would have been near impossible for me to do. Occupational Therapy has enabled me to do that and I cannot tell you how grateful I am that I can do things like that.

Most people think that an occupation is a job. But an occupation is anything which occupies someone. It might be doing something to relieve stress, it might be picking up a piece of paper, it might be listening to music – a whole range of things. Occupational Therapy is a term as wide as the term disability and like disability does not concentrate on any particular area and does not describe any particular need. It describes the whole spectrum of needs, from emotional needs and physical needs through to mental health needs. It covers children, young people, adolescents, adults and the elderly. It is split into upper and lower body with specialization as detailed as the right or left arm. It can get so specific as to be impossible to comprehend.

Walter: What is going through my mind is that my book will include a chapter on the Waldon Approach, which Katrin and Alan call Functional Learning. It is the same thing. I will describe the philosophy behind the lessons that Katrin would have done with you; probably sitting at a table with her behind or to the side of you.

Larry: I do remember her being to one side of me.

Walter: And perhaps getting you to move bricks around and picking up things with tongs, putting them in buckets.

Larry: Sorting things.

Walter: Yes. Sorting and matching.

Larry: Also solving puzzles so if the squirrel has four nuts and there are six nuts in the tree how many nuts does he have. It may start with a puzzle with a simple answer but then get very gradually more complicated as I remember.

Walter: Did you do intersectional sorting, where you have a grid with say a tree along the top and a mouse along the side and you have a card with both a tree and a mouse on it and you have to place it correctly on the grid?

Larry: Yes – I think so.

Walter: One chapter will describe that kind of education – the development of understanding which you will have benefited from. It will probably be interesting for you to read it and when you are in the OT world you may see how that fits in and it may lead you in that direction.

Larry: That is entirely possible. You probably have not started thinking about this yet but things like having a large print version, speaking as a person with a visual impairment, would be hugely beneficial. It will be very interesting to see the finished product.

Walter: You will certainly get a copy. Anyone who has given me an interview will receive a copy from me. [Larry's father Robert has now joined us.] Robert – how did you first meet Katrin Stroh?

Robert: It was a time when we had taken Larry out of the first special school in 1999 when Larry was about eight and we felt that the teachers were having a deleterious effect. They were punishing him as if the behaviour was bad when it was really a manifestation of anxiety or frustration or not understanding. At this point Anne and I started sitting in on lessons at the school to find out what was going on and were shocked to see how cruel and punitive some of the teachers were being with children who had special needs. They were routinely shouting at the children and being quite unpleasant.

We kept Larry at home while we tried to see what would be the best way forward. We found some home tutors and there were various organizations which supported home education. We were looking at all the options and then my sister-in-law Pamela, a psychotherapist, heard Katrin speak, was very impressed and thought that this might be something useful. We looked into it; found that Katrin was very local, arranged a meeting and after interviewing us she took us on.

At this time Larry was really quite troubled; he made a lot of involuntary noises with some facial grimacing which were related to his anxiety. They wanted to label him with Tourette's syndrome. As far as we were concerned it was just a symptom related to his anxiety. There had also been an Asperger's label and other labels were flying around but they were all just reflections of these symptoms. It is probably not happy to remember all these things, Larry; it was a painful time for you.

Coming back to Katrin, I remember that she wanted to involve Anne and myself, particularly me, and so I was with Larry for most of the sessions. Sometimes I would be sitting and watching, but sometimes I would be brought into the work. As we talk it comes back to me. There were several different things that we would do. She presented Larry with little exercises, there would be various objects and we would do things like sorting and sequencing, and my feeling was that she was working not only about learning a skill but more about processing the feelings that came up in the course of the learning process. There might be drawing things as well and I particularly remember an exercise I did with Larry, in which we were both at a very long piece of paper with coloured felt tips. Maybe Larry was drawing lines, perhaps some pattern and my job was to follow Larry. It was about getting in tune with one another.

There were difficult moments when Larry got cross or whatever and Katrin would work with that. I remember her being very boundaried and very firm and also very caring. [Anne has now joined us.] Anne, do you remember any more?

Anne: I remember the room being set up in a particular way. In the very early days Larry was putting things in and out of a jar and making sure he always used two hands and crossing the midline. Do you remember, Larry?

Larry: I am afraid I seem to have blanked out those memories; it was such an upsetting time.

Walter: The things that would have been typical with those lessons would have been banging, sorting, matching, and a lot of sequencing.

Anne: I don't remember banging but there may have been. Sorting and matching – yes. Sequencing yes and what you said about the midline was new because what we had done in conductive education was to make sure that everything was symmetrical and now this was about crossing the midline. I remember you would tear up the room in frustration at not being able to do it. It was good in a way Larry because you could express your feelings.

Walter: Larry has said to me absolutely clearly that without the help of Katrin and Alan he would not be the person he is today.

Larry: It is extraordinary to think about all of this. I have not thought about it really for a long time. I have travelled a million miles since then.

Anne: Despite both being doctors we found that the outlook from the medical¹ profession in the early days was grim. That Larry would probably not see very well; he may not sit up and if he did, he probably would not walk and if he did, it might be with a calliper on one leg. Life was going to be exceptionally difficult. I remember standing there with this professor who was saying: 'He has optic atrophy' and thinking: 'If I don't hold on to the cot I am going to faint'.

Anne and Robert: We would both like to say how enormously grateful we are to Katrin and Alan for their work with Larry and with ourselves. The work was neither easy nor comfortable and was sometimes emotionally tough. But their belief in Larry (and in us), the idea of his going to university which we never forgot and which now has become a reality, was such an inspiration to us all.

PS (six months later): It would be great to add a paragraph about Larry's first two terms at university. He has done really well and enjoyed it a great deal. Of three study assignments, he has passed two and failed one (by 5 marks), and is receiving support in bringing the failed assignment up to a pass. He says he has made more friends at uni in half a year than he did in 19 years at home in London. He was elected as 'rep' for his floor at the Hall of Residence and nominated 'rep of the year'. He has also been a rep for disabled students at the Students Union. He has been involved in peaceful student demonstrations against 'the cuts' and is growing in political awareness. He is managing independent living well, only seems to need contact with us once a week or so, and has only needed one or two small top-ups to his allowance. Next term he will do his first six weeks work placement in a hospital.

Freddie

Father

At the time that I met Geoffrey I was working at Meanwood Hospital for adults with learning difficulties, mainly with quite severe problems. I was unhappy with the approaches being practised there which seemed to me to have a weak foundation in developmental theory.²

I met Geoffrey in 1984 and suddenly here was somebody who demonstrated other ways of thinking about development. It was a kind of Socratic dialogue. Instead of telling things he would ask you to think about a particular question. I would struggle with the question and only after that struggle would there be any real discourse. Then in the course of the conversation all sorts of lights would go on, and I would realize that previously I had been labouring under a misapprehension about fundamental aspects of learning and development.

There is a real distinction between this and the 'training' which I had been used to in the social services where a short course would 'qualify' one in something. With Geoffrey; it was much more to do with 'education', but not in the sense which reduces education to the accumulation of certificates. There is an emphasis in our society on what Waldon would call Cultural or Particular Understanding but it may be based on a weak foundation of something more fundamental which he called General Understanding. Education in our society is primarily concerned with Cultural Understanding.

Having been introduced to the Approach and been to a couple of Geoffrey's courses I was very keen to know more of the theory that lay behind the practice. The theory expands as you get to know it. It is not finite and the more effort one puts into understanding the theory the better one can comprehend its scope.

Freddie was born about two years after I had met Geoffrey, which was very fortunate because I had somewhere to take Freddie. There was virtually nothing offered from the medical services – no real help or advice at that time. Freddie had all the symptoms of the rare Prader-Willi syndrome. He was a very floppy baby. He did not move much in the womb and had very poor muscle tone.

Without movement there are few opportunities for learning and so initially, when I took Freddie to see Geoffrey, he would move him about quite vigorously – surprisingly so for a tiny baby of six or eight weeks old. Freddie went to see Geoffrey every week and I did my best to continue the work on a daily basis. I was a facilitator of sorts, but I was hardly confident in what I was doing.

One of the problems with Prader is lack of muscle tone but there is also a deficiency of muscle forming tissue, leading to a circular problem. You are less inclined to move and because you don't move your ability to move is reduced further. Add to that a failure of the sense of being sated and massive weight gain is a real danger. More weight leads to even less inclination to move.

Moving Freddie around gave him familiarity with movement pathways that he would not have explored by himself and having experienced them they were more likely to be repeated outside the lesson. Geoffrey believed that the only thing that really mattered is what happened outside the lesson. Nothing is learnt during the lesson because learning is from your own behaviour. The idea of the lesson is to encourage familiarities with certain pathways which will later be spontaneously reinforced outside the lesson environment.

I worked with Freddie for several years. He went to the local mainstream school and had developed enough muscle strength to walk and get around. Freddie became mobile but he was always very interested in food and was never skinny; he didn't become obese although he certainly was a bit chubby.

Prader children have a tendency to have tantrums because of a low threshold towards emotional strain and the feeling that their understanding is put under too many demands. This can lead to frustration and tantrums and behaviour breakdown and this happened quite quickly with Freddie. He was absolutely lovely, until he was about two but his behaviour started changing about that point. It was classic Prader syndrome.

At age two he was developing at the appropriate rate and he was accepted at the nursery section of the school – and did very well there. As he progressed through school it became more and more difficult as Freddie's needs came into conflict with what was being offered. The school did their best, but eventually, in what would have been his last year at school, they found him too difficult and certainly he found them difficult. He was about 10 at the time.

The Waldon Lessons helped in all sorts of ways. They facilitate the student's acquisition of General Understanding through the learning-how-to-learn-tools. I do believe that Freddie's General Understanding was both broader and deeper than could be expected of a child with his syndrome. I am totally convinced that his understanding of himself and of the world around him increased enormously through the Waldon Lessons.

Freddie left school at about 10. He was tutored at home for a while, partly by me and I took some days off work. The local authority had a part-time peripatetic teacher who came round from time to time to do schoolwork and that went on for a while. Then of course the question was: where does he go next? The nearest school that I could find that would take Freddie was a special needs school in Dorset, 250 miles away. They had had someone there with Prader syndrome so they did have some experience. Most schools found Prader children too difficult because of their attentional behaviour. He went to Dorset where distance prevented his receiving any Waldon Lessons.

After school he went to a college where he worked with animals on a city farm. He really likes animals and enjoyed that for a few years. He was kept on as a volunteer after the course had finished.

Freddie is now 22 and lives at home with his mum (we are separated). He volunteers at a museum on a time-limited basis and goes to a dogs' home where he walks dogs and introduces people to dogs – a kind of matchmaking. He spends a lot of time playing computer games, watching videos and that sort of thing. He does not have many friends but is pretty good on his own. He has an elder sister and an elder brother who have both moved out now.

He functions very well in all areas although he is still a bit fragile from time to time as perhaps we all are. His defensive behaviours are much less frequent and rarely develop into full blown tantrums. He does not drive but he is pretty independent in most respects. He can take care of himself. He is attractive as an individual, has a certain charm, a good sense of humour and sense of fun and a good attitude towards other people. I don't know about getting married possibly; he has had girlfriends certainly. Whether he would ultimately get married I don't know, but I certainly would not rule it out. It may or may not be a goal in Freddie's life.

Parents of a newborn child with some difficulties are immediately faced with all kinds of problems. One thing everyone wants to do is to help their child. But the overriding feeling for me was that I did not want my child to suffer. I did not want my child to go through life with any more problems than was necessary. It almost haunted me that I had brought somebody into this world who because of their disability was going to suffer. And that applies I suspect to a lot of people who have disabled children. So what do you do? What is the best way to go about reducing the possibilities for suffering on the part of your child? That means helping your child become more independent and to better understand themselves and the world around, to operate within it and to have a richness of experience.

One can create environments for people with disabilities which are soothing and place few demands on them but the problem there is that there is no encouragement to develop and so their whole experience becomes impoverished. The great benefit of the Waldon Approach is that experience becomes richer. What makes life worthwhile is ultimately how we experience things, and that is dependent on how we understand things.

Mother

Having seen [Freddie's father] Jack's theoretical perspective, I think that I can talk a bit more emotionally and socially about Waldon, which may be a bit more antipathetic towards him, but that is how I feel. Freddie was a very tiny baby and it was obvious from birth that there was something wrong with him. He was very floppy, had not moved very much in the womb and there was a lot of concern about him in the hospital. We were given a list of the things that were wrong with him but obviously no diagnosis at that point.[3]

Jack was very keen to get him to Geoffrey as quickly as possible which we did. I think he was only about 10 days old and I was horrified. I had heard a lot about Waldon but never met him and I suppose that as a mother with a child who had obvious disabilities and facing what could have been a very challenging and possibly terminal diagnosis, Geoffrey represented a lot of hope. But I was emotionally very upset at the time and was not really ready for Geoffrey's way of dealing with things. Geoffrey stripped him naked and started moving his limbs around and I found it utterly distressing because he seemed to me to be so vulnerable in that situation.

Geoffrey would lay him on a hard table, sometimes with a towel on it, but no padding but he did not have the strength to lift his arms. Geoffrey would hold him by his arms, almost all of his forearm because Geoffrey's hands were so huge and Freddie was so small. He was 8 lb when he was born and by then 10–12 lb at the most. He had a very high-pitched cry at that time, a sort of mewling, not like a proper baby's full throated cry. He had poor muscle tone so his lungs were not that brilliant at crying. Geoffrey would pull him up so that he would begin to develop some strength and movement and he could go through the range of movements that Geoffrey thought he should be going through at that stage of his development.

It was quite shocking. It was quite painful as a parent to watch. It was painful because you felt that you wanted to rescue him and yet something told me that it was my emotions wanting to stop Geoffrey; that it was not in Freddie's best interests to follow what I wanted at that time. I knew we had to go with the lesson and I did not have the courage to rip him away from Geoffrey and say: 'We are not doing that any more. Don't do that'.

I am happy that I didn't stop him and I am sure that the lessons made a big difference. But they were quite something to see and I don't think people who did not understand would have been able to cope with it. Geoffrey was always gentle and made sure the room was warm. He was not interested in making sure Freddie had had a drink, that was my job, but you did not interrupt the lesson with those minor concerns. They really did not bother Geoffrey at all.

It seemed to me to make absolute sense to put him through the range of movements that he should typically be going through on his own. Later we did arms up and banging all over the place. Whenever I talk about Geoffrey's lessons I start flinging my arms about in all directions because of how effective it is. If you can't do those movements then everything else is restricted.

I agreed with continuing to see him because in that situation any parent wants somebody who appears to be aware of what they are doing and gives you some hope. So we persisted. But there was a split between us. Jack just believed in Waldon and it was an obsession. He became completely committed to it and it did not matter what was going on, that was what he wanted to do. And I found that difficult. I don't have any regrets about it but it was difficult at the time.

Four or five months later we were given the diagnosis of Prader-Willi syndrome (PWS) and this was a genetic condition. It was quite difficult because PWS has very specific things attached to it. Babies are very floppy for the first two years but then things change and they do achieve their milestones and so I often felt in some kind of conflict in my own head. It was not overt. I found it quite difficult to deal with Geoffrey's very dispassionate and objective approach to my child and looking back on that now I can recognize that part of it was a definite process – having a disabled child and dealing with it. Geoffrey's bluntness and kind of totally emotionless approach because he was so convinced – and he was right. Freddie did wonderfully, and exceeded expectations through the lessons. But speaking as a parent, I found it very difficult because I didn't have the theoretical understanding to get on Geoffrey's wavelength and see Freddie as an organism rather than my child. That was very difficult for me.

But we did carry on. Jack was really driving it and if it had been left just to me I don't know what I would have done. I have a much more eclectic personality and I looked into all sorts of approaches. We went to physiotherapy, and I looked into the Doman Delcato method in America. Jack was convinced all the way through that all we needed was Waldon. It was more difficult for me to just accept Waldon as I am not by nature a one-track person. I tend to have a lot of different things going on, which I do not regret, but Waldon was our consistent approach until Freddie was about the age of 10.

Jack gave the daily lessons and Geoffrey gave one every week until he died which was when Freddie was only two. After that the alternative Waldon group from Leeds used to come over to Manchester on a Saturday and we booked a local play centre in a park where parents came with their children and their siblings and we would organize activities for the siblings and three, four or five people would give lessons to different children throughout the afternoon. I have got some really nice photos actually. The group was called 'Place for Learning' and then it developed into a small school which ran twice a week for two or three years. Jack gave most of the lessons with Andy from Leeds. And Terry or Marilyn or Ann would come over sometimes to support it. That was great because I met lots of other parents and children met other children who had disabled siblings. We did lots of nice things so they enjoyed it as well, but meanwhile the children got lessons. It was absolutely fantastic. It petered out as children got older; 10, 11, 12, and they got different schooling, moved away, went to residential schools. It just drifted really.

Reverting to Freddie – PWS is a genetic syndrome which is not very well known but which has a clear developmental path. Freddie well exceeded the average achievement of those children. It is hard to say that it was all down to Waldon but that was such a big part of his life that I can't see how you could deny it. He is talking; he can read and write very well. Many children with PWS have scoliosis and have speech difficulties. He does not have either.

He has a reasonable level of functioning in the low, mild learning difficulty range. Physically he can walk, run, swim, do the sort of things which perhaps we were not sure that he would be able to do. We still have all the battles with his weight, with his eating and things like that but he has a better quality of life than we could have hoped for; although life is still very challenging for him. He volunteers at the museum and at an animal sanctuary. He would love to work but we have been advised that he would have to give up his benefits and because he has got challenging behaviour you can't rely on a workplace where he could fall out with whoever was employing him and have lost both his job and his benefits. It is too risky. He has fallen out with a few volunteering projects just because of his behaviour. He is always right. You can't correct him very easily no matter what he does, which is difficult for people to deal with.

I remember Geoffrey's lessons very clearly. I can put myself back in that room with him and Freddie was only two when he died, and it was just awful for everyone who was investing so heavily in him. People felt abandoned and it all pulled together when teachers started coming over from Leeds. The only way people could keep it going was by doing it themselves and using the practice notes of the very committed people in Leeds.

I don't think you could ever say that Waldon was not useful and when you see a normal baby develop the theory does make sense.

From our family perspective, we had Waldon stuff all round the house and Jack would do the lessons. We had a high chair set up especially for it and sometimes there would be time for Jack to give Freddie a lesson at home; at other times he would just cart him off with all the gear and then come home, tip it all out and start him off again.

The other two children are older and they loved the family stuff at the weekends. It was brilliant. Loads of our friends came and supported it; both those with and without disabled children – a lot without. And their kids really enjoyed the experience and just accepted children being worked with, and physically disabled children just being a part of the group and doing things. There was lots of play activity, music and drama, nothing very organized, just keeping them busy and in the midst of all of that Waldon Lessons going on and disabled children just lying around. I think it was very valuable. Today it would be called being 'inclusive'. Freddie was at the local school with a lot of the kids up to the age of 10 and a lot of the children knew him and just grew up with him.

To sum up I would say that I believe that without Waldon we would have never got to where we are today. Waldon was absolutely central to Freddie's development and his achievements. In the early days it gave us structure, something to do, something to focus on and some hope. Somebody was saying: 'You can get on with this. If you do this, things will start to come together'. I think the tendency for parents with a disabled child is not to feel that, but to be passively accepting of mainstream whatever.

As well as Waldon, we tried physiotherapy, massage, reflexology – we would give anything a whirl – but nothing with the consistency or intensity of Waldon. Everything else was provided by social services or we would go off and do a one-off session with somebody. Waldon was the one consistent thing that we did over the years.

Roy (assumed name)

Father[4]

I first met Geoffrey in 1988 when Roy was about four and we went over to see him every fourth Saturday for about a year until the Leeds Waldon people set up here in Leeds and Roy would see them once a week or once a fortnight. My ex-wife found Geoffrey through a colleague and it was only later that we found that there was a contingent of Waldon practitioners here in Leeds.

Roy was handicapped from birth. His birth was normal but after about six weeks he started having fits so we took him to the infirmary where there is an excellent paediatrics department. It was a big challenge. He could not stop having fits, at one point up to 80 a day. He was an extreme case. They tried every kind of anti-convulsant medication and nothing would work.

I had the greatest respect for the doctors there but I had to say to them that we were not getting anywhere so I suggested a transfer to Great Ormond Street. To their credit they said 'yes' right away and they took him down by ambulance and he stayed there for a couple of weeks.

As he got older, mainstream anti-convulsants did begin to work and he has been on the same medication now for many years. It keeps them under control although he does still have fits, usually early in the morning. His medical diagnosis today is epilepsy, profound developmental problems and cerebral palsy. He is stiff down his right side; he can walk short distances but with a pronounced limp. He is very reluctant to use his right hand, and his right hand and foot are smaller than his left ones. His right leg is also thinner and weaker than his left. He is very reluctant to use his right hand, so the Waldon people have spent a long time trying to integrate the use of both arms and hands across the space in front of him. And also I did a lot of that with him.

I tried to give lessons myself and still have various Waldon tools here at home. It was a tough life just looking after him on a day-to-day basis so I did not do a lot of Waldon at home; there was not enough energy left over for that. My ex-wife did see the value in the lessons but was never as keen on them as I became.

Roy was originally at a special school in the north east of Leeds and then we got him transferred to a special school nearer home. They were both schools for children with profound or moderate learning difficulties. The council arranged the transport for him, either in a shared van with an escort or a taxi with an escort. Every year his statement of special needs would come out and every year we refused to sign it. We insisted that he should have one-to-one Waldon Lessons in his normal curriculum and they always refused to accept this. They would not even guarantee one-to-one lessons under their own approaches – let alone for Waldon. They just would not commit themselves to anything.

When Roy was about 15 we got him a residential place and when he had to leave at 18 we got him a place at Home Farm Trust, a charity set up to run residential care for handicapped people. They have centres all across the UK. It has all the usual residential care problems with difficulties in doing any proper learning. They are not too bad at everyday care but considering they are not specialists they are much better than the educational departments at understanding the learning needs of handicapped people.

Roy was also at Blenheim College in Leeds until he was 18. He went there part-time from his residential care home and he did get some Waldon Lessons there. Terry Buchan was one of the managers for the West Leeds Inclusive Learning Centre and it had several sites including Blenheim College. So if Terry and the other Waldon teachers were not able to give Roy lessons at Blenheim, then transport could be arranged for him to go to the Leeds Waldon Centre to have the lessons there. But once Terry retired the others were at the mercy of new managers and the whole thing petered out.

Roy is now 26 and with a mental age of about two, and to an outside observer it would be very hard to quantify the benefit of the Waldon Lessons. As a parent I can say that it has on many fronts, in very small ways, improved the quality of his life. He is able to feed himself, if you are willing to put up with the mess; he responds to basic commands such as come to the table for a meal or go to the toilet – he will get up and do those things. He is more attentive in terms of social interaction; if he likes people he will make eye contact and smile or make gestures towards them; if he does not like them he will ignore them. He is very clear about who he does or does not like. He will sit down, relax and concentrate on things; he loves and listens to music, he watches TV. He is better co-ordinated. It is all hard to quantify but I would just say that his quality of life is OK in terms of his handicaps.

Without Waldon he would have gone early into residential care and I believe people would have given up on him ever being able to learn anything. It is very unlikely that he would have developed even the basic skills I have described above. When Roy was younger he often looked miserable, pasty and under the weather. Now that happens very rarely and he is generally of a quite pleasant disposition and seems happy. If you came across him now without any pre-knowledge you would say that he is obviously handicapped but seems quite happy and relaxed in his own world. You would never have thought that of him before he had the lessons. He was always moaning, crying and very miserable.

Who can say how the Waldon Lessons changed all that but my gut instinct, watching him over the years, is that that side of his personality has definitely improved. That is why we persevered with the lessons. I always noticed, even from a very young age, that after Roy had had a lesson he was much more alert – you just felt that there was something about him that was more settled and awake. He was more interested in things and for several hours afterwards you just felt that he was a different person. There was something about his being that was more focused. It was as though he had a little boost and felt more alive.

In the best of all possible worlds after we had started the Waldon Lessons; if we had had an institutional set up where Roy could have had good one-to-one Waldon every day of his school life, I am convinced that he would be much more advanced now than he is. But we only had one hour a week and that is not enough. Every form of cognitive therapy requires working every day. If Roy and other people like Roy could have a daily dose of Waldon Lessons then there is no doubt that they would come on in leaps and bounds; that they would learn and develop incrementally.

Elinor (real name)

Father

Elinor is now 24. When she was a couple of years old we recognized that she had learning difficulties and like many middle-class parents wanted to do something about it. We knew Elinor Goldschmied who died recently but who was very big in play for the under fives and she recommended two therapists who practised the Waldon methods.[5]

What attracted us was that it was not behaviour therapy and that it actually grew out of how children learn to play. It made sense to us as a concept. Elinor would have been about three then (about 1988). She is characterized as having moderate to severe learning difficulties and at one time she was said to have autistic tendencies. That related to her inaccessibility and remoteness as a child and is no longer true at all. We saw these therapists periodically and did our own lessons daily. We did two lessons a day at one time – I did it in the morning and my wife later in the day. At some point we went to see Geoffrey, which I remember vividly. We went twice and what he did was certainly consistent with what we had been doing with these two therapists.

I do remember how Elinor's initial reaction was distress. It was difficult and painful. Why we persisted I am not sure any longer – but I am glad we did. It took a while before we saw any improvement but the concept made sense to us and that was important. At some point we began to see some return and could see that Elinor was beginning to engage and to understand elements of what was actually happening to her. At some point we stopped giving her lessons ourselves – I don't remember why or when – and she started seeing Mary Jo [Middleton] once a week for a while and then once every couple of weeks. She saw Mary Jo until about a couple of years ago and now she no longer has lessons.

When she started she cried a lot and hated the lessons. When you have invested so much of your life in the Waldon Approach you need to believe that it did do some good. I am conscious of that. Elinor was disengaged from the world. A better way of putting it is that she had no understanding of it. It was like a wall and she understood very little about what was happening to her; who was around her, what was going on and she did not relate very well.

We were told that Elinor's capacity for learning was very limited, but the thing that stuck was that her capacity to learn would diminish over time. It would slow down. The implication was that she had better learn quickly. That has turned out to be absolute nonsense.

Elinor lives between me and her mother. She is at risk in the street because she does not understand traffic, her mobility is limited and she has no speech. But from being a child who was quite withdrawn and unresponsive she is now a person who engages with the world, engages with objects and with activities and enjoys life. For me and for her mother Waldon is a very big part of that development.

She enjoys being with me, her mother and other people but does not have friends in the ordinary sense. What I do with her now is still informed by Waldon. She has always been interested in food and she will engage in activities related to food. She will pour, she will stir, and she will chop. Her understanding of those activities is a direct link with Waldon. Her world when she started was always closed in like this [Ian looks down and draws his arms around his body]. You could feel the resistance to her reaching out for things. As soon as you went beyond a close area – she wouldn't. We did all the banging, reaching, extending, using space, and rings on sticks. She reached down here and over there; and a stick with a ring on it; and transferring from the stick which you held in your hand onto a stick which was on the table. It is my sense that those activities helped Elinor come out of herself and use a wider space. Gradually Elinor's world got bigger by inches and feet and yards. The world got bigger for her. That is real, that happened.

The question might be how much the lessons had to do with that. I personally am convinced that they were a big part of it. She understands some speech. She understands some activities and contexts. She will get the saucepans out of the cupboard and transfer them to the stove. You can tell her to do this and she will do it and she understands that that is what you do at that particular point in time. She will take an apron from the door, she will open a cupboard and get a cup out of it and put it down and pour a drink into it. She will do all of these things which are all directly related to her Waldon Lessons

She enjoys life very much; she is passionate about music and besotted with Eric Clapton. Swimming – she has always been more comfortable in water than on her feet. She sings without words and has a considerable range. She is fervent about the guitar. Elinor's natural state is happiness.

Abigail (real names)

A conversation with her parents

Peter: The Waldon Approach helped us with Abigail and with our other children because we really appreciated the concept of facilitating learning, the ability to distinguish between motivation and incentive and it has been instrumental in how they have all developed.[6]

Sarah: Abi is the second child in the family of four children She has an elder brother and younger twin sisters. She was born a week late and was a lovely baby, very bonny, very content and smiley. I became pregnant with the twins before we realized that there was perhaps something wrong with Abi's development. She seemed a little bit aloof when she was about one year and it was only when I was pregnant that they started, very rapidly, to try and find out what the problem was with Abi and whether there was likely to be a problem with the babies.

We had a fraught time with the child development unit over two weeks; they thought Abigail might be deaf and I felt quite relieved. I thought that if that is all that the problem was it would be wonderful. But that was not the case and we eventually saw a kind paediatrician who said that it was none of the major things that they could think of as possibilities; that it was often the case that you could not give a child a diagnosis or label. So he pretty much said we should go away and enjoy her.

It was very disturbing, an awful period in our lives really. We just did not know what was going on; we did not know what was best. Things were hectic at home because in effect I had three babies by then. The twins had been born but Abi was still like a baby, but bigger. We had to spoon feed three babies, change three bottoms, and so on. We managed to get Abi into a local school which had a little pre-school diagnostic and special needs unit. She quite liked going, it was not far away. Then we met Di Morley who had been to several of Geoffrey's lectures and felt that we should meet him. So immediately Peter went.

Peter: I just went along, met Geoffrey and could not fail to be impressed with what he said. It was a revelation. I left feeling that I knew more about life than when I arrived. That is a very rare occurrence.

Sarah: I remember Peter rang me up and said it all makes sense. He is a wonderful man. We have got to take Abigail. When can we go? And we made the first appointment that we could for the first assessment. This was quite distressing because Abi hated everything which he did with her. I think she probably cried full time. I remember Geoffrey even said that we needed to go out of the room; that not to worry this often happens. We did go out. I did because I could not bear to see her so distressed but, that aside, everything that he said just seemed to make sense. She was only three and we thought that everything Geoffrey was saying made sense and we were prepared to take it on board and give it a try.

Peter: I really do feel that it has made a difference for Abigail. A lot of what Geoffrey said in the early days when we were talking to him, we can now see still working out for Abi. Geoffrey's position was that one of the significant points was that Abigail had an eight-month-old mind in, at that time, a five- or six-year-old body. So everything was out of synchronization; her physical development was far ahead of her mental development, and that was making everything more difficult.

In the last few years, her physical state has stabilized and you can see development in Abigail's cognitive abilities. And it is not something that just we see in Abi; everybody involved with Abi over the last two or three years agrees that Abi is continuing to develop. This is what Geoffrey indicated would happen once her mind was becoming more in sync with her physical development. Over the last few years she has become far more aware of her interaction with the world around her; far more confident; she is more engaging with people and you can see the continuation of what Geoffrey had forecast.

Sarah: We were very anxious when I was carrying the twins that we should get some kind of diagnosis but having met Geoffrey it became less and less important. He did say that he felt that she might have had an encephalitis in the early stages of life which as a parent we would not have particularly noticed, perhaps induced by some kind of viral infection which might have created some form of brain damage.

We were quite happy with that but as she got older there was all the form filling to get the help or allowances to which you were entitled. We still had an annual appointment with a paediatrician and he kept talking about Rett's syndrome. It affects mainly girls and is to do with a faulty gene but, in the days that Abi was in her teens, the only diagnosis was a checklist of behaviour. And Abi did have all those behaviours – you could tick them all off. She had small hands, small feet; she did hyper-ventilate a lot in those days (but not any more); she had epileptic seizures which again she no longer has. So from our point of view filling in all these forms for the Department of Health and Social Services (DHSS) we just wrote down Rett's Syndrome. Because it was a recognized condition it was easier than trying to explain something else.

Walter: So you are saying that you don't think it is Rett's?

Sarah: No – we don't really. One of the things with Rett's is that it is a degenerating condition and Abi isn't degenerating. She is making slow steps forward. A lot of the Rett's people by now would be confined to a wheelchair.

Walter: So perhaps the movement exercises that I am sure you did in the lessons, helped to change the course.

Sarah: Definitely. I do think that. Five years or so ago I had a letter from a geneticist to say that there now was a blood test that they could do to verify Rett's. So Abi had the blood test but she did not come up positive with it.

We put our energy into Waldon and I am convinced that is the reason Abi is as she is now with her mobility – we still can get her to go up and down stairs, she walks and steps into the bath, all these physical activities she can still do and is improving at. She will be 27 this year. And I am sure that her development is to do with the early years and the amount of work that we did then.

Peter: We continue to challenge Abi. We make sure that she walks wherever she can walk and that she walks up stairs. The physical challenges that we give her are in line with what Geoffrey would have suggested and are designed to extend her mobility. We continue to make her work hard at her own level of understanding which she enjoys. When she is not challenged then she becomes fretful. Although she seems very content sitting there at the moment, after a while she won't be. She will start to agitate for a walk, to go up and down things, to stretch and generally to be challenged. Geoffrey used to comment on how people very quickly learn to manipulate their environment and how that can be a great restriction. Abigail has learnt to manipulate her environment as far as we are concerned. She knows that we will bring her food, that we will look after her, and she will try to play upon it for anything she likes so we do try to get her out of that and I think she enjoys it.

Sarah: We take her for a walk and if she really does not want to go she will start crouching as if she wants to sit down. It does not work with us. We just carry on. But she does enjoy a sense of achievement. We go every year to the same place in North Wales, and there are long walks down to the beach – difficult walks, over rocks and through the shingle and when we get to the bottom of the beach you can sense a feeling of achievement that she has done it. And then we have got to do it all the way back.

Walter: How does she express that? By smiling at you?

Sarah: Yes, an: 'I am pleased to be here' look about her. 'I've done it and I've joined you all and we are all together' sort of look. And certainly when we get back you can feel a real buzz in a way. She is a part of it all.

Walter: What level do you think her understanding is at?

Peter: Because the cognitive abilities of her brain are so far removed from her physical status it is very difficult to make a judgement on that. Probably, in the last two years she might have come on maybe a month. It is interesting the way she interacts with people. She does interact whereas before she didn't; she does understand conversations a bit more and can be quite intuitive or aware when the discussion is going to involve her somewhere along the line. She is consciously quite clued up about what is going to happen; you can see her smile; you can see her move towards the door or wherever it is that she knows that the action is going to be next. In the evenings she knows that she is going to get her medication and she will mimic me. I will take a vitamin tablet and I will give her one of her medication tablets and she will look at me swallowing it; she will laugh and swallow hers; I will pick up my cup of tea to wash it down; she will take her mug of drink to wash it down. Then she will look at me and smile.

Two years ago this would have been totally unheard of. So she is getting a great deal of reward from actually joining in with something, and she certainly does enjoy it. She does not do it every day but more days than not and this is a tremendous improvement for her. She recognizes people and voices; she recognizes occasions; she is generally more aware of what is going to happen.

Walter: Would she know if she were having a birthday?

Peter: No, I don't think she would know it. But she would know that there were a lot of people here for her. She would pick up on that, rather than that this is that particular 'special day'. She would certainly pick up if the gathering was all about Abigail. She would be very smiley, very engaging with people. She is probably aware that we are now talking about Abigail – playing it by ear; seeing what comes of it all.

Sarah: Another thing which was really good was the other contacts we made later on. I always used to feel that I would go for my hour and a half session and I never met anybody else, and that it would be nice to meet some of the other parents who were going there. After Geoffrey died, we did then all get together. I am not sure who first suggested it; perhaps it was Annabel who had this idea of setting up a parent support group. We called it 'Space for Learning' and it became really valuable. We had heard some of these names and because while I was busy with the family at home Peter tended to go off for the weekend courses that Geoffrey would run, he met the Leeds people long before I met them. After Geoffrey died everybody came together and I started to meet some of these people through Space.

We ran this as a support group and the parents met in the evening and also met as whole families some weekends. The Leeds people would come over and work with the Waldon children while we put on activities for their siblings – painting, puppet making and that sort of thing, and we managed to get some funding for that. We met once a month on a Saturday and it was very successful. Our children still talk about those days.

Walter: Going back to Abigail, can you sum up how Waldon changed her quality of life; how it might have been and how it is?

Sarah: I don't know where to start. Abi is very dependent on other people. She cannot dress herself. She can finger feed but cannot spoon feed. She can pick up a cup; pick up sandwiches, bananas or other fruit. I think from our point of view the most significant thing is the fact that she is mobile and still increasingly aware of her surroundings. If we had never come across Geoffrey's ideas she would still be living with us but we would probably be sitting her down in a corner for the day. I don't think that we would have understood that we had got to give her these challenges. She would have been with us but would have been less mobile, probably less content and less happy really.

Peter: Yes. Certainly the way I regard Abigail now is highly influenced by Geoffrey. I suspect that if we had not met Geoffrey, as Sarah said, we would probably see Abigail as something or someone to accommodate rather than seeing her as a young daughter still, who is going through that part of life where she is developing. It makes it very easy for me to look at Abigail and say yes, she still needs developing and ask myself how we are going to do that; rather than looking at her as somebody of no potential or just someone who needs permanent care. It is not so final. We can see our role with Abigail far more clearly and it makes our relationship with her far more meaningful.

Abigail is just really a little baby in an enormous body who is just progressing a lot slower than all our other children; so that my relationship with Abigail is not as an adult but as the only daughter who has not yet grown up. [They laugh.] I don't know about Sarah but that is the way I see and feel about Abigail. Geoffrey took us away from this concept of chronological age and chronological expectation and taught us to see development as a progression; where you progress next is dependent on where you are now and not due to any artificial benchmark of chronological age.

So we see Abigail in terms of where she is, rather than how old she is and this has given us some very interesting run-ins with more conventional establishments. [Sarah giggles.] It always impressed me when Geoffrey was explaining how difficult life is for Abigail with a young mind in a large body which is problem enough without anything else that we might chuck in her way. Many years ago when the school was going to take all the children to Skegness for a week, we said no. They thought that we were being very cruel and unreasonable.

I can remember a mischievously enjoyable conversation with them, trying to explain the cruelty of putting a 12-month-old mind trapped in a 12-year-old body, in a bus for eight hours all the way to Skegness! I think we made a little bit of progress and it certainly made them rather more aware that they had to explain whatever they did to Abigail to us. Through that they began to focus on Abigail a bit more and think about what they did with her.

The young lady is tuned in now and she is listening slightly because she is smiling and I think she knows that we are talking about her.

Walter: It is a challenge for me, when there is such a clear and dramatic difference in Robert's outcome, and with all that effort going in you still have a baby. And it is interesting to hear how that does impact on you as a family and how you do get pleasure from your relationship with Abi.

Peter: Abi is still developing and whilst she is still developing there is always tremendous hope of further growth in understanding. I certainly feel that any exposure to Waldon will alter your understanding of the world at large.

Sarah: It has certainly altered my approach to teaching. I teach secondary school, 11 to 18 years, and it has given me a different outlook to the way I teach – trying to get students more involved and motivated.

Peter: Geoffrey was such a fascinating person, one of the few real polymaths that I have been lucky enough to meet. Any time with him was priceless.

Bodhi (real names)

A conversation with his mother

Ruth: The exposure that Geoffrey has had to his work has generated two diametrically opposed responses. One has been from the people who have experienced it, and is just joy at his insight and gratitude for the results he has produced; and the other has been derision basically from people who do not understand.[7]

Bodhi had meningitis at 11 months and was really badly damaged. The prognosis was that he would never speak or hear or move much. When he was first recovering the only movement he had was a very slight dither with his left hand and he was constantly having fits and almost unconscious for most of the time. It took three months of trying different epilepsy medication before he would stay awake for any part of the day. During all that time I had no consciousness of anything but nursing him day by day, going to the hospital, sitting with him, nursing him, feeding him, changing him – it was a blur of moments with no resolution coming out of it. The rest of the time we just had to try to cope with the situation. We had two older boys and we just about managed.

When Bodhi came home we had no support for his care whatsoever. We did have support for his epilepsy from a neurologist who was trying to assess which cocktail of drugs was going to work and not cause him to be docile and drowsy all the time and that was a very useful professional input but it was the only input that we had.

We were eventually assigned to a consultant in paediatric development who sat in his office with four other medical professionals and talked about us – not to us but across us – and by this time both my husband Kevin and I were absolutely exhausted and at the point of collapse, and this treatment of our presence as an absence just completely infuriated us.

We finally managed to get someone else to help us, Jane Wynn was based at the Belmont House Paediatric Centre. The first consultant had not asked to see Bodhi at all and did not want Bodhi there whilst he was discussing him. Jane immediately asked us to bring Bodhi in and while he was sitting on my knee, Jane squatted down and while talking to us she played with his face, moved his arms about and generally observed him. We suddenly felt comfortable with her. She could not do a great deal herself but she was more of a referee to other agencies. We stuck with her for a number of years until she had to pass us on because of Bodhi's age.

As time went by it was obvious that Bodhi was seeing; he developed an absolute obsession with anything to do with string, which he would fiddle with for hours. Sometimes health professionals visited and if we did not notice where a handbag had been put we would very often look down and find Bodhi chewing the strap!

At about age four he could shuffle about. He did not really crawl. He only really had the use of his left side, so he would propel himself with his elbow. He could sit and was fairly sturdy.

He started at a Social Services nursery school called the Herb Garden which had a unit for extra help. It had its own space which you could shut in – basically separate the children who needed extra help. The main teacher in the unit was tremendous. He was full of life, full of enthusiasm, and had what I recognized as the touch with children. He did pretty much what I believe was the way that one does things – contacting the children in their own place, in their inner selves and finding the paths that the children would use to come out into the world, and encouraging that.

I was friends with Terry Buchan and Marilyn Crook at that time. Terry had found Waldon and was chatting about it and the description that he was providing of how Waldon worked with children; how he taught the facilitators to work with students, chimed closely with my understanding of what any child needed. They had started to go over to Manchester on a regular basis and they suggested asking Geoffrey to see Bodhi.

He was now around seven and Geoffrey was well aware of the limitations in Bodhi's potential; but he had no difficulty in saying that there were things which could be done. He was not saying that we would cure this boy but that there would be some differences to Bodhi's life from having the therapy.

Soon we were going over once a month, which was all that we could afford.

Let me describe Bodhi at that time. His main difficulty was that he was closed very tightly into an enclosed space in front of his body. His arms were tucked around himself into his chest and his head was also tucked down into that same space. You could almost see a ball of his world somewhere in front of his chest. That was his entire world. You could get him to turn a little bit to a noise beside him or behind him that was interesting, like a feeder cup he had which made a particular noise when you put the top on or took it off. That would interest him. The crinkle of cellophane packaging would interest him. But the most movement you could get was this very minute turning of his head, and sometimes his eyes going round into the corner.

After the first few sessions with Geoffrey and the additional sessions which were being provided here in Leeds, it must have been after three months at the most, we were beginning to see movement out from this sphere. His arms were becoming freer and looser, his head was becoming more relaxed from its stooped pose. He was turning his head in both directions which was something new. Previously he had only ever turned to the left and now he turned to the right which was his more damaged half. This was all within that first very short period of time. I was running round telling everybody that there was this therapy which was just the most tremendous thing. I just could not stop talking about it. The changes were just so dramatic. These were things that for us were massive progress.

Although Bodhi could walk he was very reluctant to walk. But because his arms and head were now freed up he was starting to walk more all over the place. We would take him out to the park and he would just walk in a straight line, his left hand would be slightly waving about but his right hand was as though he was gripping something in front of him. His reach upwards was increasing and increasing. Because his head was up he was seeing the world a lot more closely, not detailed, but he could see what he wanted to see wherever it was. His interaction with the world was giving him something more than he had up to that point.

We had a game we played with him where we put something that we knew he wanted in a position where he could see it, but he would find it only if he looked around. He liked bread so we would leave a pack where he could see it and his effort would go into grabbing the pack. Then we started to put things out of reach to see what he would do and he started to reach. He was about two-thirds the height of a normal child his age; he had great difficulties in eating so never really grew. He had previously had this closed tight sphere of existence and within three months he was reaching up above his head, at full stretch, to try to get the bread from a high shelf way above his head.

At that stage we were going to Waldon once a month and trying to give lessons at home. Terry and Marilyn were also giving him lessons. There was also an attempt to get a number of people involved to come and work with Bodhi and we tried to create an appropriate lesson environment. Kevin built a table top which Bodhi would be raised up at, so that the facilitator would be standing fairly straight and not bending over too much, as he or she attempted to use the Waldon Approach.

As time went by it became clear to Terry and Marilyn that the rest of us were really not able to follow the approach closely enough and that we were confusing Bodhi. That was considered counter-productive so it was cut back to just the sessions which the professionals could do with him. At that time they had started a centre in Leeds and offered sessions on a regular basis. They charged for it because in that way they could maintain the centre.

This meant that some of the people who had been helping us with trying to do the work felt a bit cut out from Bodhi's care. So their teaching contributions became financial contribution to Bodhi's lessons at the centre, which was just wonderful, because we did not have a lot of leeway on the state benefits which we had been on all this time.

This was the period just before Bodhi was going to school and Jane recommended the school alongside Meanwood Park Hospital. The Head there was willing to have Bodhi as a sessional student which meant a couple of mornings and an afternoon or so a week.

This was the first time that I came across negative responses to Geoffrey's work. It could be a wonderful opportunity as Terry and his team were actually working at Meanwood Park Hospital. Perhaps they could come across to the school or Bodhi could go across to them and he could have some sessions on that basis. But the Head would not have anything to do with it. She had this all too common, as I have now come to recognize it, negative response to the Waldon Therapy.

I just could not work it out. They had not seen the work. They had not seen anybody giving lessons, so they judged it on two particular things that they disliked. The facilitators were not praising people as they worked. The behaviourist model had always been that in order to get somebody to repeat an action, they had to be told that it was good; that they had done it right. From Geoffrey's perspective there was nothing in the outside world that could possibly reward them as much as what goes on inside them. Secondly the whole emphasis on working with a student within their own space rather than within the facilitator's space was being judged as coldness. That came as a shock to me. It was the last thing that I thought that people would see it as. To my mind the quietness and the unobtrusiveness of the facilitator in the lesson gave the person the opportunity to come from themselves in the 'truth' of their own capacities.

So the whole resistance to the Waldon therapy from the education authority was on the one hand that the facilitators were not praising the students but were remaining in the background and being judged as cold. Secondly they thought a student would be forced to do things. I knew that that was just not so and that you helped the student to do something by giving a gentle impetus.

A facilitator had to find the movement which was possible for the student and help to make it happen. And you could see the musculature in the student becoming tense and tight and resisting and not wanting to do the thing and the facilitator moving within that space. You could see it and there were times when I was watching a lesson and my heart was just pounding with joy that this thing was there, that somebody had found this way of making something happen with a person who was trapped within this – as with Bodhi – little ball with his scrunched up arms and scrunched down head. I was just astonished at the resistance that the education authority had to this work.

But the two things which were valuable for him there were firstly that he was in a physically different environment and secondly there was something to be said for the physical contact he would be having with other people. The Waldon Lessons are part of somebody's life but are not the entirety of somebody's life and physical contact, whether it was someone holding a hand and walking around or sitting on someone's knee or cuddling somebody is another section of that person's life. And he was getting some of that in the school.

He was there until he was 19 and during all that time he had been having weekly sessions with the team. When he became 19 he moved to the adult services, which meant that he could access continuing education. The adult education authority had no objection to the Waldon work so he was now able to access that three times a week. He had three Waldon Lessons a week at Meanwood Hospital until that closed and then he went wherever the work was based. It moved around a bit but when he went as a day student to an adult training centre he continued to have these three sessions a week of Waldon Lessons throughout the first 10 years of his tenure there. He was doing very basic things such as physical co-ordination, placing, bilateral co-ordination, involvement of the head in the actions and all the things which are crucial for the synthesis of perception and the forging of linkages with the world.

The fact of it being three times a week made such a difference. Within the first year of having three sessions a week I could see a difference in his understanding. Up to that point I had not seen a great deal of growth in his General Understanding but even by the end of that first year I could see the difference.

His understanding of his own life started to become obvious not just to me but to other people watching him. You could see him finding things out like: where did he go to eat. I go to this place. That is where I go now. Where can I sit down? There is a place. I don't like that cushion, I'll throw it out of my way.

Walter: He developed a sense of self.

Ruth: Absolutely – not just self but self in place. He was still intolerant of people's very close presence but I always used to insist on him letting me sit very close to him. I would push him into the corner of the sofa and he would squeal and push me away. But that was all interaction, and I would not persist enough to upset him but we would always maintain some intrusion into his self-defined personal space which he would want to be free.

Bodhi is now 33 and still goes to the same centre. We have had difficulties with the new authorities who took over. The sessions were cut down to two a week, then one a week and this is now his second year of having no Waldon Lessons at all. I worry about regression. I do my best with him but that is not anything like enough and the day centres do not have anything like that sort of approach – nor would I expect it.

Walter: Could you sum up in a few words how you feel about the Waldon Lessons and what you think they have given Bodhi?

Ruth: His interactions are increasing and the big thing that I think has happened for him, and it was happening through the years when he had three sessions a week, was that at some level he understood that he had learnt something. He would not have known that is what it was but the fact of picking something up and placing it by himself, even with his poor hand, meant that there was an awareness within him that this was something he could do.

Walter: Are you saying that he begins to understand some continuant behaviour?

Ruth: Absolutely – that is the exact phrase. One of the things that he had which was an absolute nightmare was self harming behaviour. The main reason was that he had nothing else. He had no connections to draw on for whatever it was that was troubling him. Or even if there was nothing troubling him, and he just needed something to happen and the main form this took was punching his head. Because he now has this connection out into the world, because there is something that he does understand about things, he has more options open to him and so self harming has fallen by the way. Regardless of the after effect of having a bad bruise on his face, a black eye or a bloody nose, the self harming did give him some pleasure but he now has other options and does not need to go to that.

So what are the things that I notice which are different? Going back a number of years you would come into the room where he was and there would be absolutely no response. He would just sit there and be rocking. Now you come in and he looks up. Always and automatically he looks up. That is a huge change.

We go on holiday every year to Centre Parks; my middle son and his family come with us and I was talking about his looking up when people come in. It does not last long and is pretty soon back to wallpaper. Well, with the children around, they are coming in, going out, noisy, moving, darting about, shouting and he is looking up and looking at them, because of all the different things that they do. I think that carries over for some weeks after we get back.

I have been talking about his picking new experiences up more quickly. The biggest thing that has been happening this year is the use of the right hand, his bad hand. He is actually opposing his thumb which is making a tremendous difference to his stability. His mobility had deteriorated dreadfully over the past 10 or 15 years. While he was at school he had three sessions a week with a physiotherapist, but none with a Waldon facilitator. Physio stopped dead after school ended and it was two years before he had any more. I could see the deterioration already in his standing and walking.

The upper body mobility has not deteriorated; in fact that is where the Waldon Lessons have continued to create improvement.

Bishopswood day school

Carol Parrey and eight children (all assumed names)

I am the nursery teacher at the Bishopswood Day School and have worked with the nursery children for 20 years now. I have the youngsters when they first come in. I was introduced to the work of Geoffrey Waldon at Bishopswood and my colleagues and I used to attend the meetings every half term with Sheila Coates and Richard Brooks where we discussed the Waldon ideas and how they could be translated for classroom use.[8]

We still use the Waldon Approach which we call learning-to-learn; we train staff. The people from the Oxfordshire Autism Support Service are familiar with Waldon and also train staff. Over the years I have seen children move on. Many of the children we had coming through with autism 20 years ago have made a lot of progress; some have gone on to do 'A' levels, and to university.

The school now takes children with very severe and complex needs, children who have usually been highly assessed before they have come here, and we are really working towards strategies that can help them to make sense of the world and to become as independent as possible. To that end we use the Waldon learning-to-learn-tools.

Children can come at two but now they tend to be three because they have to be 'statemented' and usually they have not used any of these techniques. There is a lot of fear now in handling children or in restraining them in any way. And when you start with the Waldon Approach you sometimes have to use physical means to get them to do what is required – sit down, helping them with the movements, all of those kinds of things – and I know a lot of schools in the community find it hard to relate to that.

We discuss everything with parents before starting, get their approval, and are comfortable doing it because we have seen the results at the other end. For a few tears and paddies early on, to see children sitting there and working their ways independently through various activities is well worth it. We use the asocial aspect of the lessons on a one-to-one basis, and we also do similar things outside the classroom so that they can become included with their mainstream peers. We have lots of pouring, mark making, sorting, matching and container play within the nursery.

Some children I can think of who have profited from the learning-to-learn include:

Sean is with me at the moment. He came at the age of three having been to a pre-school and they were really not able to do much with him other than allowing him to just run around and spend all his time just playing with his dinosaurs. If they tried to get him to do anything else he would kick and bite. They could not get him to sit on a chair. I started to become involved with him as I also have an outreach role and it was quite clear to me that he could benefit from a lot of the things which we can offer here.

He met the criteria for being statemented and he transferred here. He has regular Waldon Lessons usually twice a week. Sean's behaviour has improved 100%. We show him the symbol for Waldon and he comes through and works through the activities and when he is out in the classroom now, he is able to engage in some of the group placing and mark making activities. He would have moved up to our next level but the family have been re-housed and are moving out of the area. The parents have six other children, live in a mobile home and have very constrained space and resources. They have been absolutely delighted by his progress. They have written so many positive things about the school. He is still very autistic, make no mistake, but within the community he can relate to other people and do activities now.

We are a 26-place nursery with eight places allocated for children who are statemented with any kind of complex learning difficulty, not just autism, and we use the Waldon Approach for all of these children. We had a very successful outcome with a child who we will call **Mary** who had cerebral palsy. Her placing, sorting and matching have all come on tremendously through starting off with banging and scraping. She is not casting stuff around; she is very focused on what she is meant to be doing.

Some parents have got very involved and have come for training sessions, and it definitely makes a difference if they take it on board. But it is quite complicated and it does take time and effort for them to understand it.

Barney came here with a diagnosis of autism at the age of two. He did not relate to other people at all, was unfocused. We did a lot of Waldon work with him. He became much more focused. He started to speak more. He went on at age five to a mainstream primary school and the last I heard from his mum was that he was doing 'A' levels in physics and other subjects and was going to go on to university. She said he has become a delightful young man, goes out with his mates – and yes – he was statemented as autistic.

Howard was in a day nursery and they were having great problems with him. They could not control him at all and he was just pushing and grabbing anything that he wanted; and was getting bigger and had no awareness of the other children – just what he wanted to do – and so he was statemented as autistic and came here when he was three coming up to four.

We had him here for at least a year. He took to Waldon extremely well. He really liked the activities because he could see where he was going with them and they were structured. His behaviour improved considerably. The only thing which did not improve with him was his relationship with other children to whom he did not relate at all. This is why he went on to Chinnor rather than to a mainstream school. He is still at Chinnor I believe and I hope he is still getting Waldon there. He would be about seven now.

Zack is a little boy that I have here now. He is not autistic, he was quite premature and emotionally and socially he is quite immature. We have been using Waldon with him to focus him and he again has taken to it extremely well. He is going to move on to a mainstream school in January, with quite a lot of support because he is still quite immature. He needs the Waldon focus because if you just leave him he will aimlessly go around, emptying things out, throwing things over hedges so that a lot of the stuff we are doing, placing, etc. is helping him to put things in things.

Another girl that was with me was a little girl **Lizzie** with learning difficulties and motor impairment and when she first came here she was not even walking and had hemiplegia with a very weak side and we did lots of Waldon with her to integrate all her body movements and she made lots of progress here – enough so that, with support, she was able to go to a local primary school and she is still there now. She must be about eight and is managing to hold on there. She was coming back to our primary department to have some extra support with Waldon when she first started there but I think she is just coming back for language work now.

Sampson and **Charlie** were both diagnosed as autistic spectrum and both of them had some degree of motor and organizational problems. Both made a lot of progress with language as well, they both had language delay. They did very well while they were here and both went on to their local primary schools, and then went on to college. Charlie is about to do 'A' levels, although Sampson is not academically able enough to do 'A' levels and he is following a different college course. I see him out and about in Henley, socializing with his friends. They both came here very young and neither was at all capable socially.

Charlie became much more social much more quickly once his language and movement skills started to fall into place and I guess that his self-confidence grew. That is one of the great things about Waldon – they feel successful because there is no externally imposed right or wrong, no success or failure. They feel that they are achieving something and it is very good for their self-esteem because there is nobody telling them that they are doing it right or wrong.

We do use the Waldon Functional Reading approach for children here who are ready to read but generally that is in the infant school. I am not sure what system they use there but we have had training in that and I certainly used it successfully with Howard, and I guess they carried on with it at Chinnor, which used to be the county's provision for children with autism, from the age of five, but with the trend towards 'inclusion' everywhere I am not sure how that works now.

Lesley Feldman, who is the Service for Autism person in South Oxfordshire, visits us regularly and both she and Sue Saville come in and help with the training. We all have copies of Katrin Stroh's book: *Every Child Can Learn*, which is really helpful. The thing that Waldon does is to give you the cognitive aspect of things, rather than keeping putting shapes in posting boxes, it gives the children a much wider experience. It could be said to be useful for all children and we will often see normal children at play, perhaps younger siblings who come in, and they are perhaps moving bricks from one place to another without any direction from anybody else and we will say: 'Look at the Waldon going on'.

Judi Stacpoole and nine more children (assumed names)[9]

I am Senior Teacher in the Primary department at Bishopswood School and have been involved with Waldon since about 1988 through Richard Brooks and Sheila Coates from Oxfordshire when they started doing the training with us. We just thought: 'Hey – what a good way of enabling children actually to learn'. Ever since then at this school we have been real advocates of Waldon and it is interesting how most of our children, and they all have severe and complex needs, have taken to it.

I can remember, when I first started, I had one little lad we will call **Duncan**, who had severe epilepsy and severe learning difficulties, no spoken language, tantrums, etc. and he took to it like a duck to water. It suited him perfectly. He really enjoyed it. He was a very challenging lad and it was very difficult to get him motivated and involved with anything. But he just really loved it. He was about six or seven. He was not actually in my class but I had just had a session with Sheila and Richard and happened to be just covering the class so I thought: 'I will have a go here'. All the piling, the placing and the sorting activities really suited him.

That was when I first started learning about Waldon and then I went into mainstream schools for about 10 years where I did use some of the Waldon ideas with children who had special needs in mainstream, particularly some of the sequencing and some of the coding activities.

Another little lass **Angie**, was also about six or seven, a very anxious child with autistic tendencies and with severe learning difficulties and minimal language. She was a child who could not do anything on her own and couldn't self occupy. When she was older, perhaps about 13 years old, she would look for the equipment and find things and take herself through lots of the games she had learnt.

Waldon Lessons seemed to reduce or eliminate some of the obsessional and repetitive behaviour and children could find activities outside the lesson, basic activities that normal toddlers would amuse themselves with, and hence used less of the stereotypical and self-perpetuating behaviours.

I get children from Carol's nursery class, and take them through primary school here and then, although I do see the children as they grow older, they move on to the senior school where they have less pure Waldon activity.

There was one autistic child, **Jake**, who left the school, quite a difficult boy with a lot of behavioural issues. He was very resistant and did eventually move into residential school. We found doing the Waldon activities was very calming for children like him – being in a quiet environment, a quiet room with very little language and just activities and games happening. You had to be very persistent with Jake to begin with but once you had got through that you could have sustained sessions of 20 to 30 minutes where he would really get involved in the activities and certainly learned the games and became quite independent in a lot of the activities. It really suited his learning processes.

I am lucky at the moment because I am well staffed and most of my children get three sessions a week. I can't get it up to five because of all the other activities which are going on. I can think of one girl in my class at the moment and she really has done so well. She used not to be able to focus on anything but she has improved in a whole range of areas. I am sure that having those very intensive Waldon games has really focused her attention. She is sorting really well now, whereas before things would just get discarded, but now she is focused and enjoying the activity.

Another lass, **Annie**, has very complex needs and over the years has learnt from the activities and is able to do some of them independently once they have been set up. She has learnt what to do. Previously she was completely unfocused and would be doing anything other than what you wanted her to do. Now she is looking and attending much more to placing activities and what is required of her. A lot of children do not focus on any sustained activity, they just sit and lose themselves fiddling, but this little girl with some gentle encouragement will sustain interest and activity much more than she was able to, say, two years earlier.

A lot of the children we have now will always need a lot of support and it will take them a long time to develop. It is quite different from your story of your son. A lot of what we aim for is having purposeful self-occupation.

Walter: Some parents have said to me that despite the fact that their child has had extremely severe and complex needs and still in their twenties have these same problems and are never going to progress from total dependence; because of the Waldon Lessons they are much more contented and happy.

Judi: That is interesting. I have noticed that when you are in the middle of a very rhythmical session you hear the children making happy type burbling and gurgling sounds. I have noticed that a lot – which is lovely.

Walter: And do they carry that over into their daily activities?

Judi: Absolutely – yes. What would be good would be to do sessions for parents. It is a problem of time and having so many different things going on. Also we have had a lot of new staff and we have had to get them trained and up to speed. Some new staff have not found it easy to work in this way and it has been difficult to help them through the initial stage when a child might show difficult behaviour and to be quite firm with the children. Sometimes I have noticed that if a child is losing momentum in a session if you suddenly really pace things up a little, and become very active and vigorous, it can make a huge difference.

I remember a child who has left the school now, **Dotty**, who could be very challenging, and she really settled and her level of abilities developed well. She was matching and doing some very simple sorting of things and she was a child who would send everything flying in her normal lessons but in the Waldon sessions, once we had got into a good rhythm, she became very engrossed and co-operative. She was making very good progress but she had to leave the school because her family moved elsewhere.

Walter: Do you enjoy giving the lessons?

Judi: Yes, I love Waldon. It is interesting and even with children with really complex needs after a time you can see progress. Having worked with some of the earlier children that I mentioned, when they were very little, and I was new to the whole concept and then seeing them much later when they were leaving the school, they were much more able and independent. One of the important things for us to achieve for these children as they approach adulthood is their ability to do things on their own and keep themselves amused.

Walter: It is really good to be here and to see how Waldon is integrated into the daily school life.

Judi: It was interesting, when I was on outreach and working with children in mainstream how some of the basic sorting and sequencing activities were what those children really needed, rather than the mainstream maths and other subjects. There are two children, **Harry** and **Simon**, now in the senior department, who were beginning to move along to Functional Reading when I had them. They were two autistic children who are on one level quite able, but although one of them developed some quite difficult behaviour, I am sure that at some level they will still be doing Waldon. They got on quite well with Functional Reading and I found it helpful. I haven't got anyone at the moment on that programme.

There is one autistic girl we will call **Sue** at the school and to get her motivated to do anything used to be impossible; she used to get so cross with me when we tried to get something started. There was real moaning and groaning but then she would do everything eventually – under protest.

We have a copy of Katrin Stroh's book in the staffroom and found it really useful. It is excellent for new staff and it includes some videos. There is that wonderful video of a little girl, really protesting, and you see her when she first starts and then again 18 months later and just loving the session. All my new staff use the videos. I have two new young female staff members and they are absolutely fascinated by them.

Slovenia

Vera (assumed name)

Father

Our daughter Vera is 13 years old and has been handicapped since birth.[10] The doctors noticed that something was wrong with her at about three months and at between eight and 10 months we as parents noticed that Vera was not a normal child. She could not walk, could not talk and was completely dependent on us. She finally started to walk at age two but there has been no possibility for her to talk. We visited many doctors who performed many tests and examinations and suggested many syndromes to explain what is wrong with Vera but still today they have not found a clear diagnosis. My hypothesis is that there might be some fault in her chromosomes and a second is that during her birth she had some oxygen deprivation which caused brain damage.

When she was three years old we started with Functional Learning with Anamarija. At the beginning I had many doubts about the efficiency of this method because I am a technical person and just moving items, collecting pairs and similar things seemed very strange to me. I was not able to imagine how she could start talking through this way of learning. Later on I did notice some progress and that she was really learning something but until today she still cannot talk. But we can communicate with her and have practically no problem in normal life and talk normally to her and she can show us with gesture and body language what she likes and what she thinks. If we are not completely sure we just ask different questions and she tells us with her hands or her head whether we are right or wrong. So we do not have any problem.

Mother

(In answer to my question), I was never sceptical about the programme. I always believed in it.

Father

I still have some questions as to whether Functional Learning is efficient or not. I would be sure if I had two identical Veras and one had Functional Learning and one did not. Then I could tell whether or not it had made a difference. But even so I believe that the time was not wasted because Vera made progress and I am sure that if we had done nothing she would never had reached this level. That is why we still insist on having this approach. Anamarija has much more experience than I do and at the beginning I could not understand what she was doing, although later on I could. We used to have a session every two weeks but it is now reduced to about one session per month.

I could see that every three months the difficulty of the tasks increased and during this long period Vera certainly learned many things. But this has been such a long period of time. At the start I thought that this was just a bad dream and that after a few years Vera would become like a normal child and everything would be alright. After about three or four years I finally came to accept the situation and I know that Vera will never be a normal child and that we will need to take care of her until the end of our lives. We can only do as much as we can to make her everyday life easier. I would like to end by thanking Anamarija who has helped Vera for all these years with all of her heart.

Bogdan (assumed name)

Anamarija Filipiè Dolnièar

Bogdan, started with me when he was three years old.[11] He came to the School for Deaf Children and was not able to do anything at that time.

We started with placing and pairing and moved on to the other learning tools and before he left the school he was able to play placing games by himself. He could choose out of toys placed in front of him, he could produce some sounds, could recognize words and pictures and could understand both the words and the pictures when presented separately. He was able to communicate with his parents and with the therapist and could use a few signs.

Bogdan still comes to see me. He uses a few signs spontaneously and during the activities. He recognizes the pictures and symbols and the words and the letters, is able to make letter sounds. He is able to do some writing by himself and can hear words, recognize them, analyse them and write them. He can communicate with the people he knows and in his school he can move around by himself and perform tasks that they give to him so that he has independence in familiar surroundings.

Bogdan has CHARGE syndrome which means that he is deaf, he has mobility problems, problems with his chest, his cognitive development is very low and usually CHARGE children have problems with the heart. CHARGE is very rare and probably there are just three in Slovenia.

Mother

Bogdan is 15 years old. When he was born he could not see, he could not hear and he could not swallow. By the time he was seven months he could see and hear a little but still could not swallow so he had to be aspirated for the first two years when he had an operation and could start to swallow with my help. It was a kind of artificial swallowing. A medical report from when he was four years old states that there was damage to his cerebellum which contains among other basic things the centre for swallowing.

When he was three he went to the kindergarten at the School for Deaf Children where we met Anamarija and I was happy because Bogdan started Functional Learning. I never doubted that it was the right thing for him and came to visit Anamarija regularly although my more sceptical husband did not come. When he saw the improvements in Bogdan he began to accept its validity but still did not come with me.

Bogdan improved considerably but had to leave this school when he was 10, but we continued to see Anamarija at the clinic in Domzale. He started to walk when he was seven and now we can communicate between ourselves. They use sign language and communicate in all kinds of ways with gestures and with pictures. We do not have any help or support from the national or the state government because there are so few children with CHARGE syndrome.

I did not have any problems during pregnancy, no problems during labour or birth so I do not know how it occurred. We help him as much as possible to make his and our lives easier. I have always worked with Functional Learning and with no other programme so cannot say what difference it made. The doctors have never made any alternative suggestions.

Anamarija

There were many children who had severe developmental delays and who other therapists were not able to do anything with. They failed to improve using other methods. Their level of cognition was so low that they could not get any benefit from learning speech. They had to have some level of understanding before they could do anything.

Through Functional Learning they began to understand speech and words and learnt to recognize pictures, symbols, etc. There was one older person who was about 30 when he started Functional Learning. On his own initiative he just did nothing but after Functional Learning he started to move around by himself, to eat by himself, to pick things up without external stimulus. He had improvements in understanding the world around him. His problems were severe so he never started speech but there were great improvements in his behaviour.

There were so very many other children ....

9
Functional Reading: A Special Orientation of the Approach

'Anxiety is the big enemy of learning to read.' (G.Waldon)

Functional Reading is a specialized orientation of the Waldon Approach and will be most easily understood and appreciated by those who already have considerable familiarity with the learning-how-to-learn-tools. This chapter provides both the theory and a practical explanation of Functional Reading and benefits greatly from the experiences of Mary Jo Middleton, a special needs teacher. She attended Geoffrey Waldon's workshops on Functional Reading and has taught children to read using this approach after they had failed to learn using conventional methods.

Development and theory

The origins

Functional Reading is a way of orienting the Waldon Approach to develop a written form of conventional language while enabling General Understanding to grow. Geoffrey Waldon developed Functional Reading as an aspect of his interest in how animals, and particularly human beings, develop the kind of adaptive ability needed for survival. His interest in adaptive capacity or what he called General Understanding grew out of his study of neurology at the time. He was also interested in language development and thought that there might be some kind of direct connection between the structure of General Understanding, and that of language.[1]

Teaching reading

Reading is usually taught in a way which relies on children's existing spoken language. Geoffrey Waldon described: 'A ritual which is called: "listening to children read"', where children produce the sounds associated with the words or the letters and someone tells them whether or not they are saying them correctly. The content of what children read at about five years is at about the level that they would have understood at least two years earlier and is linguistically simpler than the language they use in everyday conversation. This seems reasonable because it allows children to easily understand what they are reading by translating the words into a spoken form. Because the level is lower than their current understanding of speech they should be able to predict the likely words with greater ease. It may be noticed that this process tends to make the student dependent on the adult who is listening to them read and can tell them whether or not they are getting it 'right'. From a Waldon point of view this is a potentially anxiety-inducing situation which may discourage the growth of independent General Understanding.

Functional Reading, by contrast, is a way of creating a shared or conventional written language, where prior understanding of speech is unnecessary. Memorizing is discouraged in favour of active searching and 'looking up', with the student ultimately reliant on their own judgement about the meaning of what they read.

Functional Reading and General Understanding

It is essential for Functional Reading that students are already working at the level of continuant behaviour (see Chapter 5), so that they are able and inclined to keep going with an activity, whatever they are making of it. The learning-to-learn-tools explained in that chapter must all be well established at around a three-year-old level. Without that level of General Understanding it would be premature to start Functional Reading or indeed any reading programme. From the point of view of Functional Reading the most important learning tools are perhaps sorting, matching, sequencing and coding. When writing starts, students will need to have established their use of tools, derived from scraping and leading to making marks and to the use of a writing implement.

Functional Reading is always a combination and development of the learning-to-learn-tools. Normally it will be incorporated within the Waldon Lesson and not emphasized as in any way different from all the other Waldon Lesson activities. The tools are always taught in a way that enables students to remain flexible. Sequencing, for example, is not always from left to right but in all directions and at every level, and will include, especially at the early stages, scanning and space structuring capabilities and effortful searching – a lot of coming and going. As always, sessions follow the Waldon principle that effortful activity well within the student's established understanding increases motivation; thus enabling the student to persist with a less familiar activity which might arise from the familiar one.

Every stage of Functional Reading operates on the same basic Waldon principle, derived from his theory of how learning occurs, of doing, noticing that you are doing, and then deliberately trying to repeat that pattern. So, initially, from the point of view of students, a new activity arises accidentally from something which they are already doing. Eventually it is noticed by the students and then they can try to re-create it.

Reading and communication

Reading in daily life is very much bound up with communication. Functional Reading is intended to be a form of reading which grows in the same way that conventional language grows, that is, dependent on our General Understanding and within a context of communication. Communication here is taken to mean influencing another person's behaviour. We actually cause students to do what we want by means of our speech and we can also do this by use of the written form of Functional Reading. That too is a communication which changes students' behaviour.

The most direct form of communication is to get someone to physically do something by moving the person in a way that causes them to do that thing. We conventionalize this by developing a language of speech. In Functional Reading the shared language is a written one and communication develops from the physical to the conventional during the process of learning.

So if one says to a child: 'Stand up', in the earliest stages the words accompany the child being helped to perform the action. When we say to a child: 'Stand up' at the same time we use and speak a lifting motion: 'Up you come' and the baby has no choice in the matter. As the action itself comes under the child's voluntary control, it becomes associated with the speech pattern of the injunction and early conventional language is almost always reinforced in that kind of way. By about six months the average baby is capable, under supportive conditions, of producing a very distinct behaviour in response to commands such as: 'clap hands' or 'wave bye bye' or whatever. By eight months most babies would produce responses to such injunctive commands with minimal support.

It may sound unlikely, but if you analyse the speech we make to small children the most effective mode is injunctive and Waldon believed that the earliest expressive speech is also injunctive, that is to say that children speak in order to influence the behaviour of people around them. Functional Reading works on the premise that written forms can also be utilized as imperatives which will tend to produce changes in the child's behaviour and this ought to be self-reinforcing.

But for this to happen it is necessary to have certain basic aspects of understanding established. Generally speaking a child will respond to an outstretched hand at about 12 months. The same child will not normally learn to respond to an outstretched hand and a held-out object implying: 'Give me another one like this' until about two and a quarter. So if one wants to employ the held-out hand in that particular way it is necessary for the child to be understanding and responding at the two and a quarter year level and beyond in a whole variety of different ways. At age two and a half it is usually well established that a child can look for something which resembles a model and that the child can utilize one thing to represent something else.

Memorizing unnecessary

In Functional Reading attempts to memorize are unnecessary and discouraged because they can lead to guessing and an attempt to get the 'right' answer – with associated anxiety – at the expense of engagement with the activity of the lesson. The emphasis instead is on active 'looking up'. The association between word and action or word and object is reinforced by the action. The more effortful the action and the more frequently it is performed, the more reinforcement it produces and the stronger the association created.

There is therefore never any demand on students to try to remember. They may remember but as there is no requirement to do so then there is no related anxiety about failing.

Movement and motivation

Adults usually try to save energy and time. By contrast children need to use a great deal of energy and time in order to maximize their gain of experience and to develop their General Understanding. Theoretically they do have all the time in the world available to them and that is the best condition for learning. Adults often aim to press knowledge onto children as quickly as possible and teach them short cuts, both of which activities are counter-productive.

Functional Reading students move themselves and other objects around a great deal – moving things from one place to another. Movement, motivation and space structuring are essential components in the development of General Understanding (see Chapter 5), and equally so in Functional Reading. Waldon often described students as tending to be 'one-or-the-other-sided': when using one side of the body, the space occupied by the other side tends to be neglected. This can be related to confusion between the two sides of the body arising from relatively poor bodily integration in the first year or so. A slight weakness in bodily integration can lead to sequencing problems which may become obvious when a child is learning to read. These problems are pre-empted by the Waldon focus on activities designed to promote integration.

Students are encouraged to alternate the use of their hands and to bring the two sides of the body together with each hand crossing the midline to encourage bodily integration. As previously discussed (Chapter 5), this helps them to develop the ability to focus attention and to shift the focus of attention while scanning the whole available space.

Extrinsic reinforcement

As in all Waldon activities, extrinsic reinforcement is never used and its use would be counter-productive. The teacher does not tell students whether they are 'getting it right'. There is no praise of any kind; the motivation for reinforcement is directly related to the pleasure derived from the activity. The more students are active, the harder they work, the more motivated they become. The less praise is given, the less desire for praise is encouraged and the less any anxiety associated with it will arise.

The process

An object will be shown and students will be prompted to discover through the gesture of the cupped hand that they have to find the one like the one offered. Although there is no speech they will learn to understand what that gesture means. One hand holds and shows a car, for example, and with a 'give me' gesture students are expected to find another car and place it in the other outstretched and cupped hand. Initially the facilitator will help students to bring the two objects together. In doing this the facilitator will take the student's hand in a journey around the available space to encourage active looking for the matching object. As the activity becomes familiar, students will need less help in looking for the matching object. That is already a communication system. The understanding is reinforced by repetition with all sorts of other objects. It is not necessary to have or to use any names for these objects. The message is clear: 'Find and give me another one like this one'. The teacher who causes students to move in a certain pattern actually communicates with them physically which is the most direct means possible. It is simpler to communicate directly in that way than through speech.

Students will later be prompted to go further and further away so that when the gesture says: 'Give me another one like this', and the matching object is further away the message becomes: 'Go and get me or bring me another one like this'. The verbal form changes even though the gesture remains the same. Sometimes the things are not easily discoverable because they are hidden and have to be looked for. The gesture remains the same but the verbal form changes again to: 'Find another one like this and bring it to me'. These are all injunctions and in time students will obey three different instructions although being unaware of that fact – which is how it should be.

The sequence of pairing starts with a game of pairing abstract objects. These are objects which are identical, and have perceptual similarities but they would be difficult to find exact names for. There might be two pink wire triangles or two wooden round circles or two green oblongs, but they do not have a social function and they do not have a name and they are identical.

Gradually students learn to pair less identical objects but still with strong perceptual similarities and then they move on to objects that are not at all identical but which are linked by name. So there might be 16 pairs of objects and those might be two dogs, two cups, two shells, two dolls and so on, and they are completely different to look at. For example a conch might be paired with a scallop shell, or a rag doll with a Barbie. Their name is not spoken and to begin with students might need the teacher's help to pair the objects, although usually they immediately know which the pairs are. The students' own General Understanding is relied on. Even though they are talked about here as named objects no words are used. General Understanding, growing out of the learning-how-to-learn-tools, is our internal language which enables us to form concepts and to accept conventionalized representations of these in learning either conventional speech or Functional Reading. As suggested above, Functional Reading is a written conventional language.

There are other things going on within these pairing games. The teacher starts to use a 'give me' gesture (a cupped hand). There is an object in one hand and the other hand performs the 'give me' gesture and eventually the point is reached where the give me gesture comes first. That is important because it is going to pave the way for the words. So 'give me' becomes what Waldon called a definer[2] in its own right as a gesture.

Also students are having to pair over a wider and wider spatial area. They have to make a considerable effort to look for and to find the match. More sets are introduced and it is made even more difficult, to build up the level of effort and motivation and organized space scanning. Eventually students will be going all round the room looking for something which might be hidden in a box or under something else, and then they have to return with the object to complete the activity. Effortful searching over increasing space enables students to start to bear in mind what it is that they are looking for over longer periods of time and regardless of environmental distractions.

Students will reach the point where they are able to pair named objects. Then starting, with a 'give me' gesture, the definers are varied and extended. At the beginning it will always be 'give me' and once that is really well established a container can be introduced. Students are shown an object and have to pick up the matching named object as before but now the teacher uses the 'put' gesture (moving a pointing finger towards). So now there are two gestures in use; the 'give me' and the 'put' and they are the two basic definers in Functional Reading. At this point students start to have to wait to see what the definer will be. Waiting is important because it is through pausing an action that alternative behaviours can be anticipated and chosen between, which is part of developing General Understanding. This is also fundamental to understanding the components of conventional language which can subsequently be separated and reorganized to make sentences with different meanings.

Use of symbols

Once pairing activities are secure the teacher moves gradually towards use of symbols and visual representation of three-dimensional objects and actions. There are various aspects to that. At the pairing level picture object pairs can be introduced. At the beginning very clear pictures are used, which are really like the object to be paired. Often photographs are used and an easy way of organizing that is first to find the pictures and then find the object to pair with them. Then move on to large detailed line drawings and then start to match the line drawings with just the photos, rather than the objects. Then the detailed line drawings are paired with picto-grammatic representations. The teacher takes as many stages and as much time as needed during that development process. At a much later stage one would develop towards reading by conventionalizing this into standard writing by introducing the letters e.g. A P P L E. Each stage of representation continues to demand the same effortful functional response.

Students will be working at pairing at many different levels with several sets of pairing cards to maintain variety so that they are not always working with just one set of cards or of objects. The whole set of learning-to-learn-tools will always be kept in mind and used to expand the working base, always making sure that the students use both sides of the body. Cards will be hidden under pots and under the table using all kind of imaginative ideas to make the game more fun and more effortful and to develop the principle of 'looking for something'. Remember that increased effort leads to an increase in the level of motivation and increases the students' need and ability to carry the image of what it is they are looking for in mind.

Waldon suggested that the association between word and object is 'cemented' by an 'overspill of reinforcant' which would be directly proportional to the level of effort expended, including, but not always, what he called emotional effort, which is experienced when an activity is somewhat frustrating and demands sustained attention. But bodily integration is essential to this and requires physically large and effortful movement. Effort does not mean effort to get something 'right' in the eyes of another but refers to the level of physical and emotional engagement involved in the activity.

Use of pictograms

When the stage is reached of using very abstract pictograms the teacher can start to introduce pictogram representations of both the gesture and the object. So the pictogram is still vaguely related to the object and students know, within the context of the game, that it has to apply to one of the objects. So they can pick the one which it is most like. There is a card that goes with the object, a card that goes with the gesture and the teacher can get students used to the cards by helping them at the same time as showing them. Students find themselves, at first with help from behind, picking up the matching object which goes with the pictogram being shown to them. They also see a gesture, which they become used to, with its pictogram representation in the teacher's hand. They are involved in playing a structured game so they know that it is going to be either a 'give me' and an object or an object and a 'put'.

Gradually the point is reached where, rather than being held, the card is placed down in front of students and they can see that it is the 'give me' gesture and an object and then they must look for the object. The teacher might work for months with the pictogram cards and the gestures and the objects. The learning time varies enormously between students. Some students pick it up incredibly quickly and with others it is necessary to keep going back to an earlier level and then work forward again.

The purpose of the games is to reach the stage where students are using pieces of a sentence: definers and directors (verbs and nouns). At the same time they are working on sequencing. They practise sequencing in different ways and in different directions and it is necessary in the context of Functional Reading for them to be able to do that, so that they can work through a list of objects or a list of instructions: 'Give me this, give me this, give me this' or 'put this, put this', which are gradually being introduced. Director cards can be spread out on the table in various arrangements to encourage multi-directional organized scanning.

Once the use of symbols, or pictograms for objects and gestures, is well established, the teacher can increase the variety and number of responses required. Many different containers can be introduced and drawn differently. Eventually the point is reached where the students are working through a list of symbol sentences using cards and later these can be written sequentially and pictogramatically on paper.

A pictogram sentence might be: pictogram 'put'; pictogram 'duck'; pictogram 'box', meaning: 'Put the duck into the box'. The student might look blankly at that and at the beginning may require help to carry out the action. The first drawing of 'give me' might be much more like a hand, becoming later a pictogram of a hand and gradually becoming a very abstract symbol. Some students go through the steps very quickly but may still need to work on general space structuring and motivation.

Use of word cards

Word cards can be introduced once it is certain that students can match at a high level where they will be able to notice the differences between different words. Pairing, sorting and matching all need to be at a high level before written words can be introduced.

Pairing activities usually utilize an 'H-board' and the student is at first helped to use this with hand-over-hand prompting to ensure that they can follow a sequence and find a match without losing their place.

The pairing levels worked through before words can be introduced are typically:

- clearly different cards which have many different features and colours
- monochrome cards which have very different images
- monochrome cards requiring more discrimination, for example outlines of various non-canonical shapes
- cards with more than one element and perhaps two colours
- cards with intersecting elements and more than one colour
- cards with small letter-like shapes

- combinations of letter-like shapes
- letter and word matching.

As with the object pairing described above, each level will be introduced with a few pairs in the student's near space. Gradually more pairs will be introduced, along with 'redundant' cards, and searching will take place over a wider space and with more obstacles.

At each level the student needs to be able to pair the type of materials being used. When they come to use written words they need to be secure in word pairing. Initially the words may be quite different from each other but the more the students advance and the more words they use the finer distinctions they will need to make. Over time the sorting and matching activities can focus on all types of letter patterns – initial letters, middle letters, pairs of letters, upper and lower case letters and so on.

Mechanical Coding and keys

While they are getting used to pairing word cards, the teacher introduces Mechanical Coding which is where students are taught to use a 'key' together with an H-board, usually with space for 10 or 12 pairs. A key contains arbitrary pairs, for example numbers paired with shapes. On an H-board the numbers on cards are arranged in a different order and the student has to refer to the key to place each shape card with its correct number. As with pairing, this activity is extended over space and the pairs may require consideration of more than one perceptual feature.

Students have to get used to looking for something on the key, finding it and placing it in the appropriate space on the H-board. To begin with, like pairing, students need hand-over-hand prompting so that they can get used to the sequence and the shifts in attentional focus without losing their place. Mechanical Coding involves pairing because when it is pointed to on the code, students have to find the match and then place it with the pair. The more difficult things are at the visual discrimination level, the more difficult it is going to be to do coding with them.

Therefore, as with pairing itself, the teacher might start with very big differences – one very brightly coloured to make it more visually distinguished and then one in monochrome. It is easier to pair two which are visually quite different rather than two which are visually similar. So the progression might be from coloured cards to monochrome cards and then code letters or numbers with little squiggles. The teacher can see how students perform at the simpler levels and decide when they are ready to move on to the higher levels which will be when they are seen to have been paying closer attention to more features. Eventually the point is reached where the student is ready to move on to the complete word. To be clear – letters and words are being paired but it is not necessary at this stage to know the alphabet or the meanings. The words are just used and seen as a pattern.

More cards are introduced to increase the complexity. The first level of Mechanical Coding is done with two sets of eight cards with two separate keys, using either one or two H-boards. That depends on whether all the cards are used or if there are redundant ones to make it harder for students to find just the one they need. The level of complexity is infinitely variable.

Introducing words into coding

The next level will be coding with words and pictograms, using the key and the H-board system. As with any progression this is introduced in many different ways. Everything is always done in multiple varieties, although a consistent pattern is maintained on the H-board because students need to follow the sequencing in an orderly way. Even at this level it is important that the increase in space is continued, so to begin with, the key will be close to the H-board and the cards. Gradually as the activity is established the cards could be placed further away and students will need to maintain the visual image for longer, but can always return to the key to check. They are asked to carry a visual representation of the word in their heads over space and time. That will have been introduced and practised at an earlier level and students have to remain motivated or they will not be able to perform the task. All the earlier work starts to come together, and soon word recognition starts to develop.

Once the student is able to pair words and use pictograms with words in coding, written words can be incorporated into the pictogrammatic instructions which the student has learned to follow. The now-familiar pictogram is retained for some time and only gradually superseded by words without symbols as it becomes clear that the student has grasped the principle of coded representation and is confident to refer to a coding key. Initially the key may just contain the directors (nouns). Later a second key can be introduced for the definers, with cards for 'give me', 'put', 'draw', etc.

It is critical that students refer to the key and do not start to guess, so they must be prompted to keep using the key until it is absolutely certain that they recognize every word. This enables students to be independent. They can find out what they need to know by themselves and will be certain in their knowledge. It is also more important in terms of their reading development for students to be constantly looking back and thinking about differences and similarities rather than just memorizing a word.

The role of the facilitator is to observe how students are responding and to adjust the activities to enable them to move forward without anxiety.

The definite and indefinite articles

When the word duck is said there is no 'the'; but on the word card the teacher writes 'the duck'. That is because, as Waldon said, whatever utterances students hear they scan for anything they can understand and make use of that, and around that other things start to make sense. It is an incidental variation and bit by bit students just get used to the 'the' or the 'an' or whatever it is. It is not taught but just comes as an 'add-on'. When the definite article with the name under the picture is included it is not alluded to and the picture does not include it. (Similarly a symbol for 'and' is introduced only *after* activities which require the student to pick up more than one object.)

Descriptive statements and questions

At this stage it is time to introduce a new concept: 'This is'. It is introduced in the same way as the definite and indefinite articles are introduced, that is by stealth. The student is caused to refer to the key and refer back to the sentence and then tick or cross as appropriate. For example 'this is a duck' under the picture of a duck will be ticked because the word 'duck' will correspond to the duck word/pictogram pair on the coding key. This enables them to practise using a tick for correspondence and a cross for dissonance. The tick and cross are easy to do and easy to understand as a symbol. (Later the student can move on to use 'yes' and 'no'.) Once this is established, the teacher can start to write sentences of the form 'Is this?' surreptitiously introducing question forms with associated punctuation. At this stage there may also be coding keys for colour words or size or prepositions, so that the student will be in a position to answer questions such as: 'Is this a red duck?' or: 'Is the cup under the table?' By now the student is being given pages and pages and pages of these settings interspersed with: 'give me' and 'put', so he is gradually building up his ability to respond differentially to sentences and learning to cope with a whole page of writing. He constantly has to break down what is in front of him.

Further development

Students are by now at quite a high level so the definers can be branched further by, for example, introducing 'go and find' in place of 'give me'. New verbs can be introduced and prepositions in any manner as long as it is clear to students how it is being done. Symbols can be introduced for: in, up, on, under, and so on. Now a written or a drawing component can be introduced because it is an easy way to branch the definers. For this to be possible students will have to work on their use of tools leading to the learning-how-to-learn-tool of drawing. Instructions like 'draw a ring round' can be introduced and initially each action would have its own pictogram. It is first done with gesture, then a pictogram for that gesture and then the word with a key. This has become the standard way of introducing any new action.

From this point on more traditional reading material can be used because students have already worked to the level where this is an obvious extension. Depending on exactly what is chosen, the facilitator may have to make introductory materials to support the text in the same way as they would previously have introduced new material within Functional Reading.

Writing

Like speech, writing may be thought of as having two aspects, expressive and mechanical. The expressive side is what we want to say, and the mechanical side is how we do it. By far the most important part of helping someone to write is developing their need for expression. Within the asocial lesson this is most often done by causing the student to complete a pattern, using a card or by drawing, as exemplified in the paragraph above about how descriptive statements and questions are introduced. At a later stage the student is gradually enabled to use writing to influence the behaviour of the facilitator, for example by using a card or combination of cards to ask a facilitator for a piece of equipment they need (e.g. 'the blue wheel' to complete a model).

The mechanical side of drawing comes out of early tool use, leading to scraping and scribbling and eventually more complex drawing patterns. Within the asocial lesson the student progresses through these stages until they are at a point where it is possible for them to copy letter shapes and words. Their ability to do this is supported, as for the reading, with sequencing and pairing activities. As with the reading, coding keys are used over increasing distance and looking up is encouraged.

With the Functional Reading approach students learn to read naturally and at the same level as their General Understanding.

A case study in Functional Reading

Edward from Chapter 7 was taught to read by Mary Jo using the Functional Reading Approach. Here is an introduction by his father followed by a general discussion of his development by Mary Jo.

Father

> Let us talk about where Functional Reading fits into all of this. Functional Reading is a very particular application of Geoffrey's theory. You isolate and emphasize certain of the learning-to-learn-tools in order to give a child a kick start to reading. I think if Geoffrey had been left to his own devices he would not have taught it separately from the asocial lesson. What is remarkable about this approach is the relating of symbols to a physical action. Edward was never wondering what was being asked of him by these abstract squiggles. He was not asked to read out loud. He was asked to perform an action that he had been carefully prepared to perform so that by the time he reached the point he knew that for example an 'arrow' meant 'put the brick in the pan'.

> The symbols become more and more abstract as he has simultaneously learnt to do coding and then the code got more abstract and then appeared with a word underneath, but his attention is not drawn to the

word. It just happens to be there. As that evolves the word is presented. So Edward never had any anxiety about reading or reading material from school and I think that is because he had done Functional Reading with Mary Jo. It never – even when he could not do it – caused him emotional distress. It was introduced to him as an integral part of his Saturday lesson – perhaps 10 minutes towards the end. Mary Jo knew that if he could not read it would cause him disadvantage at school and over the last six months it helped with some great things he has achieved. It appeared that he could suddenly read but he had been slowly building up to that through Functional Reading. He understands and enjoys what he reads. He reads all the bedtime stories, he insists on reading to us at bedtime.

Mary Jo

I started to see Edward when he was about three when he was quite withdrawn and inclined to want to lie on the carpet and roll around and not do anything else. He had a very marked pattern of running out of steam; he would literally run a few steps and then stop, and he flapped his hands and did not really do anything constructive with them. He did not play in any of the usual ways and I don't think that he was speaking at that time.[3]

He was very anxious about being asked to do things that he was not used to doing so that it took a long time to get him used to banging, for example. He would get very angry and not want to do it. But that was actually a plus because he developed what Geoffrey would have called a head of steam which eventually could express itself in banging, in scraping and in really vigorous picking up and putting in. It became more and more the case that his rage against doing something translated into a much more active form of doing and he gradually settled down.

For a long time, until Edward was about five, there were occasions when he would get really agitated and that made it very difficult for him to do things and not to be able or to want to do things by himself. I remember both parents telling me that he had terrible tantrums when they took him out and how difficult it was to manage that, particularly as he got older and it was more obvious.

By the time he was six or seven Edward developed an astonishing level of emotional equilibrium with an ability to stop and reflect. He would do something to express that he was angry but it would be a very specific, limited, almost a sensible thing to do. He might cast his shoe to the floor in an angry manner, knowing that eventually he was going to pick it up and put it on again. He became a very balanced child.

When he started the lessons he was very one-or-the-other-sided. Generally he tended to be right sided and to neglect his left side space. He found it very difficult to do things with both hands. That still is evident and I still give him tasks, like using tongs, which force him to maintain a grasp and hence attention in both hands. This was really marked when he was young but has improved considerably now. Two-handed tasks were really difficult for him, whether they were complementary or reciprocal movements, that is each hand in turn. He used not to like crossing his arms across his body. He was a slightly floppy, low toned child and he found it difficult to sit and if he did sit he tended to lounge and lean. All those things still persist but in a much less prominent form.

At the beginning his space scanning was incredibly weak and he really could not find things; if he had a box of objects to search in it would upset him straight away. He would feel threatened by that so we had to do a lot of things where I was helping him to find objects and bit by bit he improved and could find something among a bigger group of objects. But he always wanted to settle for the nearest object and not keep looking for whatever it was that he was originally setting out to look for. I had to structure equipment to avoid his picking up the first thing he came to.

However, over the last three years Edward has become incredibly persistent. I can give him the most difficult things to do, that we would all struggle with, and he just pegs away at it until he has got there. I think that has come through the lessons. In the beginning he wanted to give up all the time and if anything was too difficult he was just frustrated and distressed. He used not to tolerate things being put away before they were finished; he wanted to achieve completion of a task and for it not to be an open-ended activity that maybe could come and go and something else could happen instead.

When separating, he had great difficulty accepting something that did not fit exactly into a category set up when we started. As soon as we went beyond a very simple two-set level, he would get confused about the actual organization of the game; the putting things into different categories. So if, for example, he started by separating out all the square things, after a while he might change to separating all the blue things because he would forget that he had been working on the square things to begin with.

There was a parallel in his understanding of speech which is still somewhat the case. I think of it as slippage although there is probably a better way to describe it. His base level categories are not clearly separate in his mind and he can easily move between putting things together because they go together in time and putting things together because they have a perceptual content which is the same; and then he has difficulty in remembering which of those two things he is doing.

That was very marked when he was little and when he first started to speak but it has improved a lot. I can remember that when he did start to speak for a long time he would occasionally speak but generally did not want to. Then his speech reached a level where it was more comfortable for him and he realized its power to affect the behaviour of others. So he got very keen on it, which he still is. Edward loved speech patterns. Before he developed any functional speech he used to repeat whole phrases from films and he still sometimes does that. But his speech now is integrated in a much more syntactically and semantically appropriate way. It is not big chunks any more, although sometimes he will still take on and quote a character from a film.

At the time of writing this it seems hard to remember that there was a time before Edward could read and when it seemed unlikely that he would be able to. I introduced Functional Reading into the Waldon sessions when I could see that Edward's matching, sorting, sequencing and scanning of two-dimensional space were at a high enough level to take them in the direction of Functional Reading. We followed exactly the sequence of activities described in this chapter and there was a rapid progression from responding to pictograms to being able to respond to writing. Particularly important for Edward was carrying visual images over increasing space and the most difficult thing for him was probably moving on to word discrimination from the single or double letter stage when he had to bear the word in mind. While he could easily identify a pair of words in his near space, he found this much more difficult to do when he had to go into a different room. Similarly with writing, he was inclined to write one or two letters then return to the key for the next one or two and this went on for a long time before he started to write whole words.

Edward can read, just as in speech he can copy what he hears, at a level which is higher than his functional expressive speech. His writing is at an appropriate level from an expressive point of view but mechanically he has less developed drawing than other children of his age and needs more space for his writing – though this is not a huge difficulty.

At school recently he read a modern version of Red Riding Hood, quite a well known children's poem all about the wolf. It is a really long ballad and he just read the whole thing by heart for a school competition fantastically with lots of expression and remembering all the words. I was struck by his ability to learn such a long sequence and perform on the stage. It demonstrates his strengths well. You can see how he might have put that together from simpler elements; he can learn words; he likes the sounds of words; he can listen to other people saying them and they can have a particular emphasis. It was different from his own speech which might not have had that level of expressiveness, which he probably picked up from hearing a parent recite the poem. Then he would have listened himself, found it entertaining, and so developed expression from the pleasure of reading. Waldon might have said learning with effortful pleasure!

Edward loves being able to make people laugh and to influence people in all sorts of ways and the discovery that this was possible was a major change for him. I can remember going round to their house to babysit and Edward said something like: 'Come into the garden and let's play on the hammock', and that was already a major change for him. For him to suggest an activity was a massive change and then when we were in the hammock he said: 'You do this and I'll do that' and whatever it was and it was a very simple game – it was his idea. I was so moved at the time because previously it was difficult to get him to do anything. All he wanted was to go into his room and hide in the corner or sit under the bed or turn on the computer. Now he could see that you could make a person do what you wanted; that you could have an idea and they would do it and that was a fantastic development. Now he has great ideas about how to move people around by talking to them. He will say something like: 'Daddy you go next door and talk to Mary Jo' by which he means: 'and I can stay in here and watch the telly'. He comes up with these great plans without disclosing what his real plan is. That is what everyone does!

End Notes

Chapter 1: Early Days 1968–1972

1 Hannah and Bruce were close friends and this was one home where we were always welcome. Bruce asked me to use assumed names.

2 After Pamela, Robert's mother, died in May 2006 our daughter Debbie found some part typed, part handwritten notes which were intended to be the beginning of a book she would write. Debbie as her mother's executor has kindly given me permission to use them, which I have done in their entirety.

3 Assumed name.

4 Dr Michael Casson was our GP and unfailingly supportive and caring. Although most of the medical professionals are referred to by their professional position Michael's widow and son have kindly allowed me to use his name.

5 Clinical note by Dr Casson: 'Mother worried because she thinks child may be deaf, but can hear sounds quite well but does not respond to human voice. Is not emotionally responsive to people. Possibly autistic. 9 May 2009'.

6 Extract of letter from Professor to Dr M.A. Casson, 12 June 1969. With the exception of Dr Casson, medical professionals referred to are anonymous.

7 Extract from the Psychological Report of the Lecturer in Educational Psychology, 26 June 1969.

8 Dr Casson, clinical note, 30 June 1969.

9 Extract from Progress Report from Consultant Paediatrician, 17 November 1969.

10 Report by Consultant Paediatrician, 22 December 1969.

11 Rodney House School is an early years' assessment provision. Children are admitted to the school because there is some concern about their development and a possibility that they may have special educational needs. At that time it was associated with The Duchess of York Hospital for Babies.

12 Dr Casson, clinical note, 15 December 1969.

13 Extract from Psychological Report, 29 January 1970.

14 Dr Geoffrey Waldon, Progress Notes, 25 June 1969 to 26 October 1970.

15 Extract from a letter from the Consultant Neurologist to Consultant Paediatrician, 30 January 1970.

16 Letter from Consultant Neurologist to Dr Michael Casson, 6 February 1970.

17 Dr Geoffrey Waldon, Progress Notes.

18 Conversation with Bruce and Janet, 19 May 2010.

19 Conversation with Gillian, 11 July 2010.

20 Conversation with Hilary, 10 February 2010.

21 Conversation with Valerie, 16 January 2011.
22 Conversation with Ella and Stephen, 20 May 2010.
23 Conversation with Heather, 9 February 2010, and letter 27 May 2011.

Chapter 2: School Years 1972–1987

1   Extract of letter from Paediatric Neurologist to Dr Michael Casson, 9 June 1972.
2   Interview with Sheila Bernstein, 18 June 2010.
3   Memo from Day Nursery, unsigned, undated.
4   Letter from Senior Educational Psychologist, Education Department, Cheshire County Council to us, 18 July 1973.
5   Letter from Head Teacher, Primary School, Cheshire Education Authority.
6   Interview with Joanne Beressi, 30 April 2007.
7   Private School Report, Autumn Term, 1975.
8   Private School Report, Summer Term, 1977.
9   Private undated special report.
10 Private School Report, Autumn Term, 1977.
11 Private School Report, Spring Term, 1978.
12 Grammar School Report, Autumn Term, 1979.
13 Grammar School Report, Summer Term, 1980.
14 Axline, Virginia M., *Dibs – In Search of Self*, Penguin Books, USA, 1964.
15 The Tavistock Clinic is a leading centre for psychoanalysis and psycho-therapy situated close to Sigmund Freud's home in London. A seated statue of Freud is outside the entrance.
16 Tustin, Frances, *Autistic States in Children*, Routledge & Kegan Paul, 1981, pp. 209–236.
17 Spensley, Sheila, *Frances Tustin*, Routledge series: 'Makers of Modern Psychotherapy', 1995, pp. 73–88.
18 Chris Holland, personal communication, 2010.
19 Tustin, Frances, 'Brief Glimpses of Dr. Geoffrey Waldon', *Koine*, 2 (3), The Waldon Association, June 1992.
20 Anne Alvarez, personal communication with Richard Brooks, 15 October 2009, confirmed by Anne Alvarez in personal communication, 31 March 2010.
21 A Barmitzvah is a Jewish coming of religious age ceremony for boys.
22 Letter from Geoffrey Waldon to the Progressive School Director, August 1980.
23 This is the first of a series of interviews with Robert in August 2009 when he and Yelena visited me in France and again in November 2009 when I visited them in Baltimore. This reference covers all of Robert and Yelena's conversations with me relating to this book.
24 A yarmulke is a skull cap worn by religious Jews.
25 A compilation from various reports from the next school, Washington DC.
26 Maths teacher report for New England Boarding School, 16 June 1982.

Chapter 3: College Years, UK and Israel 1987–1998

1   Students are selected for the Dean's List in recognition of superior scholastic performance.
2   Debbie was at Brown University, Rhode Island at the time.
3   se•ed is a Jewish adult education programme.
4   A Yeshiva is a Jewish Rabbinical College and Or Sameach in Jerusalem is a Yeshiva which is specifically organized for non-religious Jews, or those who have not come from a strong orthodox background, to begin their studies.
5   Tzaddick means a righteous one. Here Robert is using a more common translation, meaning to be wise.
6   Simcha means gladness or joy.
7   Letter from Professor Bodenheimer to the author, 15 May 1994.

Chapter 4: Work and Marriage 1998–2011

1   Personal communication, 11 June 2011.
2   Personal communication, Rabbi Diskind, 11 June 2011.
3   Winnicott, D.W., *The Family and Individual Development.* London/New York: Tavistock/Routledge, 1965.
4   Spensley, Sheila, *Frances Tustin*, p.86.

Chapter 5: The Waldon Theory of Child Development and the Waldon Approach

1   Jonas Torrance who co-ordinates the therapy team in the Oxfordshire Service for Autism gave me an interesting interview about movement theory and how movement can be broken down into time, space, weight and flow and how specific rhythms arise in repetitive work (17 March 2010).
2   I have used the words child(ren)/student(s) and teacher/facilitator interchangeably and they will have the same meaning in this context.
3   Waldon, Geoffrey: 'A Personal Note' – Preface to the *Processes of Sorting and Matching*, The Centre for Learning to Learn More Effectively, 1985.
4   Maxine Sheets-Johnstone was a professor of dance for a number of years prior to her professorship in philosophy at the University of Oregon.
5   Rudolf Laban (1879–1958) was a dancer, a choreographer and a dance/movement theoretician.
6   Milne, A.A., *Winnie The Pooh,* Methuen: London, 1926.
7   Pennyhooks is an organic farm in Wiltshire that runs courses for young people with autism spectrum disorder. The farm manager, Lydia Otter, previously a special needs teacher, was trained in the Waldon Approach.

8 John Bowlby in *The Making and Breaking of Affectional Bonds* (1989: 87) also used the differentiation of primary and secondary impediments, albeit with a slightly different emphasis.

9 Chris Holland, personal communication, 2010.

10 Before a lesson can start the student must be sitting expectantly in a chair of the appropriate size at the uncluttered table.

11 The mother of Dan from Chapter 7 wrote this mother's-eye view.

12 *The New Shorter Oxford English Dictionary*, Oxford: Clarendon Press, 1993.

13 *The New Shorter Oxford English Dictionary.*

14 Personal communication, 2010.

15 Chris Holland, personal communication, 2010.

16 Chris Holland, personal communication, 2010.

17 Katrin Stroh, personal communication, 2011.

Chapter 6: Centres Influenced by Geoffrey Waldon

1 Ann Clark, personal communication, 24 June 2009.

2 Interview with Terry Buchan, Marilyn Crook, Eileen Armstrong, Ann Clark and Pat Brown, who were teachers at Meanwood Hospital in Leeds and subsequently at the Leeds Waldon Centre, 24 June 2009.

3 Meanwood Park Hospital was a residential institution for people then called 'mentally handicapped'. It contained a 'special school' within its grounds which closed in 1989.

4 Interview with Sheila Coates, 22 October 2009.

5 Tinbergen, Nikolaas, Nobel Prize in Physiology or Medicine, 1973.

6 Tinbergen, Nikolaas, *The Herring Gull's World*, Collins, 1953.

7 Interview with Jenny Wager, 24 May 2010.

8 Interview with Sue Saville, 17 March 2010.

9 Interview with Alan Proctor, 7 February 2010.

10 Functional Learning was the name chosen by Dr George Stroh to describe the Waldon Approach. I have used whichever name is used by the institution I am describing. As Alan Proctor said: 'If you see any of us giving a lesson under the name Functional Learning it will look identical to a lesson under the Waldon Approach'.

11 Chris Holland, personal communication, 2011. In one conversation with Geoffrey I could not help saying: 'What you have described is just what Winnicott would have called a transitional object'. Geoffrey was confused as he had come at the same understanding of child development from such a completely different direction – except that both Waldon and Winnicott had spent years very carefully studying children.

12 Interview with Dr Breda Sustersic, 1 April 2011.

13 Author's note. It seems to me that the Waldon Approach, indeed the whole Waldon philosophy, would be a useful method in the teaching of deaf,

especially profoundly deaf, children. The emphasis on movement and the de-emphasis on speech make it the ideal vehicle for the development of understanding in the hearing impaired.

14 Interview with Anamarija Filipiè Dolnièar, 1 April 2011. Anamarija was responsible for the introduction of Functional Learning into Slovenia.

15 Interview with Irena Roblek and Anuška Kovač, 4 April 2011.

16 Jiri Berger, *The Waldon Approach to Educating Developmentally Backward Children: A Feasibility Study Within a School Setting.* Final Report, November 1985, unpublished.

Chapter 7: Case Studies of Children on the Autistic Spectrum

1 Interview with Edward's father, 19 October 2009.

2 Interview with Edward's mother, 9 October 2010.

3 Interview with Peter's parents, 22 May 2010. Subsequently revised by Peter's father.

4 Interview with Peter (in the presence of his parents), 29 May 2010.

5 Email from Dan's father (from Australia), 20 October 2009.

6 Interview with Christopher's mother, 10 September 2010.

7 Pat was a teacher who worked at the Waldon Centre in Manchester.

8 Interview with Barbara Šömen, Marko's Functional Learning therapist, 5 September 2011.

9 Interview with Anamarija, Kaspar's Functional Learning therapist and later with his parents, 3 and 6 September 2011.

10 Interview with Michael's parents and sister, 21 May 2010.

11 The Newsom Report (1963) *Half our Future. A Report of the Central Advisory Council for England.* London: Her Majesty's Stationery Office.

Chapter 8: Not Only for Autism – More Case Studies

1 Interview with Larry, 15 September 2010, followed by a discussion with his parents who arrived later.

2 Interview with Freddie's father, 26 June 2009.

3 Interview with Freddie's mother, 22 March 2010.

4 Interview with Roy's father, 23 March 2010.

5 Interview with Elinor's father, 13 October 2009.

6 Interview with Abigail's parents, 23 May 2010, Abigail was present.

7 Interview with Bodhi's mother, 23 March 2010.

8 Interview with Carol Parrey, 24 May 2010.

9 Interview with Judi Stacpoole, 25 May 2010.
10 Interview with Vera's parents, 5 April 2011.
11 Interview with Anamarija, Bogdan's Functional Learning therapist, and his mother, 5 April 2011.

Chapter 9: Functional Reading: A Special Orientation of the Approach

1 Geoffrey Waldon gave weekend workshops on Functional Reading in Leeds and in Oxfordshire during 1987. This chapter is based on the notes, memory and practical teaching experience of Mary Jo Middleton who attended these workshops.
2 Waldon used the terms definer and director for verbs and nouns.
3 Interview with Mary Jo Middleton, Edward's Waldon teacher, 10 October 2010, subsequently expanded by Mary Jo.

Bibliography

There is an immense bibliography on the subject of autism so this is a personal selection of the books on my bookshelf which I have found interesting and/ or useful.

Books on autism

Acquerone, Stella (2007) *Signs of Autism in Infants: Recognition and Early Intervention*. London: Karnak Books.

Alvarez, Anne (2002) *Live Company: Psychoanalytic Psychotherapy with Autistic, Borderline, Deprived and Abused Children*. London: Routledge London.

Alvarez, Anne and Reid, Susan (1999) *Autism and Personality: Findings from the Tavistock Autism Workshop*. London: Routledge.

Anderson, Margaret (2007) *Tales from the Table: ABA Intervention with Children on the Autistic Spectrum*. London and Philadelphia: Jessica Kingsley Publishers.

Asperger, H. (1994) 'Die "Autistischen Psychopathen" im Kindersalter', *Archiv für Psychiatrie und Nervenkrankheiten*, 117: 76–136.

Aston, Maxine (2003) *Aspergers in Love: Couple Relationships and Family Affairs*. London and Philadelphia: Jessica Kingsley Publishers.

Axline, Virginia M. (1964) *Dibs: in Search of Self*. New York: Ballantine Books.

Baron-Cohen, Simon (1995) *Mindblindness: an Essay on Autism and Theory of Mind*. Cambridge, MA and London: MIT Press.

Baron-Cohen, Simon (2003) *The Essential Difference: Male and Female Brains and the Truth about Autism*. New York: Basic Books.

Catalano, Robert A. (1998) *When Autism Strikes: Families Cope with Childhood Disintegrative Disorder*. New York: Plenum Press.

Collins, Paul (2004) *Not Even Wrong: Adventures in Autism*. London: Fusion Press.

Fein, Deborah and Dunn, Michelle (2007) *Autism in Your Classroom, A General Educator's Guide to Students with Autistic Spectrum Disorders*. Bethesda: Woodbine House.

Feinstein, Adam (2010) *A History of Autism: Conversations with the Pioneers*. Chichester: Wiley-Blackwell.

Frith, Utta (2003) *Autism: Explaining the Enigma*, 2nd edn. Malden, MA: Blackwell.

Gallese, V. and Lakoff, G. (2005) The brain's concepts: the role of the sensorimotor system in conceptual knowledge. *Cognitive Neuropsychology*, 21: 1–25.

Gillberg, Christopher (2002) *A Guide to Asperger Syndrome*. Cambridge: Cambridge University Press.

Greenspan, Stanley I. and Wieder, Serena (2006) *Engaging Autism: Using the Floortime Approach to Help Children Relate, Communicate, and Think*. New York: Perseus Books.

Hamilton, Lynn M. (2000) *Facing Autism: Giving Parents Reasons for Hope and Guidance for Help*. Colorado Springs, CO: Waterbrook Press.

Harris, S.L. and Weiss, M.J.(2007) *Right from the Start: Behavioural Intervention for Young Children with Autism*, 2nd edn. Bethesda: Woodbine House.

Janert, Sibylle (2000) *Reaching the Young Autistic Child: Reclaiming Non-autistic Potential Through Communicative Strategies and Games*. London: Free Association Books.

Keenan, M., Kerr, K.P. and Dillenburger, K. (2000) *Parents' Education as Autism Therapists: Applied Behavioural Analysis in Context*. London and Philadelphia: Jessica Kingsley Publishers.

Lytel, Jayne (2008) *Act Early Against Autism: Give Your Child a Fighting Chance from the Start*. New York: Penguin Books.

Maurice, Catherine (1993) *Let Me Hear Your Voice: A Family's Triumph Over Autism*. London: Robert Hale.

Nazeer, Kamran (2006) *Send In the Idiots: Stories from the Other Side of Autism*. London: Bloomsbury.

McCandless, Jaquelyn (2003) *Children with Starving Brains: A Medical Treatment Guide for Autistic Spectrum Disorder*. Putney, VT: Bramble Books.

McCarthy, Jenny (2007) *Louder than Words: A Mother's Journey in Healing Autism*. New York: Penguin Books.

Richman, Shira (2001) *Raising a Child with Autism: A Guide to Applied Behaviour Analysis for Parents*. London and Philadelphia: Jessica Kingsley Publishers.

Seroussi, Karyn (2002) *Unraveling the Mystery of Autism and Pervasive Developmental Disorder: A Mother's Story of Research and Recovery*. New York: Broadway Books.

Siegel, Bryna (2003) *Helping Children with Autism Learn: Treatment Approaches for Parents and Professionals*. Oxford and New York: Oxford University Press.

Spensley, Sheila (1995) *Frances Tustin*. Makers of Modern Psychotherapy Series. London: Routledge.

Tinbergen, N. and Tinbergen, E.A. (1983) *Autistic Children: New Hope for a Cure*. London: George Allen and Unwin.

Tordjman, S., Ferrari, P., Sulmont, V., Duyme, M. and Roubertoux, P. (1977) Androgenic activity in autism. *American Journal of Psychiatry*, 154: 1626–7.

Trevarthen, C., Aitken, A., Papoudi, D. and Robarts, J. (1998) *Children with Autism: Diagnosis and Interventions to Meet Their Needs*, 2nd edn. London and Philadelphia: Jessica Kingsley Publishers.

Tustin, Frances (1981) *Autistic States in Children*. London, Boston and Henley: Routledge & Kegan Paul.

Tustin, Frances (1986) *Autistic Barriers in Neurotic Patients*. Newhaven and London: Yale University Press.

Williams, Donna (1996) *Nobody Nowhere: The Remarkable Autobiography of an Autistic Girl,* revised edn. London and Philadelphia: Jessica Kingsley Publishers.

Wing, Lorna (1996) *The Autistic Spectrum: A Guide for Parents and Professionals,* new updated edn. London: Constable and Robinson.

Books on child development

Bowlby, John (2005) *The Making and Breaking of Affectional Bonds.* New York: Routledge. (First published 1979.)

Forbes, Ruth (2004) *Beginning to Play: Young Children from Birth to Three.* Maidenhead: Open University Press.

Gerhardt, Sue (2004) *Why Love Matters: How Affection Shapes a Baby's Brain.* Hove and New York: Routledge.

Hegarty, S. and Alur, M. (2002) *Education and Children with Special Needs, From Segregation to Inclusion.* New Delhi: Sage Publications.

Roberts, Rosemary (2010) *Wellbeing from Birth.* London: Sage Publications.

Stroh, Katrin, Robinson, Thelma and Proctor, Alan (2008) *Every Child Can Learn: Using Learning Tools and Play to Help Children with Developmental Delay.* London: Sage Publications.

Waldon, Geoffrey (1980) *Understanding UNDERSTANDING: An Introduction to a Personal View of the Education Needs of Children.* The Centre for Educating Handicapped Children at Home. (Slightly revised 1985). Available at: www.autismandunderstanding.com.

Waldon, Geoffrey (1985) *The Processes of Sorting and Matching: As Mental Operations Generating New Experience in Child Development.* The Centre for Learning to Learn More Effectively. Available at: www.autismandunderstanding.com.

Weiss, Lawrence G., Oakland, Thomas and Aylward, Glen (2010) *Bayley-III: Clinical Use and Interpretation.* Burlington, MA: Academic Press.

Whitfield, Graeme and Davidson, Alan (2007) *Cognitive Behavioural Therapy Explained.* Oxford and New York: Radcliffe Publishing.

Books on neuroscience and movement

Begley, Sharon (2007) *The Plastic Mind: New Science Reveals our Extraordinary Potential to Transform Ourselves.* New York: Balantine Books.

Doidge, Norman (2007) *The Brain that Changes Itself: Stories of Personal Triumph from the Frontiers of Brain Science.* New York: Penguin Books.

Greenfield, Susan (2000) *The Private Life of the Brain.* London: The Penguin Press.

McGilchrist, Iain (2009) *The Master and his Emissary: The Divided Brain and the Making of the Western World.* Newhaven CT and London: Yale University Press.

Ramachandran, V.S. (2003) *The Emerging Mind: The Reith Lectures 2003*. London: Profile Books.

Ramachandran, V.S. (2004) *A Brief Tour of Human Consciousness: From Imposter Poodles to Purple Numbers*. New York: Pearson Education.

Sheets-Johnstone, Maxine (2009) *The Corporeal Turn: An Interdisciplinary Reader.* Exeter, UK and Charlottesville, VA, USA: Imprint Academic.

Stern, Daniel, N. (2010) *Forms of Vitality: Exploring Dynamic Experience in Psychology, the Arts, Psychotherapy and Development.* Oxford: Oxford University Press.

Index

Author's note: There are no index references for Geoffrey Waldon as his philosophy and approach are embedded in every page.